SAUDI ARABIA
ON THE EDGE

Also by Thomas W. Lippman

Understanding Islam: An Introduction to the Muslim World
(1982, third revised edition 2002)

Egypt After Nasser: Sadat, Peace, and the Mirage of Prosperity (1989)

Madeleine Albright and the New American Diplomacy (2000)

Inside the Mirage: America's Fragile Partnership with Saudi Arabia (2004)

*Arabian Knight: Colonel Bill Eddy USMC and the Rise of American
Power in the Middle East* (2008)

Related Titles from Potomac Books

Crisis and Crossfire: The United States and the Middle East Since 1945
BY PETER L. HAHN

High-Value Target: Countering al Qaeda in Yemen
BY AMB. EDMUND J. HULL (RET.)

Radical Islam in America: Salafism's Journey from Arabia to the West
BY CHRIS HEFFELFINGER

*Shadow of the Sultan's Realm: The Destruction of the Ottoman Empire
and the Creation of the Modern Middle East*
BY DANIEL ALLEN BUTLER

Simple Gestures: A Cultural Journey into the Middle East
BY ANDREA B. RUGH

SAUDI ARABIA
ON THE EDGE

The Uncertain Future of an American Ally

Thomas W. Lippman

A COUNCIL ON
FOREIGN RELATIONS BOOK

Potomac Books

Washington, D.C.

Library of Congress Cataloging-in-Publication Data
Lippman, Thomas W.
    Saudi Arabia on the edge : the uncertain future of an American ally / Thomas W. Lippman.—1st ed.
        p. cm.
    "A Council on Foreign Relations book."
    Includes bibliographical references and index.
    ISBN 978-1-59797-688-6 (hardcover : alk. paper)
    ISBN 978-1-59797-876-7 (electronic edition)
    1. Saudi Arabia—Politics and government—21st century. 2. Saudi Arabia—Social conditions—21st century. 3. Saudi Arabia—Economic conditions—21st century. I. Title.
    DS244.63.L56 2012
    953.8054—dc23

                                                            2011028495

Potomac Books
22841 Quicksilver Drive
Dulles, Virginia 20166

First Edition

10 9 8 7 6 5 4 3 2 1

CONTENTS

SAUDI ARABIA

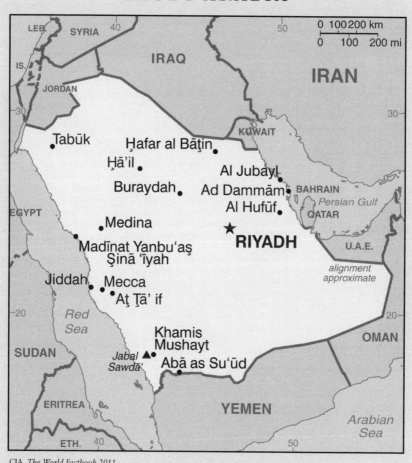

CIA, *The World Factbook 2011*

A FEW WORDS OF
GRATITUDE

In the thirty-five years I have been going to Saudi Arabia to write about the country, its people, and its long-standing alliance with the United States, I have gratefully accepted the assistance of innumerable people, both Saudi and American. My conversations with them all have shaped the perceptions reflected in this book, and I am grateful to all of them for sharing their time and their insights. In researching this book, I received invaluable assistance from a host of friends and colleagues, including Gary Samore, who brought me into the company of fellows at the Council on Foreign Relations; his successor, Jim Lindsay; and my colleagues at the council: Dan Michaeli, Janine Hill, Amy Baker, and Patricia Dorff. Others who deserve special mention are Usamah Al-Kurdi, Caryle Murphy, Kim Pringle Al-Sahhaf, Nail Al-Jubair, Louis Aboud, Jay Balasubramanian, Samar Fatany, Ibrahim Al-Muhanna, Patrice Flynn, Hassan Al-Husseini, Saleh Al-Aswad, Pat Ryan, Ibrahim Al-Beayeyz, Awadh Al-Badi, and Abdullah Alshamri. A special word of thanks is due to Ismail Nawwab, who has shared his considerable wisdom over many years.

I am indebted to John T. Chen for his assistance with translations of Arabic documents. I appreciated the enthusiastic support of my editor on this project, Hilary Claggett; of my longtime agent, Susan Protter; and of my long-suffering wife, Sidney, who cheerfully put up with the indignity of wearing the abaya.

A NOTE ON ARABIC
WORDS AND NAMES

There is no universally accepted standard for the transliteration of Arabic words and names into English. The Arabic alphabet contains letters for which there is no English equivalent. The way a particular word or name is written in the Roman alphabet sometimes depends on whether the original transliterator wrote in English or in French. In spoken Arabic, the article *al-* is elided before some consonants—for example, as in *an-Nahar*, a Lebanese newspaper—and is sometimes transliterated that way, sometimes not.

I have used the transliteration style that has become standard in American print media, with no attempt to reproduce the no-equivalent consonants or glottal stops of the original through orthographic markers, as is done in academic writing. Where an individual's preferred transliteration of his or her name is known, I have deferred to that form. An example is an official of the Ministry of Education whose name is Fahad Al-Tayash. On his English business card he runs the article into the family name and becomes Altayash. That is how his name appears in this text. Similarly, many men named for the Prophet of Islam spell the name Muhammad, which has become the English standard, but others use different versions. When these versions are known, I have used their preferred spelling.

In quotations from the writings of others I have retained the style of the original. Thus Jeddah sometimes appears as Jidda; Abdul as Abdel; sharia, or Islamic law, sometimes appears as shariah. The prefix *Al-* is capitalized in the names of individuals, otherwise not.

The names of individuals consist of a given name, a middle name (sometimes a patronymic such as bin Abdullah, or "son of" Abdullah), and a family name. The patronymic is often omitted in normal usage, as in Abdullatif Ahmed Al-Othman. On second reference, he would be Al-Othman. In the index, he would be listed by family name: Othman, Abullatif Ahmed Al-.

In a name that contains the word Abdul, as in Faisal Abdul Rahman, Abdul is not a freestanding name; it means "servant of" and is a preface to and part of the word that follows: Abdul Rahman is one name, meaning "servant of the Merciful One"—that is, of God. On second reference and in the index, this person would be listed as Abdul Rahman, not Rahman. "Abdul" is sometimes elided into the following part, as in Abdulrahman.

Princes of the Saudi royal family, however, are always identified by their given names. Thus Prince Faisal bin Turki bin Abdul Aziz—Faisal, son of Turki, who is a son of Abdul Aziz—is Faisal or Prince Faisal on subsequent references, and is listed in the index as Faisal bin Turki, Prince.

The prefixes *bin* and *ibn* are interchangeable. The founding king of Saudi Arabia was Abdul Aziz bin Abdul Rahman bin Faisal Al-Saud. For many years American and other Western writers referred to him as Ibn Saud, but it is now standard to follow the Arabs and refer to him as King Abdul Aziz.

INTRODUCTION

The Kingdom of Saudi Arabia is transforming itself. Weary of the world's antipathy, eager to escape from a controversial past, and spurred by economic urgency, the country's leaders have embraced dramatic plans to overcome the flaws of their society and join the global fraternity of advanced nations.

Saudi Arabia has set a national goal of becoming a major industrial power and full participant in the international system, a nation in which the education of its people and the sophistication of its decision making match the economic power derived from its natural resources. It is possible that it will achieve that goal; it is also possible that it will fail to achieve it and slide backward, overpowered by the regressive internal forces that have always constrained the kingdom's development and tarnished its reputation. Either way, it is incumbent on Americans to know more about this mysterious land.

Of the many countries that are vital to the strategic and economic interests of the United States, Saudi Arabia has been the least understood by the American people. Even after a decade of intense interest prompted by the terrorist attacks of September 11, 2001, the kingdom is viewed largely as a stereotype, defined by oil, terrorism, and veiled women. The dynamics of a complicated society facing a daunting and uncertain future are perceived only dimly, if at all.

This gap in Americans' knowledge of the forces that will affect their future is unfortunate and unnecessary. Saudi Arabia is not a static society encased in some religious amber. It is more open to visitors, researchers, and investors than it was in the past; its economic and intellectual engagement with the

1

world is increasing every day. The kingdom's odd life as a reclusive twilight zone of world affairs is coming to an end.

It is possible to imagine a world in which Saudi Arabia is not central to American interests. It would be a utopia in which the United States has freed itself from dependence on imported oil. It would be a world in which Israel has achieved a durable peace with all its neighbors; extremism and the appeal of violence have been extirpated from Islam; Iran is a friendly partner of the United States and its allies; Iraq and Yemen are stable, responsible countries; and nations are cooperating instead of competing in the allocation of water and food for their growing populations. In that imaginary world, the vast, opaque, largely uninhabitable country known as the Kingdom of Saudi Arabia might not be important to Americans, except perhaps as a place to make money. But in the real world, the world of today and of the next two or three decades, the stability, security, and reliability of Saudi Arabia are vital to the well-being of America and its allies.

Many tens of thousands of Americans have lived and worked in the kingdom since Chevron discovered oil there in the 1930s, but relatively few of them learned the language and only a small percentage experienced sustained cultural and personal interaction with the Saudi people. Historically, Americans have derived their culture—their ideas, religion, literature, food, music, and art—from European and, to a degree, Asian roots. Except as anonymous providers of oil, the people of Arabia have had only marginal impact on the lives of most Americans. And yet Saudi Arabia is critical to the security and prosperity of the United States and, to some extent, of Europe as well. If Saudi Arabia fails to manage the many threats and overcome the many challenges that it faces in the next decade or two, the damage to American and other Western interests is likely to be extensive.

Those who have not experienced the kingdom in person find it difficult to comprehend the scope and pace of the changes that have already transformed Saudi Arabia in every material sense. In seven decades, a single lifetime, an impoverished backwater has become a mostly urban society of computers and air conditioners. There are Saudis living today who remember the isolated life before oil, in an agrarian and nomadic subsistence economy where education was almost nonexistent and life was constructed on the foundations of the family, the tribe, the herd, and the faith. Now Saudi Arabia is a country of superhighways and skyscrapers, having undergone a transformation without historical parallel in its speed and totality. Meanwhile, Saudi Arabia's society has not changed nearly as fast as the country's physical entity, nor has it wished to do so. Now it must, if it is to prosper.

Beginning in the earliest years after the modern kingdom's unification in 1932, Americans enabled and shaped the modernization of the vast, mostly arid land. When mechanized agriculture, aviation, medical care, and electric power plants came to Saudi Arabia, it was Americans who brought them.

American interest in a stable, friendly Saudi Arabia has gone well beyond oil ever since President Franklin D. Roosevelt persuaded its founding king to declare war on the Axis powers in 1945. Saudi Arabia is a vast market for American industrial and consumer goods. General Electric has selected Saudi Arabia as its manufacturing hub for the entire region. The world's biggest Ford and Caterpillar dealerships are in Saudi Arabia, and the kingdom is a major market for such giants of the American economy as Boeing, Mars, Cisco Systems, Raytheon, McDonald's, and Bechtel. During the Cold War, Saudi Arabia was a reliable ally in the worldwide effort to contain communism. Today it is a central player—sometimes in accord with U.S. policy, sometimes not—in Arab-Israeli peace negotiations, in the quest for stability in Iraq, in Persian Gulf regional security issues focusing on Iran, and in the global struggle to promote a peaceful vision of Islam over jihadist violence. Saudi Arabia's historic primacy in Islam makes it indispensable to a constructive relationship between the non-Muslim West and the Muslim world.

At the same time, the kingdom is a central arena in the worldwide struggle within Islam between forces of tradition and xenophobia, which oppose all change and wish to turn backward, and advocates of modernization who believe that Islam must adapt to a changing world and can do so without surrendering its ideals and values. Balancing the country's unique and deeply embedded religious tradition with its headlong drive toward modernity has long been, and remains, the most important and difficult challenge confronting the society and its rulers, the princes of the House of Saud.

From the time oil was discovered in 1938 through the end of the twentieth century, the engine of the country's development and modernization was money from the export of crude oil. Lacking other resources, the kingdom relied on oil revenue to finance its astonishing progress in education, public health, housing, transportation, and infrastructure. What Saudi Arabia wanted, it simply bought, including the imported expertise to build what the country needed and the manpower to do the work that the Saudis lacked the skill or the desire to do.

Now in the twenty-first century the kingdom's needs—and its economic aspirations—are different. Oil will remain the principal source of state revenue for the foreseeable future, but Saudi Arabia is no longer content—and soon will no longer be able—to function as a classic "rentier" state, that is, living off the export of extracted natural resources and doling out fiscal sugarplums to its population. The country has embarked on a hugely ambitious effort to reconstruct itself as a powerhouse of petrochemicals, aluminum, communications, and services that would rival South Korea or Australia in the diversification of its economy, educational levels of its people, and overall quality of life. In effect, Saudi Arabia is conducting a giant, long-running laboratory experiment on itself to determine whether it can modernize its economy, its style of living, and its relations with the rest of the world without abandoning its cherished traditions. While it probably can, the outcome is not assured. The people of Saudi Arabia argue every day over how to participate in the global system without being culturally overpowered.

A prominent Saudi anthropologist, Saad Sowayan, a student of poetry and folklore, has written that in social and intellectual matters—as opposed to material matters—his country is "going through a slow process of evolution," so slow as to be almost imperceptible on a day-to-day basis but real nonetheless. The process is inevitable, he wrote, but also frightening because its end point is unknowable.[1] That uncertainty is why resistance to change is sometimes as great as the desire for change.

I first went to Saudi Arabia in the mid-1970s, when I was the regional correspondent for the *Washington Post*. In that era of great oil price increases following the 1973 Middle East War, the kingdom was drowning in a Niagara of cash. Those were gold rush days, when the shortage of hotel rooms was so acute that visiting businessmen sometimes paid the owners of taxis with air-conditioning to drive around all night so they could sleep in the back seat. I have spent a good bit of time in Saudi Arabia during the ensuing years in several capacities. I have always been received generously and courteously, and I am privileged to count many Saudis as friends. It is not a society in which I would want to live, nor would most Americans, but the Saudis are under no obligation to run their society as Westerners might prefer. Their obligation is to provide security and decent living conditions for their own citizens and to do so in accordance with the people's deeply held beliefs about human society, God, and the moral order. For the most part the kingdom's rulers and technocratic elite have succeeded in doing that, but it is getting harder all the time.

Saudi Arabia is both rich and vulnerable, a unique combination of the modern and the backward. It is, of course, the world's leading exporter of oil and will remain so for decades to come despite media-inspired fears about the potential decline of its reserves. Yet for all its wealth the country lacks the tools to meet the challenges that confront it: a restless, young population; a new generation of educated women demanding opportunities in a closed society; political stagnation under an octogenarian leadership; religious extremism and intellectual backwardness; social division; a flawed education system; chronic unemployment; shortages of food and water; and troublesome neighbors.

Statistics about Saudi Arabia are notoriously unreliable, but clearly its population is young, with a median age of about twenty-two, and is growing at a rate that has outstripped the country's economic growth and ability to provide food, water, and housing. The country is wealthy, but many of its people are not. A leading newspaper reported in the fall of 2010 that a third of the sixty thousand beggars arrested by the police in Riyadh, the capital, during the preceding twelve months were Saudi citizens.[2] According to World Bank and United Nations calculations, Saudi Arabia's per capita income in 2009 was less than half of what it was in 1980. It ranked fifty-seventh among nations, falling behind most of Europe, even Slovenia and Cyprus. A year later, using population figures from the kingdom's 2010 census, economic analysts at Riyadh's Jadwa Investment Group calculated that Saudi Arabia's per capita gross domestic product (GDP) of $15,734 was about fortieth in the world. Either way, the country's relatively low standing reflects the fact that its population growth has been outrunning the growth of its oil revenue for three decades.[3]

The country runs on the labor of millions of foreign workers while many of its own young people go without jobs. Its industrial ambitions exceed its management capabilities. It is locked into a narrow-minded and anti-intellectual version of Islam, yet it aspires to enter the modern world of knowledge and science. The Saudi people, far better informed now than in previous generations, are looking for new political institutions that will enable them to be heard, but these aspirations often conflict with the kingdom's strict traditions and with the House of Saud's determination to retain all true power. The country wishes to remain under the protection of American security while clinging to a political and social system that is antithetical to American values. Its rulers have been closely aligned with the United States since World War II and remain so, but that position is now more difficult to sell to the Saudi people than in the past. Although they admire American achievements, they have become disenchanted with America because of its invasion of Iraq and its inability to forge an acceptable peace arrangement for the Palestinians.

Despite all that, the future is promising because over the past decade the Saudis have recognized their problems, acknowledged them, encouraged public discussion of them, and marshaled resources to confront them. The Saudi rulers, the business elite, and most of the intelligentsia want to engage with and be part of the modern world without abandoning their traditions of family and faith, and they want to be accepted on their own terms. The Saudis are not isolated primitives in an unexplored wilderness; they do not want to be regarded as exhibits in some human zoo, looked upon by outsiders as scary, zealous freaks in strange clothing. Indeed, the most striking feature of the Saudi scene for a visitor today is its ordinariness. Differentiated only by their attire, Saudis go to work and school, play with their children, eat at McDonald's, shop at malls and big-box stores, and get stuck in traffic as people do everywhere. And yet Saudi Arabia is different from any other society. Those fast-food restaurants, as with almost all business establishments in the kingdom, are segregated by sex. The Koran, rather than any modern document or legislation, is the fundamental law of the land. In a country of about 28 million people there are no churches because the open practice of any religion other than Islam is prohibited. The declared purpose of the Saudi state is the advancement and protection of Islam rather than the advancement and protection of the individual. To change that mission would be to invite upheaval.

One of the earliest books about Saudi Arabia by an American who had lived there was titled simply *Kings and Camels*. It was published in 1960.[4] If the title had included the words "veils" and "oil," it would have pretty much summed up Americans' understanding of the kingdom at the time and for decades afterward. The catastrophic events of September 11, 2001, added another word: "terrorism."

In the aftermath of 9/11, Americans were suddenly bombarded with books and articles about Saudi Arabia, most of them hyperventilating demonizations of a dimly understood country. Terms such as "jihad" and "Wahhabism" were thrown around as if they explained the catastrophe of that dreadful morning. But it is no longer useful or even possible to assess Saudi Arabia with a handful of nouns. It is a complicated and changing society with profound problems and many moving parts, and despite all that has happened, the United States retains its responsibility for the kingdom's security despite losing its economic monopoly there as the kingdom has diversified its commerce.

With each passing year, Saudi Arabia has more citizens who are educated, well traveled, and linked to the world though satellite television and the Internet. Some of these people have responded to the exposure by turning backward to radicalism, but most of them, even if they remain quite conservative socially and religiously, understand the value and the necessity of engagement with the world and acceptance of new ideas. Some are striding into the future, some are being dragged into it, some are rejecting it entirely, but whatever the outcome, the Saudis will determine their own future. They will take it in their uncertain hands. We Americans cannot control it, but we can influence it to our benefit or our detriment, depending on our behavior and our attitude. It is time for Americans' thinking about Saudi Arabia to progress, as the Saudis are progressing, beyond kings and camels.

1

KINGS AND COUNTRY

The wave of uprisings that redrew the political map of the Arab world in 2010 and 2011 barely lapped at the shores of Saudi Arabia. After decades of political stagnation among the Arabs, the rulers of Tunisia and Egypt were forced from office virtually overnight. Antigovernment protests and demonstrations broke out from Algeria to Syria to Yemen. Civil war erupted in Libya. Weeks of sectarian strife paralyzed Bahrain, the tiny island state off the eastern coast of Saudi Arabia, which felt compelled to send in troops and shore up the regime.

Some analysts concluded that the Kingdom of Saudi Arabia itself was ripe for upheaval. With its autocratic political system, geriatric leadership, disenfranchised citizenry, and youth unemployment bulge, it seemed to share many characteristics of the other troubled Arab states, especially Egypt, and to be vulnerable to a similar upheaval.

There were indeed a few small demonstrations, especially in the east around the city of Qatif, home to the kingdom's restless minority of Shia Muslims. A few petitions seeking democratic reforms circulated on the Internet. Some intellectuals wrote articles asking for changes in the system; they did not call for an overthrow of the monarchy but sought greater public participation in the institutions of the state. Otherwise, not much happened. No serious challenge to the Saudi regime emerged.

There were many reasons for that. King Abdullah is popular, unlike the reviled rulers who were ousted in Egypt and Tunisia. The Al-Saud rulers, whose family has labored since the eighteenth century to create a unified state in Arabia, are widely accepted as legitimate. They have the support of the country's religious establishment, which commands wide respect in a deeply religious society. Having lived through three years of shoot-outs in the streets during an assault on the state by al-Qaeda that began in 2003, the Saudi people did not relish the prospect of more violence; they were not in an insurrectionary mood. Religious extremists, whose efforts to provoke mass demonstrations alienated large segments of the population, outmaneuvered the relatively few legitimate dissenters; meanwhile, the official, state-sponsored religious establishment proclaimed that Islam prohibited such protests. The kingdom's security forces, hardened by their struggle with al-Qaeda, banned demonstrations and showed that they were capable of enforcing the rule. (The few reformists who announced their creation of a political party were arrested.) Saudi Arabia has an impoverished underclass, but they are far outnumbered by the citizens who have benefited from the existing system—through government jobs, state-funded benefits, and business ventures with the ruling family—and have no incentive to overthrow it. The expanding Saudi economy does provide some opportunities for energetic young people, and though these are not enough, by far, they exceed what existed in Egypt or Tunisia. And unlike Egypt, Tunisia, and Yemen, Saudi Arabia has the money to provide for the well-being of its population, as evidenced by the packages of housing, salary, and education benefits worth more than $100 billion that the king bestowed at the height of the regional unrest. In fact, the region's upheavals prompted a worldwide surge in oil prices that immensely benefited Saudi Arabia, which marketed its exports at ever-higher prices and thereby enriched the treasury even as the king was handing out the new welfare.

In a perceptive analysis of the multiple uprisings of the "Arab Spring," George Mason University's Jack Goldstone, a student of revolutions, notes that most of them fail. The few that succeed do so only when a number of conditions come together:

> The government must appear so irremediably unjust or inept that it is widely viewed as a threat to the country's future; elites (especially in the military) must be alienated from the state and no longer willing to defend it; a broad-based section of the population, spanning ethnical and religious groups and socioeconomic classes must mobilize; and international powers must either refuse to step in to defend the government or constrain it from using maximum force to defend itself.[1]

None of those conditions exists in Saudi Arabia.

Thus the reign of the Al-Saud family continues, and King Abdullah's successors are likely to remain in control for years to come. That is not to say, however, that the people are entirely content with matters as they are. During a visit in the spring of 2011, I found Saudis more willing than ever before, even eager, to complain about corruption and inefficiency in the government and about their inability to make public officials respond.

The language of one of the petitions that circulated that winter, titled "A Declaration of National Reform," summed up the grievances and aspirations of the regime's critics. In part, it said,

> The status quo is cause for concern. We are witnessing with the rest of the Saudi people the decline of our country's regional role, the stagnation of the government, the deterioration in the efficiency of the management, the prevalence of corruption and nepotism, fanaticism, and the increasingly widening gap between the state and society, especially the new generation of youth. This could lead to disastrous consequences for the country and the people, and it is something we cannot accept for our homeland and our children.

> Addressing this situation requires a serious review and an immediate adoption of large-scale reforms by both the state and society, focusing on fixing the fundamental flaws in our political system, and leading the country to a well-grounded constitutional monarchy.

> The people's acceptance is the basis for legitimacy of authority, and it is the only guarantee for unity, stability, the efficiency of governance, and protecting the country against foreign interference.

This petition, as with others from this period and the past, refrained from calling for abolition of the monarchy. It asked that the monarch's powers and his responsibility to the people be defined by a written constitution and that the existing Majlis ash-Shoura, or Consultative Assembly, a quasi-legislative body appointed by the king, be elected.[2] The academics and reform advocates who circulate such documents are under no illusion that the king and his brothers will read them, suddenly find them persuasive, and order the requested changes. The purpose of the petitions is more to educate the country's politically uninformed people and to show them what they should want.

The regime is well aware of the need to do some business differently. The underlying motive for the grand plans for economic development and education reform that the government has adopted is to provide the jobs and personal opportunities that are required to keep its subjects pacified.

To the extent that those plans are fulfilled, the solutions they will bring are years in the future. In early 2011 King Abdullah returned to the kingdom after a long convalescence from back surgery in the United States and dealt with the here and now by dispensing economic and social benefits. The packages included salary increases, bonuses for civil servants, new unemployment benefits, money for housing construction, additional scholarships for university students abroad, funds for medical care, sixty thousand new jobs in the security services, more funding for religious institutions, and the establishment of a National Commission on Combating Corruption. Nothing the king did altered the country's fundamental structure of authority; the measures represented palliatives, not structural reform.

ILLUSION AND REALITY

Appearances are often deceiving in Saudi Arabia. Nowhere is the gap between appearance and reality wider than in the area of human rights and personal freedom.

It is possible to spend weeks, even months, in Saudi Arabia without being aware of the extent to which individual freedom is limited or is granted only on conditions set by the state. Saudi men are free to travel abroad, live where they like, take whatever jobs they find suitable, make money and keep it, interact with foreigners, attend any university they can get into, have as many children as they want, take their families to the park and the beach, and surf the Internet. In any coffee shop or hotel lobby, Saudi men can be seen reading one of the many newspapers or engaging in lively conversation, unwatched by the police. They mostly look comfortable, not fearful. Life is considerably more constrained for women because of restrictions on dress, travel, and contact with men, though the range of activities open to them is expanding.

But Saudi Arabia is not a "free country," not in the sense that the United States is a free country. The regime grants those freedoms that the Saudi people enjoy, and it can revoke them at any time for any reason, or no reason. The freedoms are not inherent rights of individuals. In all ways that matter, the Al-Saud rulers run the country, and the citizens defy the rulers' dictates at their peril. To the extent that this or that king is a generous or kind-hearted person, his attitude is reflected in the atmospherics of daily life. The avuncular, devout King Abdullah is popular because he has opened up the space around individual citizens, but he or any of his successors could tighten that space just as easily, because they own the country.

The Saudi system is the fundamental opposite of the American system. The purpose of the state is not to protect or enhance the rights and freedoms of the individual; it is to promote Islam, instill a culture of obedience into the population, and ensure stability. Individuals are expendable; people can be arrested without explanation and locked up for years in appalling conditions if someone in authority thinks they were out of line. Over many years human rights advocacy groups and the U.S. State Department have issued innumerable reports documenting arbitrary arrests, grotesque justice, torture in the jails, cruel punishments, and the absence of political freedom, but they have had little impact on the regime.

It may seem to Americans that such a system must inevitably break apart because it is a historical anachronism, a throwback to the era of the "enlightened despot," but there is no reason to think that the Al-Saud cannot go on running Saudi Arabia for many decades. The regime's leaders have been skillful and diligent at extending their power and building loyalty in every important constituency, through ties of blood, money, and patronage, all wrapped in the green cloak of Islam. Other than the extremists of al-Qaeda and their sympathizers, who have been suppressed if not expunged, the regime's critics operate within a narrow band and seek mostly to reform the system, not overthrow it. The few who want to get rid of the House of Saud altogether are in prison or in exile.

It is wrong to assume that the Saudi public always opposes or resists the government-imposed restrictions on liberty. The Saudis by and large do not want pornography, or for that matter Christian sermons, to be available on television or the Internet. They are devout people who believe in the primacy and inviolability of Islam, and they therefore endorse its immunity from challenge. In those respects the rulers are representative of the ruled, not out of step with them.

It appears to be true even among the younger generation of reform advocates, who seek to open up the system without displacing it. Khalid Al-Dakhil,

a reform-minded political scientist at King Saud University and a signer of
the Declaration of National Reform petition, wrote:

> The "new liberals" assume from the start that the Saudi monarchy is le-
> gitimate and reflective of the social and political reality and history of Saudi
> society. Thus, it provides a badly needed framework for maintaining na-
> tional unity.
>
>   While they accept the monarch, liberal reformers object to the govern-
> ment's insistence on ignoring the fact that social reality is not constant.
> Saudi society has been transformed dramatically over the last three decades
> and these changes need to be reflected in the political and legal institutions
> of the state and in the government's internal and foreign policies.[3]

"Nobody is against the system," he told me. "They want to change the
system from within."[4]

His observations pretty much summarize the sentiments of most of the
publicly stated critical comments in the past twenty years or so: The monarchy stays, but outdated social and legal practices should go, even if people
do not agree on which social and legal practices should be considered outdated and which should be retained.

As king, Abdullah proved to be far more flexible about "social reality"
than his predecessor was, with the result that after five years on the throne
he was popular with the public and his authority had been strengthened, not
diminished. Abdullah will leave to his successors a better-organized, more
stable country than he inherited and under the control of a regime that has
a greater degree of public acceptance.

"There is absolutely no doubt in my mind or in anybody else's mind that
we enjoy the support of the majority," said Prince Turki Al-Faisal, the former ambassador to the United States. He is probably right, if only because
no one has offered a viable alternative to the Al-Saud.[5]

There is abundant evidence that the people of Saudi Arabia want more
personal freedom, and King Abdullah has bolstered his popularity by doling
it out in small measures. There is scant evidence that any substantial portion
of the Saudi population wants to replace the regime with a different political system. A slow evolution toward greater citizen participation in public affairs is likely, but a drastic upheaval is not.

Through their control of the country's historical narrative and the flow of ideas, the Al-Saud have created a compliant political atmosphere in which "being Saudi is to be devoid of political power, its distribution and its use," as the American scholar Gwenn Okruhlik put it in a perceptive essay. "All people value the primary subjects of society and economic citizenship—family, Islam, social relations, and welfare—but the regime has borrowed the potency of these ideas and used then to devalue the explicitly political components of citizenship, such as fairness, accountability, and freedom of expression."[6]

THE KING IS NOT THE SHAH

Ever since the Shah of Iran was overthrown in the Islamic revolution of 1979, I have often been asked when—not whether, but when—the House of Saud will follow the shah out the Middle East's political door. The underlying assumption is that one monarchical dictatorship is like another and that all are doomed. My response is that Saudi Arabia's political system and social contract under the Al-Saud bear little resemblance to those of Iran under the shah, and the experience of Iran is largely irrelevant to that of contemporary Saudi Arabia. Iran and Saudi Arabia are large Muslim countries and major oil producers, but those similarities do not mean their contemporary histories must be parallel.

First, many Iranians viewed the shah, with good reason, as a creature of outside creation, installed on the Peacock Throne by the British and the Soviets and kept there by the Americans during the political crisis of 1953. He was a strutting autocrat whose overblown titles and delusions of empire were built on the authority of his secret police. The Al-Saud, by contrast, are of Arabian tribal stock like the other citizens of the kingdom. They created the modern kingdom of Saudi Arabia, are the only rulers the country has had, and are widely perceived as the glue holding it together.

Second, the shah, with his pretensions about Persepolis and the glories of Persian culture, was perceived to value Iran's pre-Islamic heritage more than he valued the faith taught by the Prophet. No such criticism is applicable to the House of Saud, which is built on a foundation of Islam.

Third, the shah ruled a Shia Muslim country in which the religious authorities, the mullahs and ayatollahs, were financially and politically independent of the government. The shah could exile clerical foes such as Ayatollah

Ruhollah Khomeini, but he could not strip the mullahs of their influence in Iranian life or silence them because he did not control their jobs or their money. In short, they did not work for him. In Saudi Arabia, as in most Sunni Muslim countries, the religious authorities—the ulama, or "learned scholars"—are employees of the state. They can be and have been dismissed and silenced when the king thought they were out of line. As a result they tend to defer to the monarch.

And finally, the shah was Israel's best friend in the Muslim Middle East. The same cannot be said about the king of Saudi Arabia, who has offered peace to Israel but only on terms that the vast majority of Muslims would accept and has otherwise kept his distance.

In general, authoritarian regimes such as the shah's survive through fear or poverty: the people are either intimidated into submission or so poor that they must concentrate on survival and depend on the government for resources. Sometimes both conditions prevail, as in North Korea, for example. Saudi Arabia is different. Its rulers do not hesitate to throw people in jail when they see a threat to themselves or to national stability, but their preferred style of rule is to persuade or bribe people to buy into the system. The entire apparatus of the state teaches its citizens that Islam and the family are the foundations of society and that the state embodies those values. To maintain that image, the regime must persuade people that it acts on their behalf in conformity with those values.

As many Saudis have explained it, the Saudi state resembles a giant family-owned corporation in which the king, as chief executive, presides over a fractious board of directors—the other members of the family—and the citizens are the workers. The workers have no voice in how the company is run, but their cooperation must be secured through generous pay and benefits.

"This is not an absolute monarchy," says Abdul Aziz Fahad, a prominent Riyadh lawyer who likes to describe himself as "the only liberal" in Saudi Arabia. "Abdullah is not the Sun King." According to Fahad, the Al-Saud need family consensus for their decisions, but he also acknowledges that they show "some sensitivity" to public opinion, that there are religious restrictions on their authority, and that "because of the sheer complexity of the modern state, the king can't do everything or even know about everything." The king sets policy, in consultation with his brothers, and sometimes acts on specific cases—to pardon a prisoner, for example, or to order that a university be built—but well-established institutions run by technocrats, such as the Ministry of Petroleum and the Saudi Arabian Monetary Agency, or central bank, conduct much of the government's business now.[7] Indeed, the very complexity of the state has become an issue with reform advocates, who say that the king who succeeds Abdullah should not also be prime minister, as he is. They say the post of prime minister requires administrative competence and technocratic skills that a king might not possess.

In the words of Jamal Khashoggi, a provocative journalist who has been in and out of favor with the authorities,

> The King is an authority, not a dictator. He rules by consensus. He has many constituencies he has to look out for. You should see Saudi Arabia as a coalition government between a liberal front and a progressive party and conservative elements. He has to see the interests of all of those groups and come about with a reform, with progress, which will accommodate the need of all sectors of the Saudi society without ending up in dissent or in a break-up situation.

He said Saudis "very much appreciate" the stability and social cohesion that the monarchy has fostered, a sentiment that is widely shared.[8]

"You can rule by consensus, or by fear like Saddam Hussein," said David Rundell, who spent years in the kingdom as a U.S. diplomat. "The king must maintain a consensus. He can't tolerate a situation where only 25 percent of the people think he is doing a good job and should remain. In the United States people may tolerate that because they know the current ruler will be gone in a few years, but the king expects to rule for life and to have a member of the family follow him."[9]

THE STATE'S UNIQUE CHARTER

Saudi Arabia operates under a "Basic Law of Government," decreed by King Fahd in 1992, that codified the informal, Koran-based system of rules that had governed the kingdom since its creation in 1932. The Basic Law is one of the most remarkable state charters ever published, both for what it says and for what it does not say.

"The Kingdom of Saudi Arabia is a sovereign Arab Islamic state with Islam as its religion; God's book [the Koran] and the Sunnah [example] of His Prophet, God's prayers and peace be upon him, are its constitution. Arabic is its language and Riyadh is its capital," the law says. The family "is the kernel of Saudi society, and its members shall be brought up on the basis of the Islamic faith, and loyalty and obedience to God, [to] His Messenger, and to guardians; respect for and implementation of the law, and love of and pride in the homeland and its glorious history as the Islamic faith stipulates." It is the duty of each citizen to defend Islam.

The document specifies that "the system of government in the Kingdom of Saudi Arabia is a monarchy" and that the monarch must be a direct male descendant of the founder, King Abdul Aziz. The Basic Law has eighty-three articles, which specify, among other things, that the purpose of education is to promote Islam, the legal system is based on Islamic law, and all power to appoint and dismiss judges, make treaties, appoint government officials, and dictate the national budget lies with the king. The king is also the commander of the armed forces and the prime minister as well as chief executive.

Autocratic rule is enshrined as state policy. Article Six says, in its entirety, "Citizens are to pay allegiance to the King in accordance with our holy Koran and the tradition of the Prophet, in submission and obedience, in times of ease and difficulty, fortune and adversity." Article Eighty-three stipulates that "this law may only be amended in the same way as it was promulgated"—that is, by the king and on his own authority.

The Basic Law's assertion that citizens must obey the king "in accordance with our holy Koran" obviously reinforces the ruling family's claim to legitimacy, but it is—in the word used by Asad Abukhalil, a California academic who blogs as the "Angry Arab"—"bogus" because "nowhere does the Qur'an urge believers to obey and submit to the king, any king." The Holy Book of Islam does call upon believers to follow the commands of their leaders, but it does not specify that the leader should be a king. Most Muslim countries are not monarchies.[10]

Saudi princes sometimes describe the Basic Law as a "contract" between them and the citizens, but that is disingenuous. A contract is a binding agreement between parties who enter into it voluntarily. The Basic Law was handed down from on high, unilaterally. It specifies many duties required of the citizens, but it does not specify any duties or obligations of the king other than to rule in accordance with Islam.

The Basic Law provided for the creation of a Consultative Council, to be convened at the behest of the king, but otherwise offers only one avenue by which citizens may have any input into affairs of state: "The King's Court and that of the Crown Prince shall be open to all citizens and to anyone who has a complaint or a plea against an injustice. Every individual shall have the right to address the public authorities in all matters affecting him." In effect, that provision writes into law the traditional Arabian *majlis* system, in which citizens who have a grievance or who need help are entitled to petition the person in charge directly. The ruler may give the petitioner satisfaction or he may not. What the petitioner cannot do is organize his fellow citizens in an effort to replace one ruler with another or stoke public demand for change.[11]

Armed with the authority codified in the Basic Law and with control of the country's vast oil income, the House of Saud has entrenched itself in the fabric of the state as few other dynasties have been able to do in modern times. The majlis system originated in the impoverished past, when the people of the Arabian Peninsula were mostly illiterate and their numbers were small enough that a ruler could pay personal attention to them. The system is increasingly irrelevant in the complex, modern state that Saudi Arabia is becoming, but it still generates the impression in many people's minds that the rulers listen to them, which is what the rulers intended.

"I think that what is recognized by the population is that consultation is the primary modus operandi that leads to decision making in the kingdom, that it's not just royal decrees that will fix things," said the affable Prince Turki, who, when I interviewed him, was teaching at Georgetown University. "It has to be taking opinion from different walks of life. Whether it is the ulama, whether it is the family, the council of ministers, the *Shura* [Consultative Council], the business people, the average citizens, and the armed forces. Even in the public majlis, the king will find members of the armed forces coming forward to express a grievance or present a petition on something that's important in their lives. And that's not counting the letters or various other means of communication through which they present their opinions to the king and the crown prince. And so, really, the consultative nature of the society precludes authoritarianism."[12]

That is all true, except for the assertion that the system "precludes authoritarianism." Everyone has an anecdote about a person who took a problem directly to Prince X or Prince Y and saw the matter resolved to his satisfaction.

But the reason all those people are taking their problems to the king, the crown prince, and their brothers, the provincial governors, is that there is no other place for them to go. The religious establishment, tamed by the Al-Saud, follows orders. The armed forces are rigorously excluded from politics. There are no trade unions. There is no elected parliament, and nobody has subpoena power over the ruling family. The king is the final arbiter of judicial matters. There are hardly any nongovernmental organizations (NGOs) that espouse positions on matters of public interest such as the environment. Princes who are not in government positions own some of the country's biggest businesses. Senior princes and their cronies own the newspapers and television stations and appoint the editors. Books, newspapers, and magazines are censored. Discussions of such problems as poverty and crime are permitted, but criticism of the king and senior princes is not.

The state tries to block Internet sources that might introduce objectionable material about religion, sex, or politics, but that is becoming harder to do as computer literacy and Internet access spread. In the summer of 2011, for example, the regime secretly circulated a proposed law that would restrict criticism of the royal family and the religious authorities and impose severe penalties on violators. Someone leaked the secret document to Amnesty International, which posted it on its Web site. The next day the government blocked access to that site, but it was too late—the text had already zipped around the country as an e-mail attachment.

Saudi Arabia has a lively blog culture, but every so often a blogger is arrested, for reasons that are sometimes obvious, sometimes not. The individual always faces the problem that the line of what is permitted is not visible, and sometimes the only way to find out where the line lies is the hard way—that is, by stepping over it and facing the consequences.[13] The reform advocate Fouad Al-Farhan, one of the few writers to blog under his own name, was arrested in December 2007 and held for six months, for reasons that were never specified. After his release, he was prohibited from leaving the country. There have been many other examples.

DISSENT THROUGH RELIGION

Because so many channels of public participation in matters of state are closed, it is not surprising that the few serious internal challenges to the authority of the Al-Saud that have arisen in the past have been based on religion and articulated in religious terms. When expressed as an evocation of religious principles, dissent is difficult to stifle. The most dangerous challengers to the regime have accused the rulers of being insufficiently religious, not excessively so.

This phenomenon can be traced back to the battle of Sabila in 1929, three years before the unified kingdom was created. The ferociously zealous warriors known as the *Ikhwan* (Brothers), who had been the instrument of Abdul Aziz ibn Saud's conquests, objected to his willingness to import infidels for technological assistance and to reach an accommodation with Britain, the ruling power in neighboring Iraq. They wanted to invade Iraq in the name of Islam. The Ikhwan fought it out with Abdul Aziz and his supporters at Sabila and were crushed. Their defeat freed the kingdom's founder to do business with infidels—including an American oil company—in the name of progress for his people.[14] Abdul Aziz was that unusual revolutionary who understood that once he was in power, he was required to run the state. To do so in a land that had neither money nor technology required importing people who brought both.

The other insurrections claiming a foundation in religion were the takeover and siege of the Great Mosque in Mecca in 1979 by a gang that included some descendants of the Ikhwan, and the al-Qaeda uprising that began in 2003. Both groups asserted that the Al-Saud had drifted away from the basic principles of Islam, were too comfortable with Western influences, and tolerated dangerously liberal social trends. The government's response to al-Qaeda has also been expressed in religious terms, labeling the extremists as "deviants" from the true, peaceful path of Islam.[15]

When Saudi security forces were shooting it out with al-Qaeda in 2005, Saudi scholar Abdulaziz O. Sager wrote:

Islamic opposition is not new; it has been the main political driving force in the polity now known as Saudi Arabia since the advent of the twentieth century (and arguably before). It is no wonder, then, that much of the current opposition embraces the same tools and discourse. The other opposition trends, such as nationalists and leftists, who were active in the 1950s and 1960s, had little impact on either state or society, and the current resurgence of opposition in the country has been confined basically to Islamists, with a small margin left to the "liberals."[16]

Because religion is the foundation of the state and the only topic of discussion that is never off-limits, the rulers of Saudi Arabia have tolerated, even encouraged, intense public debate about fine points of the faith. These arguments become a substitute for debate about real political issues, which the rulers do not encourage.

"People in our country are focused on how to pray and how long is your beard," observed Ali Al-Ahmed, a dissident journalist who lives in exile in Washington, D.C. "People's political understanding is very weak. I call it political villagism, a village mentality."[17]

The centrality of religion to public discourse and the fact that the regime bases its power and legitimacy on the faith have resulted in a more or less continuous struggle for control of religious rule making. That is the reason King Abdullah issued a royal decree in the summer of 2010 barring the issuance of fatwas, or religious edicts, by anyone other than the senior ulama, or the official religious authorities who, of course, are appointed by the king. The king can brush off criticism from exiled reform advocates, but opposition expressed in religious terms by people with religious credentials is harder to rebut.

Inevitably, as the country's octogenarian princes leave the scene in the coming decade, the relationship between the rulers and the ruled will evolve because the new rulers will be younger and better educated than their predecessors. The Saudi people are also better educated than in the past, have more means of communicating and organizing, and have much greater contact with other societies. Saudi citizens are demonstrating in many ways that they want more avenues of participation in decision making. They want more accountability from public officials, greater freedom of artistic and cultural expression, more predictability and protection from the legal system, and more opportunities to band together in civic causes—all of which King Abdullah has been giving them, but in small doses. Yet the critics of the regime who are collectively described as Islamists probably outnumber the supporters of the liberal reforms. While they differ in tactics and in their overall vision of the how the state should function, in the aggregate the Islamists represent a formidable barrier to secular tendencies and social overhaul. In these matters, as in education and religion, the challenge confronting the Al-Saud is to encourage modernization without unleashing forces that could bring them down. The regime's first goal is always its own survival.

Religious conservatives who resist all change speak out all the time in

Saudi Arabia, but the advocates of political liberalization do so only spo-
radically. The reformers' numbers are small, their tactics cautious. They
rarely attempt to organize. As Charles "Chas" W. Freeman Jr., a witty former
U.S. ambassador to Saudi Arabia, put it, "The problem in Saudi Arabia isn't
political, it's anatomical: the liberals are born without backbones."[18]

PETITIONS FOR REFORM

Every so often, advocates of liberalizing the political system submit petitions to
the king in which they state political requests. The Declaration of National
Reform, in the spring of 2011, was only the latest example. In general they have
called for modifications to the existing system that would give citizens a voice
in how the state is run: an elected assembly, a constitution that circumscribes
the king's powers, term limits for government officials, and an independent judiciary. These documents rarely have more than a few hundred signatures, and
the petitioners have no means to compel the ruler to pay attention to them.

As the American journalist Caryle Murphy accurately observed, "The petitioners are acting in a generally unresponsive environment." Murphy, who
lived in Riyadh, said that "most Saudis are pleased by the greater social and
press freedoms they have enjoyed since Abdullah became king, though many
express frustration that social and economic reforms are not going faster.
But few Saudis are vocal about pressing for democracy, which does not seem
to be high on their wish list. This is particularly so because of what they see
when they look at their neighbors."[19] They see sectarian violence and political deadlock in supposedly democratic Iraq and Lebanon, an election outcome that split the Palestinians, civil war triggered by an election in Algeria,
and political paralysis in Kuwait brought on by a running feud between the
emir and an elected parliament. To people conditioned to value stability,
those conflicts diminish the appeal of election-based democracy

Similarly, Abdulaziz Sager wrote that "the project of reform has not yet
transcended the elitist discourse and is confined to the intelligentsia. It has provided a general framework without presenting a comprehensive and precise
reform agenda . . . the reformists have been drawn from a wide political spectrum; consequently, they still retain their suspicions toward each other and have
not so far been able to form a solid front." Nothing much has changed in the
power structure, he wrote, because "both jihadists and reformists misjudged

the strength and position of the regime. The jihadists see the regime as highly vulnerable and ripe for collapse," which it is not, "while the reformists see it as essentially still strong but in need of rejuvenating its legitimacy."[20]

Abdullah was the country's de facto ruler for several years after a stroke left his half-brother King Fahd incapacitated. In that position Abdullah began a limited program of political innovation with the creation of the so-called National Dialogue in 2003. It consists of televised public conversations among different groups and constituencies to express views that might otherwise not be heard and among people who would otherwise not be talking to each other. "The gatherings represented a potential break from a decades-old tradition of monolithic discourse," according to a report by the Brussels-based International Crisis Group. "They brought together Saudis from diverse religious backgrounds and political orientations—in itself a first—to discuss with unusual frankness sensitive issues linked to religious differences, education and the causes of Islamic extremism."[21]

Participants in these sessions included some representatives of the long-scorned Shia Muslim community. One session was devoted entirely to the status of women. The gatherings produced some surprisingly ambitious recommendations, including conversion of the Consultative Assembly into an elected legislature and permitting the establishment of labor unions and other advocacy groups. In a speech to the nation announcing that the National Dialogue would become a formal institution of the state, with its headquarters in Riyadh, Abdullah called those recommendations "constructive," but as king he proceeded cautiously.[22]

He has exercised full power only since 2005, when he became king after Fahd's death. That period was difficult in the kingdom: The country had drifted economically for years, security forces were battling the al-Qaeda insurgency, and relations with the United States had frayed after September 11. Some liberal voices were calling for political restructuring. Corruption and extravagance among the princes and their cronies were drawing increasing criticism. Abdullah, already an octogenarian when he became king, was a lifelong product of the system he was called upon to preserve and restructure at the same time.

Abdullah responded to these various pressures with a combination of firmness and symbolic gestures that give the appearance of structural reform. He authorized the nationwide armed crackdown on advocates of violence and allowed hundreds of suspects to be tried in secret. Sheikhs and imams whose public utterances appeared to encourage or condone extremism lost their jobs. Some petition signers and provocative bloggers were arrested and held for months.

At the same time, Abdullah curbed corruption and the atmosphere of impunity around the privileged classes. In one popular gesture, he ordered members of the royal family to pay their cell phone bills instead of ignoring them. He invited women to be part of his official delegation on foreign travels. He appointed the first female deputy minister in the government. He overturned a few embarrassing travesties of justice in the courts and ordered a substantial overhaul of the legal system. And in 2005 he authorized elections for half the delegates to the country's 178 municipal councils, reviving a practice from the era of King Saud in the 1950s.

The elections attracted a great deal of attention because of their novelty. Campaigns were lively, but voter participation was skimpy, apparently because the municipal councils have little real power. A second round of elections, originally scheduled for 2009, was postponed until the autumn of 2011. Both times women were excluded as candidates and voters, but a few days before the 2011 balloting King Abdullah announced that women would be allowed to vote, and run, in future rounds, probably in 2015. The symbolic and social implications of that step greatly exceeded their political impact, because these elections, while billed as part of the king's overall commitment to reform and greater citizen participation in public matters, are an exercise in pseudodemocracy. Like the National Dialogues, they derive not from the rights of citizens but from the sole discretion of the ruler. The elections are not embedded in the institutions of the state, and Abdullah's successors are under no obligation to continue them. Essentially, they are a public relations gesture, as was another of Abdullah's innovations, the creation of an official Human Rights Commission.

This organization, consisting of eighteen members appointed by the king, "shall seek to protect and promote human rights in conformity with international human rights standards in all fields, propagate awareness thereof, and help ensure their application in a manner consistent with the provisions of the Islamic Sharia," according to its charter. "The Commission shall be the government competent body to submit views and counseling on human rights issues."

How could a government agency, appointed by the king, be a credible watchdog? The commission's president, Dr. Bandar Al-Aiban, was not defensive about this paradox during a long conversation in his Riyadh office. The commission's mandate, he said, is "to ensure that human rights agreements that the government is party to are adhered to, that government agencies follow the rules with regard to human rights," and "to initiate human rights reports and represent the kingdom in international forums." Members of the commission make unannounced visits to prisons, he said, and investigate reports of human trafficking. The commission is also mandated to investigate complaints from individuals, he said, and to "help the complaining party with whatever means we can if rights were violated."

Al-Aiban, whose doctorate is from Johns Hopkins University, said it is "wrong to think that people live in a state of apprehension. The real story is that people are going about their business, going to jobs, shops, schools, taking kids to the doctor, living their lives," which is all true. "There are people making extraordinary achievements, in business, science and the economy, well-educated men and women running huge companies," he said. "This is a competitive, fast-growing economy, employing more and more of the Saudi population every day. There are twenty-five universities, and KAUST [King Abdullah University of Science and Technology], an incredible institution, is making an incredible leap into the future. Are we satisfied? No. We still have plans to realize the vision set by the King and princes. There is a lot to do. We have problems, like any other country, but not huge problems."

Al-Aiban objected to the suggestion that Islamic law is responsible for unjust treatment of individuals in Saudi criminal and family courts. "Human rights are spelled out in sharia law," he said. "Anything that is not prohibited and doesn't impinge on the rights of others is permissible. The right to work, to enjoy life and family, to engage in trade, schooling, health care, privacy, travel—all these rights are protected."[23]

King Abdullah also authorized the creation of a nongovernmental, nominally independent National Society for Human Rights, which is headed by a member of the Consultative Council. This organization has done some useful work in opposing underage marriage, advocating women's rights, and exposing the exploitation of laborers, but it has not challenged the governing system itself.[24] A planned public demonstration to demand greater rights in 2010 was called off in the face of stern warnings from security authorities.

MODERNIZING THE LEGAL SYSTEM

Whatever the eventual impact of these human rights organizations, Abdullah's effort to overhaul the legal system may turn out to be the most meaningful and lasting structural reform of his reign. In the past, the court system was essentially an enforcement mechanism for the dictates of Islamic law, as interpreted by judges who were primarily religious scholars. No rule was too archaic or cruel for them if they deemed it a requirement of the faith; no judgment, however illogical or absurd, was too outlandish if they found religious support for it. To attract foreign investment and comply with World Trade Organization requirements, Saudi Arabia has made substantial progress in updating its commercial laws toward world standards, but family law and especially criminal law are cruel and arbitrary throwbacks based on interpretations of the faith that were laid down centuries ago. A Human Rights Watch team that was permitted to visit the kingdom and scrutinize its courts and prisons conducted an extensive analysis and produced this assessment in 2008: "We found pervasive injustices in the Saudi criminal justice system and systematic and multiple violations of defendants' rights. . . . The violations of defendants' rights are so fundamental and systemic that it is hard to reconcile Saudi Arabia's criminal justice system, such as it is, with a system based on the basic principle of the rule of law and international human rights standards." Defendants were held for weeks or months before getting to court, and faced a presumption of guilt. They did not have the right to be represented by a lawyer. Judges were not bound by precedent. There was little consistency in sentencing. There was no right of appeal. The Saudi justice system, the report said, "imposes the death penalty after patently unfair trials in violation of international law, and imposes corporal punishment in the form of public flogging, which is inherently cruel and degrading."[25]

None of that information could have surprised the Human Rights Watch investigators; it was not news. In Saudi Arabia, authorities traditionally have not been motivated by considerations of international standards or constitutional protections for the individual. Their objective is to enforce Islamic law as they interpret it. Any deviation from this tradition is risky for a Saudi ruler, because the conservative religious establishment, whose values the kings claim to share, cherishes the sharia-based legal system. Saleh Al-Lohaidan, former chief of the sharia courts, defended what he called "the most distinguished judicial system in the world, though that does not please some parties, because it is based on an understanding from the book of God, the Sunna of the Prophet and the sayings of his companions."[26]

Abdullah has taken a broader view. He apparently recognized that the Saudi Arabia of his ambitions, a country that aspires to a full place in the community of nations, cannot achieve his vision if the world's news media are constantly reporting travesties of justice and bizarre cruelties in the Saudi courts. After all, under the Basic Law of Government, the king is the person ultimately responsible for what happens in the courts.

In 2007 Abdullah issued a decree that eliminated the Supreme Judicial Council—the clerical body that Al-Lohaidan headed—and established a three-tiered court system, nominally at least independent of the Ministry of Justice. Defendants have a right to appeal verdicts, with the power of final review vested in a Supreme Court consisting of legal scholars. Some judges are to be sent abroad for legal training. The decree ordered the creation of specialized courts for matters of personal status, labor issues, and commercial disputes, raising the possibility that those issues might be judged by people who actually know something about them. The Ministry of Justice has also undertaken a project to codify sharia law and develop a written penal code, eliminating the uncertainty that individual defendants have faced in the past. Abdullah set aside nearly $2 billion to build courthouses and train judges.

According to Andrew Hammond, a British journalist who knows the country well, "No one has said it publicly, but these judicial reforms all aim to train judges in some specializations outside the Hanbali school of Sharia as interpreted in the Saudi context—Wahhabism—and in some specializations outside the realm of Sharia altogether. They thus constitute a direct challenge" to the authority of the clerical establishment.[27] The reason the king wants to limit the authority of the religious establishment is to enhance his own, so the religious establishment will remain a powerful tool of control over the society but not a rival center of power.

In an address to the UN Human Rights Council in Geneva in March 2009, Bandar Al-Aiban summarized the human rights and justice reforms under Abdullah:

During the last ten years, the Kingdom has witnessed reform and qualitative developments through the updating of basic laws and dozens of other legislative instruments, such as the Statutes of the Judiciary, the Code of Criminal Procedure, the Code of Civil Procedure and the Code of Practice for Lawyers, the establishment of numerous institutions and bodies such as the Human Rights Commission and the adoption of a National Strategy to Preserve Integrity and Prevent Corruption. In furtherance of this reform and development process, a few weeks ago a number of Royal Decrees concerning the restructuring of important organs of the State, including the judiciary, the Ministries of Education and Health and the Consultative Council, were also promulgated.

Regarding the court system specifically, he said,

All the judicial institutions underwent far-reaching structural and organizational development, including the establishment of a Supreme Court, appellate courts and specialized criminal, commercial, labor, personal status and other courts. A President of the Supreme Council of the Judiciary was appointed, as well as nine members of the Supreme Court with the grade of President of a Court of Appeal; a Council of the Administrative Judiciary was formed in the Board of Grievances; and seven judges were appointed to the Supreme Administrative Court with the grade of President of a Court of Appeal.[28]

It will be several years before all the changes that Abdullah ordered are implemented and before it becomes clear whether these changes in the legal system will insulate arrested individuals from the arbitrary and sometimes cruel judgments common in the past. These changes may depend in part on who becomes king after Abdullah. The restructuring did not bestow a presumption of innocence on suspects, assure release on bail, or prohibit secret proceedings. Suspected terrorists are locked up in a parallel legal system run by the state intelligence service, and hundreds have been convicted in secret trials and imprisoned with no apparent recourse. Nor did the judicial changes eliminate the institutional bias against women that still pervades the system, devaluing the testimony of females in trials and favoring men in family and child custody cases. There is no prospect of jury trials. As Human Rights Watch noted in another extensive report in the fall of 2010, "The country still lacks a penal code, allowing judges near total discretion to decide what behavior constitutes a criminal offense. For example, judges have continued to jail and sentence people for 'witchcraft.'"[29]

Abdullah provided a substantial amount of money for the court restructuring, but most of the new judges have yet to be recruited and trained, and the new courthouses have yet to be constructed. What can be seen already, however, is that the legal restructuring fits into the overall pattern of the changes he ordered: they have strengthened, rather than diluted, the power of the Al-Saud. The regime has forcefully reasserted its authority over a religious establishment that had become an impediment to the country's modernization, reining in the religious police, shaking up the ulama, and limiting the ulama's control of the legal system. It has also appeased a restive public by expanding personal freedom and accepting previously taboo topics of public conversation, acknowledging the place of human rights among the state's responsibilities, cutting down on corruption and extravagance, and offering conciliatory gestures to previously marginalized elements of the population, including Shia Muslims and the urban poor.

Through these measures, the Al-Saud have created an illusion of liberalization without yielding any real authority. The king still rules by decree. Abdullah's decrees have generally been popular, but the bottom line is that the Saudi people still get what the monarch gives them. If they attempt to organize or demonstrate, the regime's response will be swift and unpleasant.

Gwenn Okruhlik wrote in 2005 that "although meaningful reforms are being implemented, none address the essential question of political power. Genuine political change is absent."[30] Five years later, that was still true. As Toby Jones of Rutgers University noted: "Abdullah's most important domestic accomplishment so far has been the strengthening of his and his family's grip on power."[31]

That being the case, the only perceptible obstacle to the perpetuation of Al-Saud rule is the possibility of an internal power struggle over royal succession and government positions that could pit some family members against others and divide public support, reminiscent of the contest between King Saud and Crown Prince Faisal in the 1950s and early 1960s. Most of the princes running the country today are brothers of those two rulers and remember the harsh lesson of that era: keep family deliberations out of public view, and always present an appearance of unity, lest you cause unrest among the people.

Abdullah is well into his eighties and his designated successor, Crown Prince Sultan, had been ill for years before his death at age eighty-six in October 2011. Their brothers and half brothers are all men of advanced years. Some of their sons, men already in late middle age, are showing signs of impatience for a transition to the next generation of leadership. Because the throne passes not according to age but according to merit and capability—as evaluated by the family—the long-term line of succession is unclear. Saudi Arabia could have three or four new kings in the next ten to fifteen years.

AN ORDERLY SUCCESSION?

Abdullah moved boldly to institutionalize the succession process and ensure that it would be carried out in an orderly way, with disputes resolved in a family council. On October 20, 2006, he issued a decree that established a formal, official succession process. It is designed first to ensure that the choice of any future king meets with the family's acceptance and that disputes and challenges are kept out of public view, and second to stabilize the succession process, which might have unraveled because of a proliferating number of claimants within the Al-Saud family. The law has not been tested, but if carried out as written, it will eliminate the ambiguities and uncertainties that have hung over the Al-Saud family since the power struggle between King Saud and his brother Faisal in the 1950s—and thus remove a possible threat to the regime's continuation.

In the Saudi system the king is also prime minister, an arrangement that dates to the 1960s. Each king has designated a successor, who becomes crown prince and first deputy prime minister. Sometimes the state has also had a second deputy prime minister, who is not automatically in line for the throne but, by virtue of holding that position, has a strong claim to it. Prince Sultan held that position, behind King Fahd and Crown Prince Abdullah, and was promptly promoted to crown prince and first deputy when Fahd died and Abdullah became king.

Under the Basic Law of Government, "Rule passes to the sons of the founding king . . . and to their children's children. The most upright among them is to receive allegiance in accordance with the principles of the Holy Koran and the tradition of the Venerable Prophet." But the law also gave the king the power to choose his successor. What would happen if other princes did not accept the designated heir as the "most upright" was not clear.

In 2009, when Abdullah and Sultan were out of the country at the same time, Abdullah designated Prince Nayef, the longtime interior minister, as second deputy prime minister. Nayef is one of the so-called Sudairi Seven, or full brothers whose mother was King Abdul Aziz's favorite wife, Hassa bint Ahmed Al-Sudairi. King Fahd was one of the seven, as are Crown Prince Sultan and Prince Salman, the longtime governor of Riyadh. Abdullah is not one of the Sudairi Seven; he is their half-brother.

Five of the Sudairi Seven were still alive after Prince Sultan's death in late 2011. The youngest, Prince Ahmed, was born in 1940. The public has long assumed that the brothers were first among equals in the ranks of the princes, and when Abdullah appointed Nayef as second deputy prime minister, some writers depicted his gesture as a way to gain more support from the Sudairis. Nayef's appointment as second deputy made him the likely successor after Abdullah and Sultan, but under the Allegiance Law issued by Abdullah in 2006 Nayef's elevation was not automatic. Nor will the kings who come after Abdullah have sole authority to designate their successors; the law created a committee of senior princes, called the Allegiance Institution, that will have the power to ratify or reject the king's nominee.

The law is intended to cover every eventuality: death of the king, simultaneous death of the king and crown prince, temporary incapacity because of illness, and long-term disability. It created the Allegiance Institution to designate future crown princes. The original members of this panel, appointed by Abdullah in 2007, were sixteen sons of King Abdul Aziz and nineteen of his grandsons. The chairman is Prince Mishaal, the oldest living son of Abdul Aziz, who is believed to have been born in 1926. When he dies, the chairmanship will pass to the next eldest.

Beginning with the first king after Abdullah, each new king will be required to nominate one, two, or three candidates to be his successor. Committee members may accept one of the nominees or reject all three. "If the committee rejects all the nominees, it will name a Crown Prince whom it considers to be suitable," according to a translation of the law provided by the Saudi Embassy in Washington. "In the event that the King rejects the committee's nominee, the Allegiance Institution will hold a vote to choose between the King's candidate and its own."

This process is to be completed within thirty days. In the past, long intervals of uncertainty have sometimes ensued while a new king delayed naming a successor.

The succession law also specifies the procedures to be followed if the king is incapacitated. This provision is clearly intended to avoid a repetition of the uncomfortable period between 1995 and 2005, when Fahd was disabled by a stroke. Abdullah was de facto ruler then, but his power was limited because he was not king; consequently, many important reforms were delayed or set aside during that vacuum. Under the new law, if a committee of doctors finds that the king's disability is temporary, the Allegiance Institution will transfer power to the crown prince until the king recovers. If the doctors say the incapacity is permanent, within twenty-four hours "the Allegiance Institution will certify that finding and invite the Crown Prince to assume the position of King of the country after receiving pledges of allegiance."

Under the Allegiance Law, future kings will no longer have sole power to designate their successors. The fact that the committee can accept or reject a king's preferred candidate may give some princes a voice in the process that they otherwise might not have had. It will allow them to feel that they at least were heard even if their opinions did not prevail and will thus ensure, at least in theory, that whoever is chosen has been accepted by the family as a whole.

In all other respects, the allegiance system is entirely undemocratic; not only does it leave sole power to select the ruler to a small coterie of princes, it excludes all non-royal institutions and individuals from the process. There is no role for the ulama, the Consultative Council, or, of course, the public. The law specifies that no information about the proceedings is to be made public other than the name of the person chosen and that no documents may be removed from the meeting room.

This procedure is more like the selection of a Roman Catholic pope, who is chosen in a secret conclave by princes of the church, than it is like any democratic system. When the cardinals assemble at the Vatican, any one of them in theory could be selected, but most of the time students of ecclesiastical politics—without benefit of actual knowledge—will have listed just a few as "papabile," or probable serious contenders. As with the king's selection, the only information given to the public about the Vatican's proceedings is the name of the new pope. In the same way outsiders reckon perhaps half a dozen of the many sons and grandsons of Abdul Aziz are in the running as future kings, but in truth no one outside the House of Saud knows who might be on the list.

The conventional wisdom among analysts is that princes whose mothers were not native citizens of Saudi Arabia are excluded, but any speculation by scholars, journalists, or think tank analysts about the line of succession is just that, speculation. No one who knows ever talks about this subject to outsiders. Has Prince A been negotiating with Prince B about what job his son might get if he supports Prince B in the Allegiance Institution? Probably, but we will never hear about the negotiations from them.

When the Allegiance Law was issued, Prince Turki Al-Faisal, then Saudi Arabia's ambassador to the United States, used the contract analogy to explain it. He said in a speech in Washington that it represents "a contract between the ruler and ruled. The ruler obliges himself to protect, promote, and enhance the lives and property of the ruled; and the ruled oblige themselves to protect, promote and obey the ruler in everything but that which counters the teachings of God."[32] He did not say how the "ruled" took on this obligation to obey; in fact, they have no choice in the matter. The objective of the allegiance system is not to expand the circle of citizens who have some voice in the selection of the head of state but to ensure that no family feud or palace coup threatens the authority of the Al-Saud regime.

The Allegiance Law does not answer all questions. It says members of the Allegiance Institution must be "capable and known for their integrity" but does not say how those qualities are to be determined. Nor does it specify what happens after the passing of all of Abdul Aziz's grandsons, but that milestone is many years away because some of the grandsons are still quite young. Nevertheless, given the way the House of Saud operates, it can be assumed that Abdullah issued his decree only after extensive discussion with his brothers, and probably some of his key nephews, and that they signed off on it. That means the family will neither allow nor encourage any aspirant from outside the allegiance system to stake a claim when the time comes.

The Allegiance Law thus reinforces the authority of the House of Saud and its prospects for survival. As Prince Turki said in his Washington comments about the Allegiance Law, "We are not in a hurry to experiment with foreign interpretations of democracy or methods of government."

STAYING THE COURSE

In terms of national policy, it probably matters only at the margins who the next few kings will be. Some will be more receptive than others to any American input, but the kingdom's basic approach to oil and gas production, regional security, economic development, inter-Arab politics, and relations with the United States is likely to remain pretty much the same. There is no sign that any prince who might have a realistic aspiration to the throne would alter the nation's course radically in global affairs.

Internally, however, the personalities of the kings to come, their social outlooks, and their willingness to accommodate opposition could determine whether the kingdom goes backward or forward. Some, especially of the grandsons' generation, have sophisticated wives who speak out on social issues. Some are more likely than others to accede to the demands of the religious conservatives. During my most recent visits, quite a few people—especially women—spoke openly of their anxiety about what course Prince Nayef, a career policeman whose primary public role has been to keep order, might pursue on social issues if he were to become king.

Assuming orderly transitions that preserve at least a facade of princely unity, Abdullah's successors will have time to manage the social and economic transitions that are already well under way, but they will have to manage them because it will not be possible to ignore them. As the Saudi people become better educated and more exposed to the world through travel, business contacts, and the media, they can be expected to demand more citizen participation and more governmental accountability. It will no longer enough be to say they can address their issues at the majlis. The country faces social problems for which effective solutions will require input from the public and more effective response from government officials. The outside world got a sense of this situation when a flood that ravaged Jeddah in 2009 was caused partly by official negligence in developing storm drainage. Outraged citizens, linked by the Internet, blamed incompetent government officials. When the press reported their complaints, Abdullah felt obliged to respond to their grievances. A video of vehicles being swept by the floodwaters through the streets was a powerful image when shown on YouTube.

Summarizing the conclusions of a group of experts who conducted an extensive study of the kingdom a few years ago, the scholars Paul Aarts and

Gerd Nonneman wrote that the most probable course for Saudi Arabia is "further reform towards liberalised autocracy" in the short to medium term. Beyond that, they said, "the fundamental status quo may ultimately not be sustainable against the changes and challenges that the system will increasingly face."[33] It is possible, in their analysis, that the incremental and marginal changes that future rulers will inevitably introduce will one day reach critical mass and result in a cumulative impact that will overpower the state and force systemic change, as happened to the Soviet Union under Mikhail Gorbachev.

But it is important to remember that ever since the time of King Abdul Aziz, the rulers of Saudi Arabia have been the ones to introduce modernization and liberalizing changes, often over the opposition of a conservative population, and their regimes have managed these innovations successfully. It was the kings and princes who brought Western technology, secular education, schools for girls, television, public libraries, and social breakthroughs, such as a gender-integrated Riyadh International Book Fair, to Saudi Arabia. The Al-Saud blundered dangerously in taking the country backward after the Grand Mosque uprising of 1979, but otherwise the rulers have displayed great skill at introducing modern technology, tolerating limited expansion of personal freedom, maintaining their religious piety, and doling out enough economic benefits to keep the population from growing restive.[34]

It is of course possible that some combination of royal incompetence, domestic intrigue, external pressure, popular sentiment, and economic failure could bring down the monarchy, as its critics have often predicted, but there is no reason to assume it will happen. The rulers are rich, tough, skillful, and well protected by the United States. They face immense economic and social challenges, but that has been true since the kingdom's founding. For better or for worse, the outside world can assume that the House of Saud will stand—provided that oil revenue continues to flow into its coffers.

2

OIL RICH,
ENERGY SHORT

Modern Saudi Arabia was created out of oil. Money from its vast pools of crude oil financed every development as the country was transformed from a semi-primitive backwater into an industrializing twenty-first-century power. Oil revenue to come is to be the lubricant of the kingdom's ambitions. Saudi Arabia is synonymous with oil; without it, Saudi Arabia is a vast but featureless space on the globe, important to the rest of the world only for its unique position in Islam. What happens if the oil runs out?

Ever since oil money began to propel Saudi Arabia into the modern age in the middle of the past century, that question has been asked most often about the country's growth and long-term stability. What does happen to a nation that derives 89 percent of its revenue from oil when that stream runs dry? The parallel question, of course, is what happens to the oil-thirsty world for which Saudi Arabia is the most important supplier?

In the short term—that is, for the next several decades—those are the wrong questions. From the Saudis' perspective now, the looming threat is not that they will run out of oil but that they will run out of customers for it. Sooner or later, they fear, supply will exceed demand, or the price will exceed buyers' ability to pay it, and the market for their crucial commodity will wither. Pushing that moment as far as possible into the future is the cornerstone of Saudi policy.

Preserving the oil revenue stream is literally a life-and-death issue for the kingdom. Oil revenue pays for the imported food and desalinated seawater that sustain the population. That basic fact of economic life will not change in the next twenty or thirty years, and in the meantime the kingdom plans to spend hundreds of billions of its revenue on an effort to transform itself into an industrial state.

Availability of oil is not an issue, at least not yet. The kingdom has enough crude oil to keep pumping at today's volume for decades, probably through the end of the twenty-first century, and the world's need for it will not diminish much, if at all, in the near to medium term. According to projections by the International Energy Agency (IEA), energy efficiency, population stability, and the development of new technologies such as electric vehicles will reduce oil consumption slightly in industrialized countries, including the United States, but demand will rise in developing countries such as India, China, and Brazil.

According to IEA projections, even under a "new policies scenario" that assumes countries will meet their promises to reduce carbon emissions, oil will remain "the dominant fuel in the [global] primary energy mix" through 2035. The IEA maintains that oil demand will continue "to grow steadily" in that time with Saudi Arabia as the leading exporter.[1] After 2035, the outlook grows murky, and the Saudis know it. Not only is the certainty of oil revenue in doubt, but the country also faces a related shortage of natural gas and electricity that is forcing the country to commit billions of investment dollars to energy projects that may not be sustainable.

On oil, what concerns the Saudis is that global trends over which they have little control will undercut market demand for their greatest asset. A combination of energy-saving technologies, alternative fuels, environmental concerns, and inexorably rising prices that make oil uneconomical raises the prospect that their customers will stop buying. The Saudis often quote a line attributed to their flamboyant former oil minister Ahmed Zaki Yamani, "The stone age didn't end because of a shortage of stone," suggesting that the oil age will not end because of an oil shortage but for other reasons.

The Saudis were not surprised when the U.S. National Intelligence Council, in a projection that reflected the consensus of all U.S. intelligence agencies, said in 2009 that "the most likely occurrence by 2025 is a technological breakthrough that will provide an alternative to oil and natural gas, but implementation will lag because of the necessary infrastructure costs and need for longer replacement time. However, whether the breakthrough occurs within the 2025 time frame or later, the geopolitical implications of a shift away from oil and natural gas will be immense. Saudi Arabia will absorb the biggest shock."[2] This intelligence assessment noted that if oil revenue declines substantially, Saudi Arabia's leaders "will be forced to tighten up on the costs of the royal establishment," but that is the least of their worries. Without oil money, they cannot maintain the schools, hospitals, power plants, mosques, and subsidized services that form the foundation of the princes' contract with the people, let alone support the armed forces and the police and border guards.

In decades past, Saudis of older generations talked airily about returning to a life without oil money. They said that if necessary they would re-embrace the life their ancestors lived for centuries, housed in tents and transported by animals. But most Saudis today have no memory of that life and would not know how to live it. They have grown up in an era of motor vehicles, electricity, and big, air-conditioned cities. It is unrealistic to talk nostalgically of returning to some romanticized past.

The Saudis understand that the oil revenue stream will dwindle at some unknown time in the future. There is not yet a demonstrably feasible plan for sustaining the country without oil money; the grand plans for transforming the economy are in an incipient stage and still untested. Meanwhile, the country has no choice but to keep the oil flowing and the consumers buying.

It is often said that oil is Saudi Arabia's only natural resource, but that is not quite true. The country has phosphates and gold, which are being mined in growing quantities, and it also has the fourth-largest reserves of natural gas, after Russia, Iran, and Qatar. But the kingdom uses all its gas domestically to generate electric power and provide feedstock for its huge petrochemical factories. Most of its export earnings come from oil, which Saudi Arabia must sell to finance the operations of the state.

One reason Saudi Arabia has invested billions of dollars to create refining and gasoline retailing partnerships in oil-consuming countries, including the United States and China, is to lock in a customer base and create a network of mutual interests with consumers. In the United States, for example, about eighty-nine hundred Shell and Texaco gasoline stations in the east and south are owned by Motiva Enterprises, a joint venture of Royal Dutch Shell and Saudi Refining, Inc. The latter is a subsidiary of Saudi Arabian Oil Company (Saudi Aramco), the state-owned oil company that produces and markets almost all of the kingdom's oil. (Unlike Kuwait, which through its Q8 brand puts its name on its retail outlets in Europe, the Saudis are discreet about their downstream operations because of possible political sensitivity.)

"At first our aim [in establishing international sales and refining links] was to make sure we had dedicated outlets for our crude," said Dawood M. Al-Dawood, Saudi Aramco's vice president for marketing, supply, and joint venture coordination and a loyal alumnus of the University of Kansas.

> When you are dealing with customers who have many sources of supply, you want to make sure that you protect your market share. Then we realized that in order for us to be more responsible and more reliable, in addition to profitability, we want to be close to the customers, speaking the language and reassuring the consumers: Saudi Aramco is committed to you, not only through direct supply but there in your own country. . . . It's public knowledge that for every barrel we send to the United States we could get three or four dollars more if we sent it somewhere else. So why are we there? We're not dumb. We are there because we are committed to be responsible and reliable to the people of the globe wherever they are. And we want to make sure that you Americans are comfortable that we are going to be there until the end of the last barrel that we have.[3]

Still, the Saudis recognize that not even ownership of refineries and gasoline stations will oblige customers to keep buying if the product is too expensive and they have other choices. That is why, contrary to the rhetoric of American politicians and contrary to what many Americans believe, the Saudis have strong incentives to keep the price of oil within reach.

For now, "oil is cheap, it is safe, it is reliable and it is abundant," said Abdulaziz Al-Khayyal, Saudi Aramco's senior vice president for industrial relations. "We have no doubt that one day there will be alternatives. It's going to happen one day. I am confident that when that day comes, there will still be oil in the ground. It's not like we run out of oil and people have to go elsewhere." In a world of expanding alternatives to oil and ever-increasing efficiency, Al-Khayyal said, "We want to be able to have our BTUs [British thermal units] compete with other BTUs. Our job is to make sure our BTUs are available, reliable, safe, and environmentally acceptable." In other words, Saudi policy is to keep the supply of oil abundant enough, and the price low enough, that customers will continue to rely on it.

The Saudis call this "energy interdependence" between consumers, who need the product, and producers, who need the money. It has actually been

Saudi policy since the mid-1970s, when Saudi Arabia briefly separated itself from partners in the Organization of Petroleum Exporting Countries (OPEC) that were rushing to drive up prices as rapidly as possible. In response to the price surge, U.S. president Jimmy Carter instituted energy conservation and alternative "Synfuels" policies that today are remembered scornfully, if at all, but they taught Saudi Arabia a lasting lesson: Do not push prices so high that consumers stop buying or turn to alternatives such as oil shale or liquefied coal. That lesson was reinforced by the price surge of 2008, when gasoline hit four dollars per gallon and ignited new interest, especially in the United States, in energy-efficient vehicles and alternatives such as biofuels.

All these concerns surfaced in a sharply worded essay published in the fall of 2009 by Prince Turki Al-Faisal, an experienced observer of American politics since his undergraduate days at Georgetown University. The prince denounced the goal of "energy independence" set by President Barack Obama, many of his predecessors, and other prominent politicians as "demagoguery."

The objective of independence "has become a byword on the American political scene, and invoking it is now as essential as baby-kissing," he wrote. Such appeals represent "political posturing at its worst—a concept that is unrealistic, misguided, and ultimately harmful to energy-producing and consuming countries alike. And it is often deployed as little more than code for arguing that the United States has a dangerous reliance on my country of Saudi Arabia, which gets blamed for everything from global terrorism to high gasoline prices."

Noting that the United States is the world's biggest oil consumer, he said that "there is no technology on the horizon that can completely replace oil as the fuel for the United States' massive manufacturing, transportation and military needs; any future, no matter how wishful, will include a mix of renewable and nonrenewable fuels."[4]

Prince Turki no longer holds any official position and does not speak for the Ministry of Petroleum, but his message reflected the ministry's concerns. Not long after his comments appeared, the ministry's economic adviser, Muhammad Al-Sabban, told an industry conference in Jeddah that the possibility of declining oil sales was "a concern that we need to take more seriously."[5]

For now and for some years to come, Prince Turki is indisputably correct about the United States, which is by far the world's most voracious consumer of oil. A country that was importing about 8.7 million barrels of oil a day when the economy was in recession in late 2009 and more than 10 million barrels a day when times were flush, not counting imports of gasoline, is not going to reduce its import stream to 0 barrels any time soon. Most of the oil that American refiners import does not come from Saudi Arabia, but in the global oil market, the point of origin of any particular barrel is largely irrelevant. What matters to the producers is that total demand remain constant.

By the time Obama had been in office a year, his administration's energy policy was articulated in terms much more in harmony with the Saudi position. In March 2010, Deputy Energy Secretary Daniel Poneman told a Washington audience that "President Obama is determined to put the United States on the path to a low-carbon future." He added:

> We recognize the continuing importance of the oil and gas resources of the Middle East to the U.S. and the world. . . . Even if significant constraints are imposed on the use of carbon, the International Energy Agency has found that global demand for oil and gas will continue to grow over the coming decades. So the United States will continue to seek to assure safe and reliable access to those resources, and to support our companies' ability to do business in the Middle East by promoting open, transparent, and stable rules of the road.[6]

That position fits nicely with the Saudi view. Nevertheless, Saudi Arabia knows it faces a monumental task in maintaining a long-term customer base in a global energy market that is plagued by economic upheavals, political violence, technological uncertainty, and the kingdom's own fast-growing domestic consumption.

Saudi Arabia already consumes the daily energy equivalent of 2.8 million barrels of oil, reducing the amount of oil and natural gas available for export. In 2010 the kingdom became "the second-largest source of expected global oil demand growth," behind only China, according to the International Energy Agency.[7] Put another way, the London-based Economist Intelligence Unit calculated that the Saudis' domestic energy consumption, which was the BTU equivalent of 114.6 million tons of oil in 2000, 153.2 million tons in 2005, and 198 million tons in 2010, will rise to 341.6 million tons by 2020.[8] In the summer of 2011, analysts at Jadwa Investment Group in Riyadh offered an even grimmer prediction: "Domestic consumption of oil, now sold locally for an average of around $10 per barrel, will reach 6.5 million barrels per day in 2030, exceeding oil export volumes."[9]

Part of that consumption is attributable to the country's development. Saudi Arabia needs more fuel every day for its factories, vehicles, electricity generation plants, and water desalination facilities. But much of the demand is attributable to profligate consumption spurred by what the IEA calls "the skewed incentives provided by very low end-user prices." Government-subsidized gasoline sells for about 60 cents a gallon, and electricity, created by burning oil and gas, is virtually given away to consumers. By IEA calculations, Saudi Arabia subsidized the consumption of fossil fuels to the tune of about $38 billion in 2009, or about 18 percent of all fossil fuel consumption subsidies worldwide. Only Iran, with more than twice the population, subsidized consumption more heavily.[10]

Like cities in the American West, Saudi Arabia's urban centers have developed in the age of the motor vehicle; everyone drives, or is driven, everywhere. Other than a new rail line connecting the principal sites of the annual Muslim pilgrimage in Mecca, the only public transportation in the sprawling cities consists of taxis, rattletrap jitneys used by foreign laborers, and some decrepit, fuel-guzzling buses. Households with multiple automobiles are common. Every office, restaurant, and shopping center, it seems, is cooled to temperatures that require sweaters, and nobody turns off the lights when leaving a room. In addition, according to a senior official at the Ministry of Petroleum, a substantial amount of oil is lost to smuggling across the country's porous borders, especially to oil-short Yemen.

Indeed, the British oil company BP distributed an analysis in October 2008 that projected that domestic energy demand and probable declines in production could put an end to Saudi exports as soon as 2025.[11] But is oil production going to decline, as the BP analysis assumed? The Saudis say no; on the contrary, they continue to find new fields and are investing billions to increase production capacity. Their commitment to investment in new fields and facilities, and to effective long-term management of their reservoirs, is not influenced by short-term market conditions. That flexibility is what makes them different from most of the other heavyweights in the industry. The Saudis have much more room to maneuver and much more investment capital than do cash-strapped producer countries—for example, Iran and Venezuela, which are eager to pump out every available barrel—and private companies, which have to justify investment decisions to stockholders and bankers.

According to an analysis published in the journal *Foreign Affairs* in early 2010,

> The security of [global] oil and gas supplies is in question not only because the existing supplies are depleting quickly but also because investors are wary of pouring money into finding new resources. The problem is not geology: technological innovation is more than amply offsetting the deletion of conventional fossil fuels. The problem lies in the massive economic and political risks inherent in new projects, particularly those that supply energy across national borders and thus face a multitude of political uncertainties.[12]

The Saudis say that may be true of everyone else but not of them. Saudi Aramco is immune to the short-term profitability issues that drive Wall Street and tend to discourage risky long-term investments. Originally a partnership owned by four American oil companies and known simply as Aramco, Saudi Aramco was nationalized in the 1970s. The current owner is the Saudi state, which means the Al-Saud family.

"Our spare capacity now is almost 4 million barrels a day," said Al-Dawood. "That's a very expensive amount of spare capacity. Nobody else does that, but we're doing it because we have in the back of our mind that we're not about short-term volatility, we're about long-term focus. . . . We know demand is coming, that's why we're not worried about these little [price] spikes. We are long-term focused, we want to be well-positioned to meet the demand when it comes, so consumers throughout the world don't have to pay more than they should." Or, he did not need to add, so they won't stop buying entirely.

"Our core business and our strength as a company lie in the resource that we have been given the privilege of managing and extracting on behalf of the kingdom in a way that serves the interest of shareholders," said Ali A. Al-Muhareb, Saudi Aramco's vice president for corporate planning. "We manage it on a long-term basis, not with a short-term view, to protect the interests of the kingdom. . . . We are not just a company that goes about doing its business in the traditional manner with some public relations activity that every company has."

According to Al-Muhareb, the oil price spike of 2008 and the worldwide recession of 2009 probably hastened the inevitable transition from oil to other fuels and provoked a bout of corporate self-questioning at Saudi Aramco.

"Where will the world be heading from here?" he asked, ticking off a list of questions.

How are consumers going to behave? People who got hurt, who lost their jobs, how are they going to look at spending? Are people going back to where they used to be on spending? How much permanent change of lifestyle is there of people in the way they conserve energy, the way they look at sources of energy?

You take the U.S. and to a lesser extent Europe. For us the transportation sector is really the key user of the commodity, and you had one event that had tremendous impact on the car industry. How are they going to get out of this, how do they see their future, what are the lessons learned about efficiency, what consumers would want in the future, what type of vehicles, what type of fuel? People who had big cars, the lifestyle they had, how is this going to change? Is it going to spring back, the decline in sales of cars? And to what extent? What are their expectations of car manufacturers?

He posed these as rhetorical questions, but Saudi Arabia requires real answers. Al-Muhareb said that on the one hand, in the industrialized nations a decline in per capita oil use is probably inevitable, but "on the other hand you have major developing economies and developing regions, with a high percentage of the population that don't even have their basic needs satisfied. They are using wood for cooking, animals for transport. They lack the basics, and you will see their energy needs grow. Is Africa going to stay like that? Even in parts of South America there are opportunities for growth, and in the Middle East itself."

Such an atmosphere of uncertainty might paralyze other oil enterprises, the Saudis say, but not theirs. They are committed to a long-term policy of price moderation to sustain demand and of investment in production to meet it. Of course, the Saudis would like to get an additional $10 or even $25 per barrel, just as the fruit merchant on the corner would rather get $1 per grapefruit than 60 cents. They don't attempt to charge the higher price unless they are convinced consumers will pay it. When prices rise in the global market, the Saudis are happy to collect the extra revenue, but they want to limit the price increases in order not to drive away customers.

TWILIGHT OF THE OIL GOD?

A barrel of crude oil contains forty-two gallons. How many barrels are brought to the surface from any particular well depends on subsurface conditions, the extent of the reservoir, the available technology, and the frequency of maintenance. Many smaller wells in the western United States produce less than 100 barrels a day out of small pools of oil that would not even be developed if discovered today because their output would not cover the cost. Giant, world-class fields such as Saudi Arabia's Ghawar, the biggest ever found, produce up to 5 million barrels daily. The kingdom's new Khurais field, which went into production only in 2009, "is the largest single crude oil increment ever commissioned, and will be capable of producing as much oil as the entire state of Texas," according to Khalid Al-Falih, Saudi Aramco's chief executive.[13]

The world consumed about 85.6 million barrels daily in 2008. It is projected to consume 105.6 million barrels a day in 2030 as rising demand from expanding economies such as China and India offsets declining demand in fully industrialized countries, where technology and environmental regulation will reduce the consumption of hydrocarbon fuels.[14]

According to Saudi Aramco executives interviewed in the autumn of 2009, the total amount of oil discovered in Saudi Arabia since the first successful well began producing in 1938 is 742 billion barrels. The total number "lifted," or produced, was 116 billion barrels as of October 2009. That leaves 266 billion barrels of "proven" reserves, or oil that has been identified with certainty, and another 360 billion classified as "probable, possible, contingent," depending on further geological assessment, developments in technology, and capital investment. This category consists of "stuff that will be left in the ground if we don't do anything about it," as one official put it.

Not all oil known to be in the ground or under the sea can be brought up using current technology. The Saudis say their current "extraction rate" in a given field is about 50 percent. Saudi Arabia's long-term goal is to increase the total discoveries from 742 billion barrels to 900 billion and the recovery rate to 70 percent.

It is difficult to know whether the Saudis' supply and reserve numbers are realistic because no outsider is in a position to verify them. The Saudi government owns the oil fields and facilities, and all Saudi Aramco senior executives except the general counsel are Saudis. It is not hard to find skeptics, beginning with the late Matthew Simmons, who before his death in 2010 was the chairman of an American oil consulting firm and a member of the National Petroleum Council.

In 2005 Simmons rattled the oil industry and global markets with the publication of his book *Twilight in the Desert: The Coming Saudi Oil Shock and the World Economy.*[15] His message was stark: "Saudi Arabian oil production is at or very near its *peak sustainable volume* (if it did not, in fact, peak almost 25 years ago), and is likely to go *into decline* in the very foreseeable future. There is only a small probability that Saudi Arabia will ever deliver the quantities of petroleum that are assigned to it in all the major forecasts of world oil production and consumption."[16]

Simmons intensified an academic and journalistic debate that was already under way about "peak oil," or the theory that all the biggest oil fields have already been found and that the world has reached or is approaching the inevitable moment when worldwide production starts to decline, no matter what the Saudis do. Two cofounders of the U.S. chapter of the Association for the Study of Peak Oil and Gas, Steve Andrews and Randy Udall, wrote in 2008 that "it is impossible to predict exactly when production will peak. But the preponderance of current analysis suggests this event is highly likely within the next eight years." The issue, they said, is not that the world is running out of oil; instead, "it's about not being able to grow production beyond a certain level."[17] Similarly, according to Herman Franssen, a prominent energy consultant, "There is no reason to believe that the below-ground and above-ground constraints on higher global oil production may change for the better. They could just as well change for the worse." Franssen cited a statement by Christophe de Margerie, chief executive of the French oil company Total, that global oil production could peak at 90 million barrels a day, which is well short of projected demand.[18]

At the other end of the "peak oil" spectrum is Michael Lynch, an energy consultant who formerly taught at the Massachusetts Institute of Technology (MIT). He dismisses the entire subject as a waste of time. He wrote in 2009:

Perhaps the most misleading claim of the peak-oil advocates is that the world was endowed with only 2 trillion barrels of "recoverable" oil. Actually, the consensus among geologists is that there are some 10 trillion barrels out there. Oil remains abundant, and the price will likely come down closer to the historical level of $30 a barrel as new supplies come forward in the deep waters off West Africa and Latin America, in East Africa, and perhaps in the Bakken oil shale fields of Montana and North Dakota. But that may not keep the Chicken Littles from convincing policymakers in Washington and elsewhere that oil, being finite, must increase in price. (That's the logic that led the Carter administration to create the Synthetic Fuels Corporation, a $3 billion boondoggle that never produced a gallon of useable fuel.)[19]

Lynch's caustic essay scoffed at the "Malthusian belief" that a downward slide in production is coming within a decade. Taking a direct shot at Simmons, he wrote, "Peak oil theory has been promoted by a motivated group of scientists and laymen who base their conclusions on poor analyses of data and misinterpretations of technical material." Peak oil exponents have been propounding their theory at least since 1989, Lynch maintained, alarming the public while ignoring the realities of the oil business.

In the fall of 2009, IHS Cambridge Energy Research Associates, a respected industry consulting firm, attempted to settle this question. Senior Director Peter Jackson wrote a lengthy paper based on extensive analysis of existing fields, known additional reserves, market conditions, and technological advances. His paper said, "Hydrocarbon liquids—crude oil, condensate, extra heavy oil, and natural gas liquids—are a finite resource, but based on recent trends in exploration and appraisal activity, there should be more than an adequate inventory of physical resources available to increase supply to meet anticipated levels of demand" at least until 2030. "There is no shortage of new projects or exploration potential to replenish the hopper. Exploration and field upgrades have tended to replace global production [in] recent years. Exploration is not yet in terminal decline, and while recently some 12 billion barrels of oil has been discovered annually, the five year moving average is actually growing."

What happens after 2030? "Ultimately there will be an inflection point when sustained growth of productive capacity will cease," Jackson wrote. It is arguable whether that "inflection point" is imminent or decades in the future, and what happens after it is reached is also uncertain, he wrote, but "the idea that oil supply will collapse after the inflection point and that oil will run out of the 'tank in the ground' confuses the public. In our view this inflection point will inaugurate a new era—the beginning of an undulating plateau of supply. That, in turn, will last for another two decades or so, before a long, slow decline sets in. . . . Is it imminent or two decades or more away?" Jackson asked.[20]

As the world's largest exporter, Saudi Arabia is naturally at the center of this discussion. The Saudis say that some current producers, such as Libya and Azerbaijan, possibly could deplete their fields in the near future because of overproduction and poor field management practices—it is already happening in Mexico—but they insist that they, along with such newcomers as Brazil and a revived Iraq, will be able to fill the gap. In this they are supported by the U.S. Energy Information Administration (EIA), which projected in 2009 that worldwide production will continue to increase at least until 2030 as new output from Russia, Brazil, Kazakhstan, and Iraq outpaces declining production from countries such as Mexico.[21]

According to Saudi Aramco's Al-Khayyal, "Our proven reserves at today's production will last us eighty years, but we keep pushing that eighty years forward every year because we discover as much as we produce. The eighty-year clock hasn't started ticking." But obviously, if Matt Simmons was right and the Saudis' reserve numbers are inflated, the entire global energy picture changes—as does the vision of Saudi Arabia's future.

Simmons said he reached his conclusions after reviewing Saudi Aramco's own published technical data and engineering reports over several years. Little evidence has emerged since his book came out to support his argument, however, and there appears to be no substantial reason to question the Saudis' figures.

The most outspoken defender of the Saudi reserve figures outside of Saudi Aramco itself is Nansen Saleri. He was a senior official of the company for many years but is now an independent businessman and president of Quantum Reservoir Impact in Houston. Saleri has no obligation to validate Saudi Aramco's numbers.

"I was the primary face of the company, and I know the whole philosophy: It was to show exactly what was going on. And 90 percent of what we were saying was corroborated by external data," he said. "The best judge of the future is past performance; Aramco has never failed to deliver what it has promised. This is not a matter of bravado; it's very much part of the company structure."

Saleri said he was the Saudi Aramco executive who briefed Simmons when the writer visited the kingdom. "I was Simmons's host. I showed him everything, but he already had an agenda. He had already concluded his opinion. What he put down in his book and his speeches was incorrect." He said that "industry people, people with no allegiance to Aramco," have concluded that the official production and reserve figures are mostly accurate.[22]

Another former Saudi Aramco executive, Sadad Al-Husseini, has been depicted in the oil industry trade press as a skeptic about the official reserve figures and projections and as a pessimistic counterweight to Saleri. But in a long conversation in the fall of 2009, he disputed that depiction, saying his views are considerably more nuanced. Husseini, who earned a PhD in geology from Brown University, has inside knowledge of all Saudi Aramco operations because he was the company's executive vice president for exploration and production before he retired. His reputation for skepticism about the country's remaining oil potential, he said, is based not on doubts about its ability to keep pumping at current or slightly higher rates but on doubts about its ability to meet ambitious targets projected by others, especially the U.S. Department of Energy.

In past years, he said, the department and others would write scenarios based on an increase in Saudi output to 20 million barrels a day, or about twice the current production. "The numbers were astronomical," he said. "It was dangerously misleading, and somebody needed to correct this misunderstanding."

That necessary corrective, however, was not the one supplied by Matthew Simmons, Husseini said. "On the one hand, we had this ridiculous inflated expectation, and along comes a banker [i.e., Simmons] who says it's nonsense," he said. "My point is, forget 20 million, it's not going to materialize, but at the same time Matt is wrong. The kingdom does have a heck of a lot of oil and there were many technical errors in his book. I credit him with having said, 'Wake up, guys,' even though I don't agree with his technical conclusion."

According to Husseini, the truth lies somewhere in between. The exploration and production targets set by Saudi Aramco are "good to have," he said, but "I don't think it's achievable, certainly not in our lifetime."

The oil that was easy to find in Saudi Arabia has been found, he said. The oil that was easy to bring to the surface has been lifted. There probably are

300 billion barrels or more still beneath the sand and the sea of Saudi Arabia, he said, but the costs of exploiting those resources will rise rapidly, perhaps to the point where the oil is priced out of the market. This situation is not much different from the experience in the United States, where the easy-to-find, cheap-to-produce oil of Texas gushers is being replaced by expensive, hard-to-produce oil from deep-sea reservoirs and the Arctic.

"When we talk about 700 billion barrels of oil in place in Saudi Arabia," he said, "the first 100 billion were obviously the best, the easiest to produce. As you get deeper into that pool and try to produce more of these resources, it has to be affordable. You're going to need the right costs at the right price. It has to be commercially successful. You have to have the market out there, with no alternatives to oil taking away market share. . . . If we are working on the last 300 billion barrels but meanwhile the world has moved on to something else, there may be no demand for it. So the fact that there is a resource out there doesn't mean that you will actually produce it."

Husseini said, "As the price goes up, it eats up more and more of local GDP [in any consuming country] to cover the cost of fuel." When the price of oil was $30 a barrel and worldwide production was 85 million barrels a day, he said, "you are basically dedicating 1.5 percent of the global GDP to oil. By the time you hit $90 a barrel, at 85 million barrels a day of consumption, you are consuming 4.5 percent of global GDP. So if you are looking at a price that keeps going up, at some point you cannot afford that oil, the global economy cannot afford it. So either the global economy levels off or you go into shrinkage of the [oil] market."

Conservation and new technologies can stave off this day of reckoning for a decade or so, he said, but "that does not remove the original issue, which is continuous growth in population, aspirations for a higher quality of life, continuous demand for modernization for vehicles and logistics, which have historically driven oil demand. You get a 1.5 percent a year [growth in] demand for oil. That is not a lifestyle model that is sustainable; that has to be reduced. People will have to readjust—you cannot live a life that is very energy intensive year after year and expect the whole world to do the same thing and yet have enough resources for everybody to do that. You have to have a reasonable price for fuel."

If the price is not "reasonable," he said, consumers will stop buying, no matter how extensive the producers' remaining reserves. The oil market will reach a point where Saudi Arabia will not be able to sell all the oil it will still have. The thrust of Saudi policy is to drive that point as far as possible into the future.

THE "PERFECT" PRICE

At an OPEC ministerial meeting in December 2009, Saudi oil minister Ali Ibrahim Al-Naimi declared that the world oil price at that time of $75 per barrel was just about "perfect" in balancing the needs of producers and consumers. That is, $75 was giving producing countries enough revenue to meet their needs while keeping the price of gasoline at a level consumers could afford.[23] The price level the Saudis were prepared to live with drifted higher as the global price rose above $100 per barrel in 2011 and consumers kept buying, but if the price stays at that level, it will soon stimulate new efforts to find alternative fuels, to Saudi Arabia's longer-term detriment.

In the view of Saudi Aramco executives and independent Saudi analysts, the price of oil is not the same as the value of oil. The Saudis believe that oil has always been and still is priced at a fraction of its true value after factoring in the costs of exploration, production, refining, transportation, and security. They are alternately annoyed and amused when consumers—especially Americans—complain about gasoline at $4 a gallon. They ask how much a gallon of cooking oil would cost, or shampoo or Starbucks coffee, noting that these products are unlimited in supply and much cheaper than petroleum to produce and ship.

But the Saudis recognize that if the market price rose to reflect the true cost of finding, producing, transporting, securing, and refining oil, it would be out of reach of most buyers, so they take what they can get. It has cost billions to increase Saudi production capacity, and the Saudis say their capacity is now 12.5 million barrels a day, though some independent analysts believe it is little more than 11 million. Either way the capacity is considerably more than actual production. The Saudis say they made that investment in order to be able to stabilize the market in the event of disruption from a conflict or a natural disaster. The Saudis fear instability and market chaos because it drives up prices and encourages consumers to look to other fuels. Even the threat of conflict in their part of the world spooks the market and drives up not just the price of oil itself but also the cost of shipping it and insuring the tankers.

"We can't solve all the world's problems," Al-Muhareb said. "People make a lot of scenarios about the closure of [the Strait of] Hormuz," the narrow exit from the Persian Gulf, where a country such as Iran could presumably disrupt tanker traffic. "But Gulf oil is so important to the world that Hormuz will not be closed for more than a limited period. Even if there are disruptions in Iran or Iraq or wherever, our role is to try to minimize the impact."

These oil company executives are technocrats; they are not entirely free agents in devising and implementing production and investment policies because, after all, the Al-Saud family owns the company. The king appoints the minister of petroleum, who is also the chairman of the company's board of directors, and two senior princes have for many years been prominent officials of the ministry.

The fact that the royal family, whose princely members might not know anything about the oil market, owns Saudi Aramco does not mean that oil policymaking is whimsical or capricious. On the contrary, as the Saudi scholar Nawaf Obaid wrote a decade ago, "Because oil policy has such an enormous effect on the political and economic health of the kingdom, it is not established by the whim of any individual but by the consensus of influential ruling family members after considerable debate and consultation with Saudi experts."[24] Final decision-making authority rests with a Supreme Council for Petroleum and Mineral Affairs, which was established by royal decree in 2000 and is headed by the king.

Most of the time, that setup means the company is allowed to run its business without interference, but there are occasional exceptions, usually when the king has some larger political or social objective that he assigns the company to carry out because he knows it is competent. For Americans, the best-known example of royal policy interference was the embargo on oil shipments to the United States and the Netherlands ordered by King Faisal to punish those two nations for supporting Israel in the 1973 Middle East War. Other instances have had more to do with domestic considerations.

In January 2010, for example, King Abdullah directed Saudi Aramco to assume sole responsibility for constructing a large refinery at Jizan, in the country's southwestern corner near the border with Yemen, rather than waiting for the foreign partners originally envisioned. Economic analysts said the company almost certainly would not have undertaken the project on its own for the same reason the anticipated foreign partners failed to materialize: It is not an economically sound investment. Jizan is on the opposite side of the country from the oil fields, and no pipelines connect the two regions. But the king is committed to economic development in Jizan, a long-neglected region with a large and sometimes restive Shiite population, so he gave the order.[25]

At least the refinery was an oil-related project. A few years earlier the king designated Saudi Aramco as the principal contractor for the development of his pet project, the King Abdullah University of Science and Technology, which opened in 2009. These out-of-mission assignments have a long tradition, going back to the late 1940s when King Abdul Aziz assigned the oil company to build the country's first railroad, because the oil company is more proficient than any other organization in the country at managing large, complex projects.

These occasional diversions may affect Saudi Aramco's bottom line, but only the king and his family care about that. The company's oil operations continue regardless. There are some influential princes and senior officials who would prefer a policy of higher prices, which would mean limiting production; others favor a policy of greater market share. In general, however, there are no extremists on either end, and the constant quest for a balanced policy takes place within a narrow range of possibilities. There is no reason to think that this balanced, technocratic approach will be jettisoned in the foreseeable future.

AN EXTREMIST TAKEOVER?

After al-Qaeda terrorists attacked New York and the Pentagon on September 11, 2001, and began an uprising inside Saudi Arabia twenty months later, there was a surge of alarmed commentary in the United States about the potential consequences if a hostile person or group seized power in the kingdom. What if the resulting government in Riyadh refused to sell oil to the United States?

Such concerns are unfounded for several reasons. First, an extremist takeover of Saudi Arabia is unlikely, as explained in chapters 1 and 8. Second, the United States is not dependent on oil supplies from any particular country. So long as the total amount being produced in the world is approximately equal to global consumption, the origin of any particular barrel is largely irrelevant. Finally, countries that depend on oil revenue have to sell their oil no matter who is running the government, as seen in Iraq under Saddam Hussein and in Iran in the 2010s. By selling what oil they can, even if they refuse to deal with any particular buyer, they maintain the global supply level, freeing up oil from elsewhere for purchase. Saudi Arabia will have to sell oil in the global market regardless of who is in charge. Prices might rise because of fear in the marketplace and some refineries might have to be modified, but oil would still be available. In recent history, when American refiners were not able to purchase crude oil from Libya, Iraq, or Iran, it was because the U.S. government prohibited such purchases and not because those countries cut off sales. Moreover, many countries, including the United States, have built strategic stocks of crude oil to tide them through any short-term emergencies, such as an attempt to block the Strait of Hormuz.

The Saudis are committed to price and supply stability. Demonizing the Saudis when prices do go up is counterproductive. Eventually, other sources of energy will be found and oil's importance will diminish. Reasonable behavior by consumers and producers alike can prolong the transition process and make it manageable, if not painless. The Saudis are well prepared to manage the transition in an orderly manner, but they are less well prepared for the surge in their own domestic electricity consumption, which is exceeding their supplies of natural gas.

TAKING THE LONG VIEW

The Saudis have long argued, with considerable justification, that they and their OPEC partners can tweak world oil prices at the margins by cutting or increasing production, but they do not actually control them. They maintain that speculators in New York and London who buy and sell contracts for oil, not the actual commodity, largely determine prices. For these so-called Wall Street Refiners, price stability is not necessarily desirable.

The Saudis obviously have some ability to influence prices—if they flood the market, prices will go down, and if they trim their output, prices will rise—but their argument about speculation was validated when prices surged in 2008. There was no shortage of supply. The Saudis raised production and promised President George W. Bush that they would increase their production capacity still further, but they could not stop the price escalation by themselves. Prices briefly threatened to approach the point the Saudis most fear, that is, when customers stop buying.

In that episode's wake, the veteran oil minister Al-Naimi delivered a long speech at a conference in Geneva in which he outlined his country's long-term energy strategy. Thematically it was similar to the campaigns undertaken by giant, private-sector oil companies such as BP ("Beyond Petroleum") and Chevron to position themselves as energy companies, not simply oil companies, and simultaneously shape and adjust to new realities in the global energy marketplace. (This phenomenon is not new. Mobil Oil had a solar energy unit in the 1970s, set up at the same time President Carter was promoting Synfuels.)

Al-Naimi has been in the oil business since he was a small, uneducated errand boy in Aramco's early days, when the American partners who owned the company spotted bright, local youngsters and sponsored their educations. Born into a poor Shiite Muslim family in 1935, when Saudi Arabia was one of the world's poorest countries, he went to work at the oil company when he was twelve years old. Coming from an environment where foreign languages and university educations were almost unknown, he earned an undergraduate degree in geology at Lehigh University and a master's degree at Stanford University. He rose through the ranks to become chief executive officer (CEO) of the nationalized company and was named oil minister in 1995. He is a powerful elder statesman of the global oil industry, reporting directly to the king and setting the policies that Saudi Aramco will be assigned to fulfill.

At the Geneva conference, Al-Naimi noted that the stated theme of the event was to "optimize the world's energy mix" in an era of rising demand in the developing world, of increasing concerns about the environment, and of "dwindling fossil fuel resources."

"At our current, average crude-oil production rate," he said, "proven reserves alone are conservatively estimated to continue for approximately eighty years. I emphasize the moderate nature of these estimates, especially in light of evolving exploration and production technologies, and our ability over many years to replace our annual production capacity with new reserves, which could extend the life of these immense resources quite considerably."

He continued, "Now let us look at the world's total liquid energy resources in place, encompassing not only conventional oil estimated [to be] six
to eight trillion barrels, but also non-conventional liquids, ranging from con-
densates and natural gas liquids to tar sands, oil shales and extra-heavy oil,
and estimated at seven or eight trillion barrels or higher." He was referring
to fuel reserves such as tar sands that are known to exist but are expensive
to extract and process and thus are economically feasible only when the price
of conventional crude rises to a point where these less-accessible reserves become competitive.

"These figures tell us," Al-Naimi said, "that while the days of easy oil
may be over, the days of oil as a primary fuel source for the people of the
world are far from over."

He warned against premature efforts to shift substantial percentages of
global energy consumption away from fossil fuels, efforts that he said undercut the incentives for investment in petroleum that make possible the supplies
of carbon-based fuels that the world will continue to need. But he also con-
ceded that concerns about the environment and about the long-term availability of fossil fuels will inspire accelerating efforts to develop alternatives.
Saudi Aramco intends to be among the leading energy companies in that effort. Further, Saudi Arabia, he said, "aims to be a leader in renewable energy
production—specifically as the world's largest exporter of clean electric energy produced from our abundant sunlight." One of the scientific missions
of the Aramco-built King Abdullah University for Science and Technology,
he said, will be to fund and guide a worldwide multi-institutional effort to
improve the technology of converting sunlight to electricity.[26]

"Saudi Arabia aspires to export as much solar energy in the future as it exports oil now," Al-Naimi said at a kickoff ceremony for a multi-ministry research program aimed at fulfilling this goal.[27]

Given Saudi Arabia's immense expanses of sun-baked empty land, it
makes obvious sense to promote solar energy, certainly for domestic consumption if not for export. Worldwide, oil is used mostly as a transportation
fuel and thus cannot be supplanted by solar energy, which generates electricity. The kingdom's desire to develop solar is prompted partly by concern
about the environment but more by a shortage of the natural gas needed to
power electric-generating plants and to provide feedstock for its critical
petrochemical industry.

The acute need for more natural gas is a relatively recent problem. For many years, the gas that came up from the ground along with oil was simply "flared," or burned away, because there was no demand for it. As the country electrified and industrialized in the 1970s, the folly of this waste became apparent, and Aramco undertook a massive project to capture the gas and distribute it to domestic consumers. The result was that gas-flaring emissions fell from 38 billion cubic meters per year in the early 1980s to 3.7 billion in 2010, according to World Bank calculations.[28] In the meantime, Saudi Arabia has committed itself to an industrial future built substantially on petrochemicals and other products that require natural gas as feedstock, so the demand for that gas is outpacing supply. As Al-Naimi told an investment conference in Chicago in April 2010, "We are entering a new phase of integration between the Kingdom's oil and industrial sectors. The early phase of developing basic petrochemicals is behind us, and we are promoting intermediate and specialty chemicals either by integrating the refineries with petrochemical facilities or investing to capture the full value added from our petrochemical potentials."[29]

The country's rapid population growth, urbanization, and commitment to petrochemical development have outstripped the supply of "associated" gas, or gas that is a byproduct of oil production. As a result, oil that ideally would be available for export is burned in some power plants. The country is now investing heavily in an effort to find freestanding gas reserves, so far with limited success.

Al-Naimi told the Chicago gathering that "our investment in the exploration, production and processing of our gas resources has led to a 27 percent increase in reserves and a 60 percent increase in production from 5.3 to 8.5 billion cubic feet per day between 2000 and 2009. Today more than half our gas production is non-associated"—that is, it is produced by freestanding wells, not as a byproduct of oil wells—"and with the completion of the Karan, Manifa and Arabiah and Hasbah fields [the industry's] processing capacity will be more than 15.5 billion cubic feet per day by 2015."

He may be right, but independent analysts are skeptical.

A U.S. Energy Information Administration assessment of Saudi Arabia's gas needs in November 2009 was blunt:

Rapid reserve development is necessary for Saudi Arabia's plans to fuel the growth of the petrochemical sector, as well as for power generation and for water desalination. According to Saudi Aramco forecasts, natural gas demand in the kingdom is expected to more than double to 14.5 billion cubic feet per day (Bcf/d) by 2030, up from an estimated 7.1 Bcf/d in 2007. . . . However, natural gas production (estimated at 2.7 Tcf [trillion cubic feet] in 2007) remains limited, as soaring costs of production, exploration, processing and distribution of gas have squeezed supply, while an estimated 13 to 14 percent of total production is lost to venting, flaring, reinjection and natural processes, according to OPEC and other sources.[30]

As the EIA report noted, the market's demand for oil and OPEC's production quotas limit Saudi Arabia's ability to generate additional associated gas by producing more oil. The Saudis cannot simply pump more oil to collect the gas that would come with it. A trade journal reported in October 2010 that a reduction in its OPEC quota had obliged Saudi Arabia to cut oil production and, as a result, gas production so much that there was an acute shortage of ethane. At that point "stricter allocations of ethane have resulted in the kingdom coming close to running out of feedstock resulting in short-term implications like disruptions to existing production."[31]

The Saudis could abandon the OPEC quota system, but as a founding member of the organization, the kingdom has continued to find OPEC a valuable forum for encouraging market discipline. It is possible, however, that Saudi Arabia will eventually be forced to discard the OPEC system for another reason—namely, its membership in the World Trade Organization (WTO), which generally prohibits price fixing and the cartelization of commodities. WTO regulations do not specifically cover energy, but some in the organization wish to revise the rules to include international energy markets.[32] In any case the Saudi Petroleum Ministry and Saudi Aramco have embarked on a $9 billion project to explore for and develop additional freestanding gas reserves, which can be produced without regard to OPEC quotas.

Still, despite Al-Naimi's professed confidence, natural gas production is barely keeping up with demand, and initial results from explorations in the vast southeastern desert known as the Empty Quarter have not been promising.[33]

"They haven't found any gas in those Empty Quarter explorations," said Brad Bourland, director of research at Jadwa Investment Group and a long-time resident of the kingdom. "And even if they did, it's not economical" for the international companies that are Saudi Aramco's exploration partners there to produce and distribute it. "You have to either pipe gas into the national gas distribution system, where it's sold at a very low price, or you have to create an industry to use your output. In the Empty Quarter?"[34]

"For industry they need gas, which they don't have," said John Sfakianakis, the chief economist of Banque Saudi Fransi (Saudi French Bank), an affiliate of Crédit Agricole. "What are they going to do, invade Qatar?"[35]

THE LURE OF NUCLEAR POWER

The Saudis' industrialization policy and need for export revenue provide strong incentives to limit their use of natural gas and oil to generate electricity. But at the same time the demand for electricity is exploding because of consumer demand, industrial development, and the expansion of energy-gobbling water desalination plants. Over the next several decades, energy from renewable sources may eventually fill some of the gap, but when all these considerations are added up, the obvious conclusion would seem to be the development of nuclear power.

In theory at least, Saudi Arabia is committed to the development of nuclear energy. In 2006 the kingdom joined all of its partners in the six-nation Gulf Cooperation Council (GCC) in declaring an intention to pursue that goal. In May 2008, President Bush promised King Abdullah that the United States would "assist the Kingdom of Saudi Arabia to develop civilian nuclear power for use in medicine, industry and power generation."

In announcing that commitment, the White House said, "The U.S. and Saudi Arabia will sign a Memorandum of Understanding in the area of peaceful civil nuclear energy cooperation. This agreement will pave the way for Saudi Arabia's access to safe, reliable fuel sources for energy reactors and demonstrate Saudi leadership as a positive non-proliferation model for the region."[36]

Two years later, in May 2010, the king issued a decree ordering the creation of a new center, the King Abdullah City for Atomic and Renewable Energy, to preside over the development of nuclear and solar power. "The City's goal," the decree said, "is to contribute to sustainable development in the Kingdom by using science, research and industries related to renewable atomic energy for peaceful purposes. . . . The City will be the concerned authority to fulfill national commitments pertaining to all agreements the Kingdom has signed or will sign regarding atomic and renewable energy. It will be responsible for supervising and monitoring all work related to the use of atomic energy and the resultant radioactive waste." The decree also stipulated that the work of the kingdom's existing Nuclear Energy Research Center would be transferred to the new organization.[37]

King Abdullah's decree appears to represent a serious commitment to moving forward with the development of a civilian nuclear energy program. If so, Saudi Arabia would face few of the constraints that have hindered nuclear power development in the United States and Europe since the 1980s. It has the money, and there is unlikely to be any serious political or environmental opposition. Unlike Japan, the kingdom has plenty of open space in remote regions where an accident would pose no threat to the public. Still, it will not be easy to find appropriate sites because some areas that might otherwise be desirable may be geologically unsuited to nuclear plant development.

Dr. Abdullah Al-Amri, professor of geophysics at King Saud University, said his extensive surveys have found that the Gulf coast is "quite unstable seismically," and indicators of potential volcanic activity exist along the Red Sea's coast. Deep in the desert between Riyadh and Jeddah is a formation known as the Arabian Shield that is "one of the most geologically quiet places in the world" and thus could safely support nuclear plants, he said, but the area has no water to cool the reactors and spent fuel ponds. Large quantities of seawater would have to be pumped at least thirty miles inland.[38]

On a smaller scale, Abu Dhabi confronts energy requirements and constraints similar to those in Saudi Arabia and has awarded contracts to a South Korean firm to build nuclear power plants. Unlike its small neighbor, the kingdom is at least a decade away from construction. In June 2010, the Finnish firm Pöyry Energy Consulting announced that King Abdullah City for Atomic and Renewable Energy had selected it to "help prepare a draft of the national vision and high-level strategy in the area of nuclear and renewable energy applications" for the kingdom. Company officials said at the time that their mandate was to help Saudi Arabia decide what its future mix of fuels would be and that nuclear energy, if included, was a long-term proposition.[39] In a trade press interview after the announcement, David Cox, a Pöyry executive based in Britain, was quoted as saying that the Saudi nuclear program could eventually include enrichment of its own uranium. That is doubtful, if not out of the question. Saudi Arabia is not known to have extensive uranium

reserves, but even if it did, it would be unlikely to undertake a domestic enrichment program because it would drag the country into unwanted contro-
versies about nuclear weapons.[40] (See chapter 10.) The kingdom subsequently
reached nuclear cooperation agreements with France and China as well.

Meanwhile, at the same Chicago conference where Ali Al-Naimi spoke in
April 2010, Ali Saleh Al-Barrak, chief executive of the Saudi Electricity
Company, said the country had 45 gigawatts of installed generating capacity at the time, but it would need 70 gigawatts by 2020 because annual demand grows at about 7 percent. Complicating the planning to meet that
demand is the immense disparity in usage between summer, when air conditioners are running, and winter, when temperatures are comfortable.

In 2010 dollars, he said, Saudi Arabia will need at least $80 billion to
build the required generating facilities and transmission lines. "We have a
long way to go to achieve what we want," he observed.

He said generating plants with total capacity of 25 gigawatts were under
contract or in varying planning stages. All of them, he said, will be fueled by
oil or natural gas or some combination of the two. When I asked him what
the fuel mix would be for later generating plants, after those already on the
drawing board are built, he replied, "We ask ourselves that every day."

At about the same time as the Chicago conference, the International
Energy Agency noted that Saudi Arabia had sharply increased the burning of
unrefined crude oil, rather than heavy fuel oil, in existing power plants. This
action reflects what the IEA called Saudi Arabia's "limited success" in finding new sources of natural gas, but it probably has some environmental benefit because crude pollutes less than heavy fuel oil does. However, the agency
said, it "effectively reduces that country's nominal spare [oil export] capacity. More importantly, perhaps, it leaves unaddressed the issue of runaway
power demand, which has been largely due to highly-subsidized end-user
prices."[41]

That bureaucratic language was the IEA's way of saying that electricity is
so cheap in Saudi Arabia that people don't care how much they use and have
no incentive to conserve. Most residential consumers are billed 0.12 riyals per
kilowatt-hour, or about three cents. Many economic analyses have concluded
that the government should raise the price, incrementally if not all at once,
to reflect the true cost of the product. The retail price is not about economics, however; it is about the country's fundamental bargain between the rulers

and the ruled. Citizens of Saudi Arabia pay no taxes. Education and health care are free. And essential commodities such as water, electricity, and gasoline are discounted almost to the giveaway point, all to allow the people to benefit from the oil wealth. The price the rulers extract for this largesse is political acquiescence. Withdrawing the subsidies would entail a risk that the rulers so far have been unwilling to take, although circumstances may soon force their hand.

And so they forge ahead, producing ever more oil, urgently searching for gas, and substantially investing in energy projects for as far into the future as can be envisioned. So long as the oil money flows in, they can probably afford it.

3

HUNGRY PEOPLE, THIRSTY LAND

On the broad highway that runs southeast from Riyadh, the capital of Saudi Arabia, it takes less than an hour to reach the beginning of farm country. The industrial zones end, and suddenly date palms are growing on both sides of the road, not in the random patterns of an oasis but in the long straight rows of cultivated orchards. Then the first chicken hatchery appears, and soon patches of green vegetables and alfalfa are visible. East of the farm town of al-Kharj are vast operations of corporate agriculture, such as Al Safi, the world's largest dairy farm, and Almarai, a dairy and juice conglomerate whose slogan—"Quality You Can Trust"—is posted prominently in English.

The landscape bears no resemblance to Iowa or Egypt's Nile Delta; it is unmistakably a desert and hardly looks promising for farming. But agriculture is big business in Saudi Arabia, from Hail in the north to the valleys near Taif in the west to the terraced hillsides of the southwest. Decades of government subsidies and irrigation with water pumped out of caverns deep underground have made it all possible. In 2008 agriculture accounted for nearly 5 percent of the country's annual GDP and employed about 12 percent of the labor force.[1] By 2011, rising oil output and changing government farm policies had reduced agriculture to 2.7 percent of GDP,[2] but paradoxically its relative importance to the national well-being was increasing.

Saudi state television's *This Is Our Country* program features a documentary celebrating the achievements of Saudi agriculture: self-sufficiency in wheat and poultry; impressive harvests of figs, grapes, and citrus fruits; increasing production of olive oil. The so-called Desert Kingdom is self-sufficient in potatoes—and that is saying a lot, given the amount of french fries consumed at the ubiquitous fast-food restaurants—and even produces flowers for export.

The vast ambitions of the Saudi government and of the country's agricultural entrepreneurs were reflected in the statistics compiled by one historian:

> Between 1970 and 1989 the annual production of fruit and vegetables increased from 706,000 to 2,600,000 tons; of dairy products from 156,000 to 500,000 tons; of poultry meat from 7000 to 226,000 tons; and of eggs from 5000 to 103,000 tons. This was more than enough to meet domestic demand. The surplus was exported. . . . Within the short period 1986–90 the area under cultivation grew from 5.7m [million] to 7.4m hectares. The wheat harvest rose from 3.5m tons in 1990 to 4m tons in 1991. . . . Agriculture's share in GDP grew from 3.3 % in 1985 to 6.6 % [of a larger GDP] in 1990.[3]

A hectare, a measure of land area commonly used outside the United States, equals 2.47 acres.

Nevertheless, only about 2 percent of the country's enormous land mass is arable, even with intensive irrigation and modern farming technology. Even in the lush decades when its agriculture was prospering, Saudi Arabia still depended at least partially on imported food. Now that dependence is increasing as the young population continues to grow at a rate that outpaces food production. Facing a probable 77 percent growth in its population by 2050, Saudi Arabia is grappling with the realization that its arid soil and dwindling water supply will be insufficient to feed all those people.[4] As a mostly barren land in a mostly barren region where populations are growing fast, Saudi Arabia faces a looming demand for food that it cannot satisfy on its own, a demand that at the very least will require a vast commitment of capital and at worst could provoke a conflict between the kingdom and its neighbors. A quest for "food security," in a world where competition for food can only increase, has moved to the top of the Saudi planning agenda.

It is easy to assume that Saudi Arabia could buy and import whatever food it needs, but it is not that simple. The global commodity crunch of 2007 spooked the Saudis when India, their main supplier of rice, temporarily banned exports because of its own shortage, and the prices of corn and other grains spiked upward. The Saudis are heavy consumers of rice, which is all imported. As prices rose for the long-grain basmati rice that Saudi consumers favor, the government granted a subsidy of $267 per ton in an effort to stabilize the market but canceled it two years later upon discovering that it was benefiting exporters more than it helped Saudi consumers.[5]

It seems obvious that given the amount of cash at its disposal per unit of population Saudi Arabia would be able to deal with such a problem better than most other countries could; but despite their oil wealth, the worldwide shortage prevented the Saudis from purchasing all the rice they needed. Imports fell from 958,000 tons in 2006 to 914,000 tons in 2007.[6] That development augmented a mistrust of markets that can be traced to President Jimmy Carter's cutoff of U.S. grain sales to the Soviet Union after the 1979 invasion of Afghanistan. In 2007 and 2008, food-driven inflation imposed real hardship on the millions of Saudis who live below the official poverty line and became a political issue, to the extent that there are political issues in the kingdom.[7] A new commodity price surge in 2011 ignited serious inflation in the Saudi marketplace, reinforcing the government's concern.

Combined with a growing awareness that the country has mismanaged its limited supplies of water, the commodity squeeze prompted Saudi Arabia to change its agricultural policies. The government has abandoned its aggressive campaign for self-sufficiency; scrapped support for crops that consume large amounts of water, such as wheat and alfalfa; and increased support for organic farming and vegetables for human consumption. The generous subsidies that enabled a country without any rivers or lakes to become the world's sixth-largest exporter of wheat are being phased out. No longer does the government support easy access to its reserves of fossil water, the underground aquifers from a previous geologic age that delivered water to a thirsty earth. The fossil water is like the country's oil; when it is used up, it is gone. There is no replenishing spring or mountain runoff.

Reducing the amount of water allocated to agriculture requires difficult choices, not just environmentally and economically but also politically. It makes little sense for Saudi Arabia to provide water for giant dairy farms, for example, when each cow requires 50 to 70 gallons a day for drinking and sanitation; but influential, well-connected families own the big dairies in Saudi Arabia.[8]

Nevertheless, the Agriculture Ministry is trying to promote scientific water management, water-conserving drip irrigation, and an end to the production of crops for cattle feed—or "more crops for less drops," as Agriculture Minister Fahd Bulghanaim puts it.[9] In a program that has stirred global controversy, the government also is encouraging private Saudi corporations to seek food security by developing farm resources in land-rich, cash-poor countries around the world. In effect, the Saudis plan to explore for land and to produce food overseas the way American and other Western companies once explored for oil in the Arabian Peninsula.

With its new policy, Saudi Arabia is attempting to strengthen its position in what seems certain to be a growing competition for food among the nations of the Middle East, including Iran and Iraq. Iran, Saudi Arabia's principal rival for regional influence, is already a major importer of rice and wheat.

Among the relative certainties that the world will encounter over the next decade or so, according to the U.S. government's intelligence experts, is that "continued economic growth—coupled with 1.2 billion more people by 2025—will put pressure on energy, food and water resources. The number of countries with youthful populations in the 'arc of instability' [including the Middle East] will decrease, but the populations of several youth-bulge states are projected to remain on rapid growth trajectories. The potential for conflict will increase owing to rapid changes in parts of the greater Middle East and the spread of lethal capabilities."[10] In the same vein, the director general of the Arab Organization for Agriculture Development, Tareq Al-Zadjali, has projected that the Arab countries collectively will need to invest $144 billion in agriculture projects between now and 2030 to ensure sufficient food production for their populations. Spending on that scale will require substantial participation from private investors, he said, because it is beyond the capabilities of the Arab governments.[11]

As Zadjali's analysis indicated, Saudi Arabia is hardly alone in its food supply predicament. All of its partners in the regional organization known as the Gulf Cooperation Council—Bahrain, Kuwait, Oman, the United Arab Emirates (UAE), and Qatar—are confronting the same perilous combination of rising population, higher per capita consumption of more sophisticated foods, dwindling water supplies, and global competition for commodities. For all six countries, "food inflation presents a potentially considerable socioeconomic risk which the authorities are poorly equipped to deal with," according to a detailed assessment issued in March 2010 by NCB Capital, the investment unit of Saudi Arabia's National Commercial Bank. "Given their high import dependency, a failure to source sufficient quantities of food represents a major security concern for the GCC nations."[12]

In a long-term comprehensive planning document, the Saudi Ministry of Economy and Planning in 2003 asserted confidently, "We managed to achieve total food security in less than a generation."[13] By 2009 that confidence had vaporized. Instead, according to a Ministry of Commerce and Industry presentation at an international conference in Austria, "the Kingdom's leadership vision is focused on facing the world food crisis by taking sustainable measures and securing food supplies for the Kingdom's citizens and residents."[14]

In January 2009, King Abdullah proclaimed a "Food Security Initiative," backed by an investment fund of 3 billion Saudi riyals (about $800 million), to support investment by private-sector Saudi companies in agricultural projects abroad. According to the government, "The King Abdullah Initiative for Saudi Agricultural Investment Abroad aims at contributing to realizing national and international food security, building integrative partnerships with countries all over the world that have high agricultural potential to develop and manage agricultural investments in several strategic crops at sufficient quantities and stable prices in addition to ensuring their sustainability."[15] In plain English, the Saudis intend to use their capital to develop farm projects in countries that have agricultural potential but lack the money to acquire the irrigation pumps, tractors and harvesters, fertilizer, farm-to-market roads, and refrigerated warehouses needed for major increases in output.

Among the two dozen targeted countries are Sudan, Ethiopia, Vietnam, the Philippines, Mozambique, Poland, and Ukraine. The prominent Saudi businessman Mohammed al-Amoudi has already committed his Saudi Star Agricultural Development Company to invest in the cultivation of rice and other crops on 1.2 million acres in Ethiopia.[16]

The crops developed through these investments would be exported, in whole or in part, to Saudi Arabia. Some portion would be used to establish what the government calls a "strategic reserve for basic food commodities"—including rice, wheat, and barley—"which satisfies the Kingdom's needs for food and avoids future food crisis."[17] The Saudi government has commissioned a team from the Agriculture, Foreign Affairs, Finance, and Commerce and Industry Ministries to implement the Food Security Initiative.

This program and similar efforts by other cash-rich, farmland-poor countries have stirred fears of a "land grab" reminiscent of the colonial era when European countries took over tropical lands to grow sugar and rubber. Media reports worldwide, circulated by the farmlandgrab.org Web site, have depicted these programs as a threat to peasants and indigenous populations of potential target countries, especially those in sub-Saharan Africa. Because some of these countries are themselves dependent on food imports, any plans to grow crops for export there are extremely sensitive politically.

When the first cargo of rice from a Saudi-financed farm in Ethiopia was delivered in March 2009, London's *Financial Times* pointed out that "in the past year the United Nations World Food Programme has helped to feed 11 million people in Ethiopia, which has suffered crop failures and food distribution problems."[18] How could food exports from such a country be justified?

"Land Grab: The Race for the World's Farmland" headlined an article in the *Independent*, another British Newspaper. "Neo-colonialists are buying up agricultural land in Africa—and local farmers could be crushed unless there are international rules to protect them." The article described what it called "a frantic rush," led by Saudi Arabia and the United Arab Emirates, "to gobble up farmland all around the world, but mainly cash-starved Africa."[19] In late 2010 the *New York Times* reported on its front page that "across Africa and the developing world, a new global land rush is gobbling up large expanses of arable land. Despite their ageless traditions, stunned villagers are discovering that African governments typically own their land and have been leasing it, often at bargain prices, to private investors and foreign governments for decades to come." The article said that "critics condemn the deals as neocolonial land grabs that destroy villages, uproot tens of thousands of farmers and create a volatile mass of landless poor."[20]

Well aware of the sensitivity of the issue, the Saudis say their intentions are benign and that their investments can help the target countries as well as themselves by increasing crop yields enough both to free up food for export and to feed the local people. What the Saudis see are large tracts of potentially productive land, with access to water, where yields fall far short of their potential because local farmers lack the capital to buy tractors and trucks, to install irrigation pumps and pipes, and to purchase fertilizer, and because the local government lacks the funds to build a road to the nearest port and storage facilities for the crops. If the Saudis provide the money to do all that work and realize a large increase in yields, they could share the increase with the local people, and both sides would benefit.

"Our policy is to help countries that have land and water," said Abdulaziz Al-Howaish, general director of the Agriculture Ministry's international cooperation department. "We have the technology and capital. We will help them to produce, for them and for us."

According to Al-Howaish, "Saudi investors are following the direction set by His Majesty: it should be a matter of mutual interest and emphasize the interest of local people. It is not just a land grab. We want it to be sustainable, to look at what the local people need. There should always be a clause that part of the output should go to local people if they need it."[21]

"We have a shortage of water and [we have] experience in agriculture, know-how, something to share with others," said Deputy Minister of Commerce for Foreign Trade Abdullah Al-Hamoudi. He described the program's objective as "to participate in feeding the world and to build our strategic reserve, and to build the local market" in target countries.[22]

"We're not talking about a land grab, we are talking about investment in food supply," said Usamah Al-Kurdi, a member of King Abdullah's appointed Consultative Council and an investor in the International Agriculture and Food Investment Company, formed in 2009 to participate in the food security program.

> Who is talking about buying land? We are talking about buying from farmers, producing food. The concept of buying land is wrong, in the same way that foreign oil companies don't own the land where they produce oil. It's investment of capital and technology. You invest, you buy from local farmers and produce there. This includes investment in infrastructure—irrigation, farm-to-market roads—and thus creates jobs. The idea is to participate in providing food for the world, not just Saudi Arabia.

In his view, the political problem of exporting food from countries that depend on food imports is manageable if the issue is explained correctly to the local people. Just as Egypt exports expensive, long-staple cotton to raise hard currency and uses the money to buy cheaper cotton for clothing and towels, he said, "The Philippines is one of the biggest rice importers, but there would be nothing wrong with exporting long grain rice if the people there prefer short grain and you import more of that."[23]

The UN Food and Agriculture Organization (FAO) prepared a framing paper for the World Summit on Food Security in Rome in November 2009 that summarized the issue:

> Certainly, complex and controversial economic, political, institutional, legal and ethical issues are raised in relation to property rights, food security, poverty reduction, rural development, technology and access to land and water. On the other hand, lack of investment in agriculture over decades has meant continuing low productivity and stagnant production in many developing countries. Lack of investment has been identified as an underlying cause of the recent food crisis and the difficulties developing countries encountered in dealing with it. FAO estimates that gross annual investments of USD209 billion are needed in primary agriculture and downstream services in developing countries (this is in addition to public investment needs in research, infrastructure and safety nets) to meet global food needs in 2050.[24]

If the world's expected population of 9.1 billion people is going to have enough to eat in 2050, FAO calculated, "food production will have to increase by 70 percent."[25]

FAO has concluded that international farm investment deals could be advantageous to all parties, but after an examination of existing projects, it has also issued stern warnings against potential pitfalls:

> Although on paper some countries have progressive laws and procedures that seek to increase local voice and benefit, big gaps between theory and practice, between statute books and reality on the ground result in major costs being internalised by local people—but also in difficulties for investor companies.
>
> Many countries do not have in place legal or procedural mechanisms to protect local rights and take account of local interests, livelihoods and welfare. Even in the minority of countries where legal requirements for community consultation are in place, processes to negotiate land access with communities remain unsatisfactory. Lack of transparency and of checks and balances in contract negotiations creates a breeding ground for corruption

and deals that do not maximise the public interest. Insecure use rights on state-owned land, inaccessible registration procedures, vaguely defined productive use requirements, legislative gaps, and compensation limited to loss of improvements like crops and trees (thus excluding loss of land) all undermine the position of local people.[26]

According to the Saudi government, King Abdullah's initiative is intended to address exactly that challenge. As government officials and potential Saudi investors have outlined, the program would be a partnership between the Saudi government and private business. The Saudi government would negotiate agreements with host countries, setting the terms of investment and specifying the conditions under which the host country could cut off exports in emergencies. Through the state-owned Saudi Company for Agricultural Investment and Animal Production, established in 2009, it would also provide aid to the host countries to build roads and other infrastructure projects needed to facilitate farm development. It would be up to private Saudi companies to lease the land, hire local workers, provide equipment and fertilizer, and move the crops to market.

According to Taha Al-Shareef, a Ministry of Commerce delegate to the four-ministry management committee, the team established the principles of this initiative.

> The countries have to have an abundance of land and water. The private sector is the main investor, supported by the government, which is willing to provide financial and credit support and make some kind of agreement with the investors, and [to negotiate] a bilateral agreement with the host countries to ensure the safety of the investment. Just like any other foreign investment in any foreign country, you have to guarantee the safety of that investment. Also leaving some of the crop or commodity in the host country; and to agree with the host country on what are the crops to be raised.

The team's "target products," he said, are rice, wheat, barley, maize, soybeans, oil seeds, sugar, animal feed, livestock, and fish.[27]

This idea is not entirely new. Egyptians have long fantasized about what they could do if they could marry their agricultural expertise to Libyan capital and Sudanese land, and the Saudis are hardly alone in their anxiety about future food supplies. In its *Global Trends 2025* report, which represents a synthesis of the view of all the U.S. government intelligence agencies, the U.S. National Intelligence Council said that "experts currently consider 21 countries with a combined population of about 600 million to be either cropland or freshwater scarce. Owing to continuing population growth, 36 countries, home to about 1.4 billion people, are projected to fall into this category by 2025. . . . Lack of access to stable supplies of water is reaching unprecedented proportions in many areas of the world and is likely to grow worse owing to rapid urbanization and population growth."[28]

Other studies have reported that competition for access to commodities is also being stoked by conversion of cropland to biofuel production and by a growing number of people worldwide with enough money to purchase food beyond their traditional diets. They will buy imported dairy products, for example, instead of what is available from family-owned livestock.

LAND GRAB, WATER GRAB

As a recent Canadian study of the farmland investment phenomenon noted, "Access to land without water is pointless for agricultural investments. In essence, what are often described now as land grabs are really water grabs: the purchase or long-term lease of land in order to obtain the water rights that come with the land under domestic law or with the investment contract itself."[29]

If there is any country that has "land without water," it is Saudi Arabia, and the Saudis recognize that they have mismanaged what little water they have. The wheat subsidy program that enabled Saudi Arabia to become the world's sixth-largest exporter, for example, sucked up billions of gallons of nonrenewable fossil water and shipped it out of the country. Some studies have found that as much as 40 percent of the water sent through the country's pipes and water mains is lost to leakage and evaporation. And with economic development has come increased use of water for modern bathrooms, washing machines, and dishwashers.

The kingdom has invested more than any other country in the desalination of seawater, but almost all water produced through desalination is needed for human consumption, which means that most of the water for crops and livestock comes from the fast-dwindling fossil reservoirs. "Today,

the Kingdom is the largest producer of desalinated water in the world, manufacturing nearly 3 million cubic meters of water daily," according to a recent report by the U.S.–Saudi Arabian Business Council, which promotes
bilateral trade and investment. But demand "is expected to reach 10 million
cum/d [cubic meters per day]," or more than triple current capacity, the report said.[30]

Water relief is not available from Saudi Arabia's mostly arid neighbors.
According to a Population Reference Bureau study, "Twelve of the world's
15 water-scarce countries"—that is, those that have "less than 1,000 cubic
meters of renewable fresh water per person per year"—are in the Middle East
and North Africa. Even neighboring Iraq, watered since the beginning of history by the Tigris and Euphrates Rivers and formerly a food exporter, is now
plagued by drought and must import food because upstream, Syria and
Turkey use more of those river waters for themselves. "Falling agricultural
production means that Iraq, once a food exporter, will this year have to import nearly 80 percent of its food," the *Los Angeles Times* reported in 2009.[31]

For all these reasons, a consensus has emerged in Saudi Arabia about the
need to recast its agricultural policies. Wheat exports have ceased, and production is being reduced by 12.5 percent a year and is scheduled to end in
2016. To reduce consumption of barley, of which the country is already the
world's biggest importer for animal feed, the government is offering subsidies
to dairy farmers and the owners of sheep and goats to switch to a high-protein
manufactured feed. Vegetable production is shifting from open fields, where
water evaporates, to greenhouses.

Eliminating the wheat subsidies was a difficult decision for the government because it represented a large-scale failure of a policy to which the kingdom had been committed for three decades. The subsidies for wheat and
other crops originally were conceived less as a stimulus to food production
than as a means of keeping rural populations in place. That battle has largely
been lost as the population has migrated to the cities. Moreover, the wheat
subsidy program was riddled with fraud. Wheat merchants passed off imported wheat, which was not subsidized, as a domestic product in order to
collect the subsidy, and city-dwelling landowners collected subsidies for
farms they rarely visited.[32]

With the subsidies on their way out, Saudi Arabia resumed importing
wheat in 2009 after a hiatus of more than twenty-five years. By 2016, when

all subsidies have been eliminated, the country will need to import about 3.5 million metric tons per year.[33]

The policy revisions do not mean that the government is reducing its overall support for agriculture. On the contrary, according to the U.S.–Saudi Arabian Business Council, it has "earmarked more than $28 billion worth of agricultural investment projects through 2020."[34] But it is changing the mix of crops and products it will support to emphasize those that consume less fresh water—"diversifying production away from water-intensive crops, such as barley and wheat, while encouraging the cultivation of dry climate foodstuffs," as the Business Council put it. One of the government's stated objectives is to become the world's biggest exporter of shrimp through aquaculture projects on the Red Sea coast—an unlikely prospect considering the amount of shrimp produced in China and Thailand.

Despite some grumbling from landowners who were cashing in on the wheat program, the big farmers appear to have accepted most elements of the revised policies. But there is a good deal of vocal opposition from business executives and economists who doubt whether the foreign investment program is feasible or even truly necessary. They say that investing in unstable countries such as Sudan is more trouble than it is worth and that the better solution would be to strike long-term purchase deals with reliable suppliers such as Canada and Australia. Saudi Arabia might well have to compete with other buyers for such deals, they argue, but the kingdom has the money to outbid them.

"In these foreign investments, in Sudan or Ethiopia or Ukraine, who is going to secure the investment against political risk or flood or whatever?" asked Fawaz Al-Alamy, who negotiated Saudi Arabia's entry into the World Trade Organization and is now a director of a major food and food-processing company. "I would love to see these projects succeed, but I don't believe it. Profit margins are already small in the food business. I'd rather have agreements with credible countries like New Zealand and Canada—they produce without help from us, we buy, we have stable arrangements with no investment risk."

According to American officials, that is also the policy of the U.S. government, which would prefer to see Saudi Arabia purchase whatever wheat it needs from U.S. suppliers such as Cargill.

Al-Alamy said WTO rules specifically permit countries to cut off agricultural commodity exports in times of shortage, so that "when you have a crisis any country has the right to prevent exportation, and [the result is] its people are eating food you paid to produce." He said his skepticism was fueled by experience. Several years ago he "helped put together" Saudi and Kuwaiti funding to build Kenana Sugar Company in Sudan. "About $1 billion has been invested and we have not seen one kilo of sugar," he said, because Kenana, while productive, does not meet all the demand in Sudan.[35]

Another skeptic is Turki Faisal Al-Rasheed, the outspoken chairman of the food conglomerate Golden Grass Inc. and a sometime newspaper columnist. He became a candidate for a doctoral degree at a university in Britain because, he said, he is tired of being told that people half his age know more about food or agronomy than he does simply because they have PhDs and he does not. Al-Rasheed thinks the farm investment program is unlikely to succeed and, worse, represents a bad policy decision by the Saudi government. In his view the country should be encouraging more farm production at home, not less, to insulate itself from political upheaval, natural disasters, inexorable commodity price inflation worldwide, and even domestic unrest. He said those are the reasons France and Germany subsidize their own domestic agriculture.

"The only way you could enhance security and fight poverty is through agriculture," he said. "You need to keep those rural areas, you have to keep them inhabited. Keep people in their villages. If they go below sustainable figures, those villages will be ghost towns. When the rural people move to a city, you have urban poverty, drugs, prostitution, crime. So agriculture is a form of social security."

Al-Rasheed argues that the country's oil industry will never employ more than 3 percent of the labor force and that the automated petrochemical plants to which the government is hitching the country's economic future will also employ relatively few workers. "So what are you going to do with the other 96 or 97 percent of the people? What are you going to with your labor, your 60 percent [of the population] below the age of 18?"

Agriculture, he said, "is not just a business, it's multifunctional. It's a social function, it's food security, [and] you are in the distribution of wealth to achieve security. Whoever wants to be there [in rural communities], you should give them agriculture jobs."[36]

Al-Rasheed will not prevail in the policy argument as long as Abdullah is king because the monarch is committed to the overseas investment initiative. Although some of the target countries, especially Sudan and Vietnam, have welcomed foreign agricultural investors as a potential source of capital for their under-producing farmers, Al-Rasheed and other experts predict that the initiative will succeed only marginally, if at all, because of political and economic realities in global markets and in the host countries. The skeptics include John Sfakianakis, a development specialist who is chief economist of Banque Saudi Fransi, and Brad Bourland, a longtime resident of Saudi Arabia who is director of research at Jadwa Investment Group. Both men dismissed the entire program as "a fad."[37]

Indeed, of the many announced and proposed deals reported in news media, only a handful are actually being implemented. According to a study by Canada's International Institute for Sustainable Development, "In 2009 many of the short-term factors that were present in 2008 (with the exception of the financial crisis) have temporarily disappeared. As a result, and combined with the impacts of the financial crisis and accompanying credit restrictions, the impetus to conclude deals is showing early signs of fading." As an example, the study said that an announced $4.3 billion deal organized by the Saudi Binladin Group in 2008 and involving fifteen Saudi investors was supposed to develop 500,000 hectares in Indonesia for the production of the long-grain basmati rice favored by Saudi consumers, but it has been scrapped.[38] (Saudi Binladin Group is the family-owned construction conglomerate founded by the father of Osama bin Laden.)

The experts' skepticism, however, applies only to the proposed solution for the problem, not to the existence of the problem itself. No one doubts that Saudi Arabia will face increasingly urgent food and water supply shortfalls in the 2030s or 2040s. As an Agriculture Ministry delegate told an international food conference in Austria in the spring of 2009, "With the beginning of the world economic crisis in the last quarter of 2008, food prices started to decline. This sign is not an indicator for future abundance in such products. Because it is a long-term strategy, King Abdullah's initiative had to go on as planned."[39] According to Taha Al-Shareef of the Ministry of Commerce, with the onset of the global recession in 2008, "food prices started to go down, so people thought that this is the end of the crisis. But we have to look into the future. This is a long-term initiative" that must go forward to "maintain the existing lifestyle of the people of Saudi Arabia."[40]

He looked prescient in the summer of 2010, when a prolonged drought and wildfires cut wheat harvests in Russia so deeply that the country banned exports from mid-August until the end of December. World wheat prices rose nearly 50 percent.[41]

For Saudi Arabia, the food numbers are already stark. In addition to the wheat it will be importing in ever-increasing quantities, Saudi Arabia is the world's second-largest importer of rice after Nigeria (Iran is fifth) and consumes 45 percent of all the feed barley traded in global markets.[42] The Saudis are meat eaters, and because of the shortage of grazing land, they must import—and feed—millions of sheep each year. And during the annual Muslim pilgrimage to Mecca, the Saudi government assumes the additional responsibility of providing food and water for more than 2 million people for up to a month.

There is nothing inherently problematic about being dependent on imports for any particular product or commodity. Japan imports virtually all its oil; the United States imports all its television sets. But the Saudis are aware that no product or commodity carries the immediacy or political sensitivity of food. As one put it in a private conversation, "You can postpone buying a TV; you can't decide you will eat next year."

Moreover, the Saudis are especially vulnerable to a global inflation of commodity prices because food accounts for a quarter of the spending in their consumer price index, and their ability to respond to the increased cost of imported food is limited by the peg of their currency to the dollar at a fixed exchange rate. Throughout the GCC, as one economic research group noted in 2010, "The food price shock of 2008 was a salient case in point, made worse by the broader backdrop of accelerating inflation. The limited monetary policy autonomy of the regional central banks, due to the Dollar pegs, created considerable challenges for policymakers who were forced to resort to a combination of short-term measures with relatively modest effects."[43]

Theoretically, the Saudi Food Security Initiative, backed by large amounts of cash, could contribute to a global solution to the looming commodity shortage problem by stimulating large increases in agricultural output in underperforming agrarian countries such as Ethiopia and Mozambique. If not, it will become increasingly urgent to create other negotiated international agreements that could stave off a competition for food that would inevitably pit countries against each other.

As alarming as that prospect might be, the scarcity of water in Saudi Arabia and the region is potentially even more destabilizing. In the Arabian Peninsula, it is conceivable that increasingly water-desperate governments in

Yemen, the GCC countries, and even Iraq could take up arms against each other in a quest for resources. But in truth there is no prize to be won in any such contest, for no country on the peninsula has a large lake or river that its neighbors might covet.

CENTURIES OF CONFLICT

Conflict over the region's skimpy water supply can be traced back at least to the seventh century BC when Sennacherib the Assyrian destroyed the canals of Babylon (now Iraq). In recent times, multiple studies and papers have reported the dismal water situation in Saudi Arabia and other countries of the region. Their tone ranges from grim to apocalyptic. The London-based Economist Intelligence Unit, for example, recently projected that overall water demand in Saudi Arabia in 2020 will be double what it was in 2000.[44]

"The Persian Gulf and the wider Middle East exist in what all statistical indicators suggest is one of the hottest, most water-starved environments on the planet," wrote James A. Russell of the Naval Postgraduate School in California. "This scarcity promises to become more acute as the world's temperature rises and the demand for fresh water increases due to population growth. Domestic water demand is projected to double in the Gulf by 2025; the demand for water required for industrial uses will increase threefold over that period." Compounding the problem is the "persistent mismanagement" of existing resources, Russell found.[45]

As long ago as the mid-1970s, the Saudi government considered a private firm's project to have icebergs towed down from the Arctic for their water content. And in 1994, the Committee for Middle East Trade warned bluntly that Saudi Arabia's water would simply run out in twenty-five years absent stringent conservation measures.[46] Many other studies have noted that Saudi consumers are profligate users of water because the government charges them so little for it; only Americans and Canadians consume more water per capita. In the spring of 2010, Saudi households were paying one-tenth of a riyal—less than three cents—per cubic meter, a tiny fraction of the cost of producing it through desalination. (In much of Europe, where water is abundant, the price is more than a dollar.) "Consumers and producers must undergo a change of mindset, while price incentives need restructuring in order to provide appropriate market signals," a report from Banque Saudi Fransi observed.[47]

As that report suggested, the water issue is not confined to Saudi Arabia's farms and rural communities. Its densely populated big cities are ravenous consumers, and the country is already struggling to meet the demand. The problem is especially acute in Jeddah, the Red Sea port city, where large areas have no piped water service at all. Drinking water is trucked in and sewage is trucked out. As another report put it, "It is difficult to estimate the amount of funds that will be needed to rectify the situation in Jeddah," a city of more than 3 million people.[48]

Aside from the questions of basic human need and the domestic political implications of serious water shortages, the national security consequences of the water scarcity throughout the region could be troublesome for Saudi Arabia as countries from Pakistan to Egypt compete for dwindling supplies. Yemen, the impoverished and fractious country on Saudi Arabia's southern border, has neither sufficient water nor the money to undertake large-scale desalination. The prospect of "water wars" hangs over the region. It was not an encouraging sign when in 2010 the countries that depend on the Nile River for water—including Egypt and Sudan, just across the Red Sea from Saudi Arabia—were unable to agree on a formula for allocating its water.

River issues are at least negotiable, but the depletion of underground reservoirs is not, the Middle East analyst Jon B. Alterman has noted. In April 2010, Alterman observed,

> The wells that feed much of the agriculture in the Middle East are a finite resource, and they are being exploited far beyond their capacity to restore themselves. Rains that fell on the earth tens of thousands of years ago are being poured into crops of cucumbers and tomatoes, figs and peaches, wheat and alfalfa. Once they are used up, they are used up . . . Once the water runs out, there are no good choices. Not only will agriculture collapse, but cities will find themselves hard-pressed to find basic water supplies to serve their populations.

Regional governments, Alterman noted, "have rarely done well allocating scarce resources, and decades of plenty have made choices easier. That time is coming to an end."[49]

Not only are the countries on the Arab side of the Gulf running out of underground water, but depleting this resource also leads to another serious problem. "For many coastal areas, the exhaustion of ground water has caused sea water to penetrate the aquifers, causing a rate of salinity such that it is becoming very difficult to find drinking water there," according to Suez Environment, a French consulting and water management firm.[50]

RETHINKING SUBSIDIES

Late in 2010 the national water company announced plans to increase the price of water for commercial, industrial, and institutional customers but not for individuals and households. Raising rates for the latter would be politically volatile in Saudi Arabia, where citizens have come to expect subsidized utility rates as part of their bargain with the rulers. Although the neighboring emirate of Abu Dhabi announced in May 2010 that it would install water-saving taps on the faucets in every home and office, no such project has been undertaken in Saudi Arabia. But there are indications that Saudi policy is finally adjusting to face reality.

Until a rate increase is imposed and enforced, the best that can be said for Saudi Arabia on this crucial subject is that the problem has been recognized and the kingdom has begun to boost capital spending on water-related projects. Money cannot create rivers or make more rain fall, but it can increase desalination capacity, add storage facilities, plug leaks in water mains, and capture wastewater for treatment and reuse. In that sense the Saudis are better positioned to confront their water crisis than are several of their neighbors. Desalination is expensive, and some Saudi officials fear the plants are vulnerable to sabotage and terrorism, but with few other options, the Saudis are committed to it. The annual budget approved in December 2009, for example, allocated to the government's Saline Water Conversion Corporation 13.4 billion riyals, or more than four times the allocation in 2006. Billions more are earmarked for upgraded distribution systems and the recapture of wastewater, which will be used in industry. The government has even commissioned scientists from Texas A & M and Arizona State Universities to study the feasibility of cloud seeding to stimulate rainfall. Paradoxically, Riyadh and especially Jeddah are vulnerable to flooding on the few days of the year when rain does fall because they lack storm drain and sewer networks. This problem also will require billions of dollars to solve.

The government has embarked on an effort to privatize the Saline Water Conversion Corporation, as it has already privatized the retail distribution system, and is encouraging private industry to develop independent water and power projects. The one certainty is that over the next two decades the government and private corporations will spend many multiples of $10 billion to cope with the water issue. According to calculations by the U.S.–Saudi Arabian Business Council, which promotes American trade with the kingdom, "Saudi Arabia will need to invest up to $60 billion over the next 20 years to meet the Kingdom's water needs." In addition to new desalination plants, some of which the government hopes to power with solar energy, "the Saudi government is committed to increasing investments in wastewater treatment, encouraging efficient water usage and expanding the country's dam network." The country generates an estimated 2 billion cubic meters of waste water per year, and the Ministry of Water and Electricity has set an ambitious target of treating and reusing 1.7 billion cubic meters of it for irrigation and industry.[51]

What Saudi Arabia is not planning to do is to take advantage of the great expertise and water management experience that is available just a short distance away in Israel. It is an example of how the failure to resolve the conflict between Israel and the Arabs is detrimental to both sides: Saudi Arabia certainly could use the knowledge of water management that Israelis have developed over the past half century, and Israeli companies would be happy to have contracts with Saudi clients. Neither will happen in the absence of peace.

Given that Saudi Arabia has access to more capital than most countries do and that desalination is a proven, if expensive, technology, it only makes sense that the Saudis will invest whatever is needed to keep the water flowing for the country's growing numbers of thirsty people. But desalination has an important downside: The process consumes vast amounts of energy. As discussed in chapter 2, energy consumption has become a matter of national concern because domestic energy use is undercutting Saudi Arabia's ability to export oil and gas.

PADDIES IN THE PAST

The state oil company, Saudi Aramco, published a coffee-table book about the kingdom that features a remarkable old color photograph of a dozen Arab men, some of them bare-chested, bent over rice seedlings in a paddy in the Hofuf oasis, which is near a present-day oil field. The photo is reminiscent of a scene from Vietnam or Indonesia. It was emblematic in its time, decades ago, but such scenes are less common now. Agriculture is still an important part of life in Saudi Arabia, but the water that has nurtured it is dwindling. Most of the rice comes from India now, and most of the farmers have migrated to cities, where they eat food that others have produced. As the text accompanying the photo in the book notes, "Natural water pressure in the oasis has been falling in recent decades as more and more water is drawn from spring-fed pools by mechanical pumping, and the area under cultivation has shrunk accordingly."[52]

It is hardly unknown for a society to transform itself from rural and agrarian to urban and industrial. The United States did it in the nineteenth century, and Americans still have more than enough to eat. Saudi Arabia's problem is that the cities and industries upon which it is building its future require more water than is available, and providing it will be a stern test of the country's financial resources, its determination, and its management skills. If it fails, it faces catastrophe; and if it succeeds and its neighbors fail, it faces potential conflict and a huge surge in illegal immigration as thirsty people migrate. As forecast by the U.S. National Intelligence Council, this problem portends a regional crisis that is largely beyond Saudi Arabia's control.

4

A NEW ECONOMIC
MODEL

"We will double the contribution of manufacturing to our economy to 20 percent by the year 2020."

> —ABDULLAH ALIREZA, MINISTER OF COMMERCE
> AND INDUSTRY, APRIL 2010

"There is no industrial future in this country. Manufacturing is not in the future of Saudi Arabia."

> —JOHN SFAKIANAKIS, CHIEF ECONOMIST,
> BANQUE SAUDI FRANSI, MAY 2010

It is customary in the Arab world to eat lunch late in the workday, often after 2 p.m., but not at the Saudi Basic Industries Corporation (SABIC), the huge parastatal foundation of Saudi Arabia's petrochemical industry. SABIC functions like a company in the industrial Midwest of the United States: The workers at its modern headquarters building near Riyadh's airport begin lining up at the cafeteria at 11:30 a.m.

Before entering the dining area for lunch, they stop at cashier stations to pay a flat fee of five riyals, or about $1.33, per person. For that paltry sum they can take as much as they want from abundant offerings of hot food, salads, sandwiches, pizza, desserts, and drinks. Many naturally pile their trays with more than they really want to eat at that hour, with the inevitable result that substantial amounts of this subsidized food are thrown away.

This way of feeding the SABIC workers makes no economic sense. If economic rationality were the objective, SABIC would give the workers modest salary increases and make them pay a realistic price for their meals. Or—

and here is a really radical idea—the workers could bring their lunches from home.

SABIC might subsidize the cafeteria meals by providing rent-free space to the caterer, as many American employers do, but a realistic price for the food itself would provide an incentive to eat less, waste less, and save money. But as with much of the Saudi system, economic sense is not the point. The point is to treat the workers well and make them feel as if they benefit from the state's vast wealth. It is the same motivation that impels the government to distribute electricity, water, and gasoline at ruinously subsidized prices, encouraging profligate consumption. For the same reason, Saudi citizens receive free education and health care but pay no taxes.

As a result, "the standard of living does not depend on the productivity of the workers," said David Rundell, a longtime U.S. diplomat in the kingdom. "It is a distributive economy. People derive their standard of living from the government—not just the 80 percent or so who work directly for the government or for parastatals like SABIC or Saudi Aramco, but everyone else in the sense that they get their share of the oil wealth handed to them in the form of entitlements and subsidies. They can't change that."[1]

These circumstances are manifestations of the rentier state that Saudi Arabia was for decades. The government, which means the royal family, collected the oil wealth and distributed some of it to the citizenry in the form of benefits, subsidies, and government jobs. In exchange, the citizens were expected to acquiesce in a political system in which they are fundamentally disenfranchised while their king and a small group of princes make all the important decisions.

The Saudis recognized long before the Arab upheavals of 2011 that the economic foundation upon which that bargain was constructed is no longer viable. It is not as if the king or some cabinet officer suddenly had an epiphany; the national discussion about the country's economic future has been going on since at least the 1970s. Now the state has lurched into action, committing its resources to a far-reaching, hugely ambitious effort to rebuild Saudi Arabia into an industrial powerhouse and prepare its citizens for the coming "knowledge society."

This challenge is daunting. Many economists are skeptical about the idea and dismissive of Saudi Arabia's ability to fulfill it. But if the amount of money the rulers have committed is an indicator, the Saudis are serious, and they have little choice because of the population's rapid growth. As rich as the kingdom is, the state cannot afford to be the employer of last resort for all its young job seekers, an estimated 400,000 of whom enter the labor market annually.

There is no mystery about how the Saudis intend to proceed. Different government agencies have described their ambitions, goals, and plans in detail in multiple documents. That overlap in itself suggests potential difficulties in coordination, but taken together these plans have one central theme: The era when a self-indulgent country could live off its oil wealth while the population proliferated is over. The long-term future will require a new model, a model that envisions Saudi Arabia—which is already a member of the Group of Twenty (G-20) advanced economic nations and of the World Trade Organization—as a fully modern, globally competitive, industrialized state. Instead of exporting raw materials and importing finished products, it will create the finished products itself and recapture the "added value" that up to now has been shipped abroad.

In simple terms, the government has committed itself to transforming the economic model that has sustained Saudi Arabia through its primitive-to-modern development phase over the past seven decades, based on government distribution of income from a single source. In the new model, the government is no longer the primary entrepreneur and primary employer. Private enterprise is to be the engine of growth. The government's role is to attract and stimulate that private enterprise by providing roads and railroads, electricity, water, raw materials, streamlined investment regulations, and a rebuilt education system that produces the skilled workers employers will want. At the same time, existing government-owned enterprises are being privatized and opened to competition. The state's mobile telephone monopoly now faces multiple competitors, the water-distribution business has already been sold off, and the national airline is being privatized in phases.

The implementation of this mammoth undertaking faces equally mammoth obstacles. But Saudi Arabia has matching resources, and it is hardly starting from scratch. Unlike such oil states as Nigeria and Venezuela, it has already built up its economic base beyond a total reliance on oil. According to economic researchers at Banque Saudi Fransi, at the end of 2008 the country already had 4,167 factories, employing 466,661 people in operations such as food processing, packaging, and the manufacture of electric cable, air conditioners, and plastics.[2] Unfortunately, the great majority of those workers are imported laborers, not Saudis.

THE OUTLOOK FOR 2025

In 2005 the Ministry of Economy and Planning issued the most comprehensive exposition of what Saudi Arabia is trying to do and how it intends to do it in a fifty-two-page document titled "Saudi Arabia: Long-Term Strategy 2025."[3] "By the will of Allah," it says, "the Saudi economy in 2025 will be a more diversified, prosperous, private-sector driven economy providing rewarding job opportunities, quality education, excellent heath care and necessary skills to ensure the well-being of all citizens while safeguarding Islamic values and the Kingdom's cultural heritage." Over the next twenty years, it says, "the per capita GDP will double from its current level of SAR [Saudi Arabian riyals] of 43,300 at the beginning of 2005 to SAR 98,500 in 2025 at constant 1999 prices."

Given the rate of population growth, which will add 9 million or 10 million people during the planning period, the ministry's goal is very ambitious, requiring an average annual GDP growth of 6.6 percent. The planning document declares, however, that "the ultimate destination is non-negotiable. Only the means to reach this destination are negotiable." The per capita GDP growth reflects a commitment to "promoting the national economy to the level of advanced economies"—that is, to make Saudi Arabia more like South Korea and less like Nigeria or Venezuela.

To reach that point, the plan establishes benchmarks for a complete overhaul of the national economy, emphasizing private investment, diversification of output, expansion of the service sector, and a drastic reduction in the relative importance of oil and gas. "The share of oil and gas exports in the structure of exports will decrease from 71.7 percent to 36.7 percent by 2024," the plan stipulates. "Oil's share of GDP is projected to be a mere 17.9 percent by the end of the planning period."

The planners devised a "Quality of Life Index" based on eleven components: income and distribution, working life, transportation and communications, health, education, housing, environment, family life, public safety, leisure, and public services. Using the years 1999–2002 as a base of 100, the index stood at 102.12 in 2005. "The target for 2025 is a minimum value of 119.61."

A separate, slightly earlier version of the economic plan said that private investment, both Saudi and foreign, is projected to increase by 10.3 percent annually and to provide the financing for the new industrial economy. Meanwhile, government investment, mostly in infrastructure, is expected to grow by only 4 percent per year.[4]

Fulfillment of these ambitions will require a coordinated effort across many government departments and agencies, including those responsible for education; water supply, which is always a constraint on development in the Persian Gulf region; electricity; and transportation.[5] The industrialization component was developed by the Ministry of Commerce and Industry and is spelled out in a "Comprehensive Industrial Strategy and Future Vision for the Industrial Sector in the Kingdom of Saudi Arabia."

This document lists the government's responsibilities in making possible and encouraging industrial development to reach the objectives of the long-term economic plan. Some of them are obvious; others represent a strong government role in industrial decision making that is reminiscent of the central economic planning in socialist states, such as "selection of production technologies and diversification of industrial products on a nationwide basis" and "regional deployment of particular technologies" with appropriate "allocation of industrial lands." Success requires "the identification of a preferred path of evolution of the industrial sector."[6] The government's objective is to encourage the development of industrial "clusters" in which groups of companies participating in related enterprises sell to and profit from each other and are attracted into geographical proximity by one dominant enterprise, as with the auto industry in the upper Midwest and the computer software industry in Silicon Valley.

Until 2011, the man responsible for the Saudi government's input into industrial development and for making the clusters happen was Dr. Ibrahim Babelli, executive director of the National Industrial Development Program, one of the most creative and unorthodox thinkers in Saudi Arabia. Babelli is the only Saudi I have ever met who said he would see me at 7 a.m., a ridiculously early hour by Saudi standards.

Babelli has a different take from the conventional wisdom on almost every aspect of Saudi Arabia's economic history. He challenges the narrative that says Saudi Arabia got rich on oil without having to do any work and that its dependence on foreign labor for the heavy lifting is somehow anomalous in the world.

In truth, he said, Saudi Arabia is following the same path to industrialization that the United States and smaller states such as Singapore and Ireland once followed. As the United States industrialized in the late nineteenth and early twentieth centuries, he said, the reason it did not rely on imported workers was that it had already imported the workers in the form of slaves. Once emancipated, they went to where the new industrial jobs were to meet the demand for labor.

"They used to work on plantations in the South," he said. "They went up north and worked in the steel factories. Cheap labor."

Babelli said it is "extremely unlikely that any country would immediately leapfrog to advanced, significantly value-added industry. Singapore started with heavy industry and gradually moved toward more value-added industry. Saudi Arabia is following the same path," including an overhaul of its education system to meet new employers' manpower requirements.

As in any other country, Saudi Arabia's investors and business leaders are primarily motivated by profit. Babelli told me, "It has become very clear to our business people that investing in sustainable economic activity—industry, manufacturing activity—is a very viable option in the face of the [economic] bubble. So I believe it is very clear for everybody in this part of the world that manufacturing should be a very attractive investment; it doesn't burst like a bubble. If you invest in something sustainable, the next year, the next decade, it's going to be around."

Babelli smiled wearily when I asked him why, if opportunities abound, it was necessary for the government to exert such strong influence over investors' decisions. "History shows that it is often necessary," he replied.

"If you look around the world, you will find very clearly that clusters do emerge organically," he said, "and other clusters emerge from a development push" by the government. "If you take the example of the United States, you will find that the majority of modern manufacturing in the U.S. was the result of investment by the government in Word War II. And thereafter the fallout was the modernization of clusters [of industrial development] in Europe following the devastation of the war [and] to a much lesser extent in Japan. In Europe, the revival of industry through the Marshall Plan was by donations in kind, not in cash; there was proactive development in industry by the U.S. government.

"Everybody talks about the Silicon Valley, the icon of organic development of a cluster. What happened there, if you put it next to the example I just gave of the manufacturing industry that was a by-product of the Marshall Plan, you will see that at times the government does proactively intervene. The enabling element of the U.S. government, if I may say so, may not be very obvious to people who do not know what is inside. Most people do not come to think of the enabling financial and regulatory framework that was in place that enabled the initial venture capital companies to help the development of Silicon Valley," Babelli said.

According to him, Americans like to think of themselves as free-enterprise capitalists and are unwilling to acknowledge the government's role in making their success possible—through road construction for example, or immigration policies that attract skilled people or tax incentives or purchasing contracts.

"The majority of people, when they think of the American dream, they don't think of it in the sense of the U.S. system is opening doors to those who are skilled in what they do," he said. "There is an important element of attracting the top talent in the world, and if you look very closely at what happened in Silicon Valley, you will find that the majority of people who contributed to its development came from countries that experienced a very severe caste system such as India and China. Steve Jobs is an Arab. Did you know that his [biological] father was a Middle Eastern immigrant? Anyway, the regulatory framework was actively developed by the U.S. government."

The Saudi government's role, he said, is not to issue orders to private companies but to "to see what works and encourage it" through coordinated policies "and see what doesn't work or has a detrimental effect on the country or the economy and discourage it."

The other component of his assignment, he said, is to encourage the giant oil, gas, and petrochemical industries that are still state owned to buy more of what they need from domestic suppliers. "Take the example of flanges, valves and fittings," he said. "Saudi Aramco pays $400 million for these things every year and only $5 million worth are manufactured in Saudi Arabia." Aramco is committed to manufacturing 40 percent of its intake in that category locally, he said, not because it was ordered to do so but because doing so is more efficient, reducing delivery times and shipping costs. The government's role is to create the infrastructure, competent workforce, and investment climate to enable Aramco to reach that goal.[7]

Especially in the oil region of eastern Saudi Arabia, he acknowledged, the kingdom faces a problem in that the industry-related businesses forming an oil-related economic "cluster," as American businesses did around Houston, do not have to be inside Saudi Arabia itself. They could base themselves in nearby places such as Bahrain or Dubai, where life is less restrictive. Boeing is among the international giants that have followed that model. It sells a great deal of aircraft and parts to Saudi Arabia, but most of its regional personnel live and work in the easygoing United Arab Emirates.

"SOCIAL RESPONSIBILITY"

Babelli said state-owned and state-supported companies have a "social responsibility" as well as an economic mission—namely, to provide jobs for the young people coming into the workforce. "We're not just talking about Saudi Arabia," Babelli said. "Those companies—Aramco, SABIC and others like them—are really part of a bigger industrial array in the Gulf region, the MENA [Middle East–North Africa] region, and the Islamic world."

It was in response to the pressure to live up to this social responsibility that Saudi Aramco developed the idea of promoting industrial clusters as a state-supported national policy, according to a long article in the oil company's in-house magazine, *Dimensions.* The company started with Oil Minister Ali Al-Naimi's instructions to find ways to diversify the national economy. It realized that "the Kingdom's petroleum industry is already highly developed and will offer only a limited number of additional opportunities in the near future," the article said.

Attempting to identify types of industry that could be feasible in Saudi Arabia, the oil company's New Business Development group rejected those that were clearly not suitable, such as textiles. It picked five promising industries that could take advantage of low-cost hydrocarbon supplies, the country's geographic location, and the relative affluence of its population: automotive assembly, construction materials, metals processing, packaging, and consumer goods.

In 2007, the government created the National Industrial Development Program headed by Babelli's boss, Prince Faisal bin Turki, one of two senior princes who work in the Ministry of Petroleum. The program's mission is to encourage the growth of the five targeted industries by seeking foreign investors, by arranging for the training that workers will need, and by scoping out the competition in other countries that are pursuing similar strategies.[8]

"We took out things that don't make sense," Prince Faisal said. "We don't make things that depend on wood because we don't have forests, or on a lot of potable water because we don't have a lot of potable water, but we can do industries that depend on the materials that we are producing and exporting."

Those selected industries, he said, "are going to create good-sized activity that will reward the country if it does what is necessary to enable them, with a good amount of jobs. Our estimate now is that if we realize a reasonable target we can create in the next 15 or 20 years maybe 700,000 jobs. That is not going to come because you talk about it. We need to mobilize the country, we need to mobilize the education system, we need to mobilize government administrators to reach out to the private sector when they come, and work with them to accomplish things. You need to mobilize incentives to offer these companies to come to Saudi Arabia and be competitive in the world. . . . If you have specific targets you can succeed, based on achieving a certain amount of progress that is measurable. This is basically what we have done with the cluster program. We have established a group from all over the world, plus talented Saudis, people that will be able to quarterback the government effort in establishing these clusters.

"The work has started. We are intentionally trying to play down the expectations. We want to talk when we have the government backing that is necessary."

Prince Faisal said Saudi Arabia has to understand that there is worldwide competition for investment. He cited the example of how American states competed, offering tax breaks and other incentives, to entice foreign automobile manufacturers to choose their sites for U.S.-based plants.

"This is what is being done in the world left, right and center, and we are not doing it in Saudi Arabia, believe it or not," he said. "And the reason we are not doing it is that people used to say, 'It's a free market.' Well, it's a free market, but in a free market you compete with other countries. It doesn't mean you sit and wait for the free market to come give you a helping hand."[9]

In December 2009, Oil Minister Al-Naimi announced that the ministry would give preference, when allocating oil and gas supplies, to industries in the five groups that the cluster program planners selected and to manufacturers of solar energy equipment. "We expect to see many products" from the country's petrochemical plants used as "feedstock for small and medium industries that will manufacture goods made in Saudi Arabia. That is our number one priority," he said.[10]

Prince Faisal said the cluster industries program is different from other government-led industrial development efforts because it has "a substantial dose of realism." I took that as an indirect shot at the grandly ambitious plans of the Saudi Arabian General Investment Authority (SAGIA) to develop "New Economic Cities," where the country's economic future will materialize.

NEW ECONOMIC CITIES

SAGIA is charged with recruiting and expediting foreign and Saudi private-sector investment into the Saudi economy. Its New Economic Cities program, the cornerstone of its efforts, is described on the SAGIA website in such lofty, ambitious language that it merits quoting at some length:

> Forget everything you know about "industrial parks" and "free zones." Saudi Arabia's *four new Economic Cities*—fully planned and under construction—are exactly that: new cities, where up to five million residents will live, work and play. Each will be an exciting metropolis, designed to maximise investment potential and deliver huge advantage to businesses located there.
>
> At a cost of more than $60 billion, Saudi Arabia's economy is being propelled onto a whole new level with the construction of four integrated Economic Cities. This visionary development project will promote economic diversification, create over a million new job opportunities, homes for 4–5 million residents—and, most significantly, contribute $150 billion to Saudi's GDP.
>
> **Unparalleled standards of living**
> Built on specially selected greenfield sites and strategically located around the nation, each city is being planned to the highest possible specification as the ultimate in 21st century urban living and working. Residents and workers will enjoy a virtually unique combination of high-quality housing, modern amenities, excellent sports and recreational facilities and world-class specialist healthcare. International schools will offer global curricula for workers' children from all over the world while luxurious malls will offer shops and restaurants featuring the finest goods and food from around the globe.

A benchmark for world-class, sustainable design

Each city will feature modern building design, world-class services and infrastructure and ubiquitous connectivity. These built-in advantages, combined with attractive investment incentives and a supportive regulatory environment will create significant competitive advantages for business. SAGIA is also working with leading environmental institutions to ensure that the Economic Cities are developed with minimum negative environmental impact and maximum energy efficiency and sustainability.[11]

Of all the Saudi government officials I have sought to interview in recent years, only two declined to talk to me. One was Labor Minister Ghazi Al-Gosaibi, who turned out to have a good excuse: He was fatally ill and died a few months later. The other was Essam Bukhamseen, executive director of the New Economic Cities program, who referred me to his public relations staff. That response did not surprise John Sfakianakis, chief economist of Banque Saudi Fransi. He is the skeptic in chief about the entire industrialization effort.

"Of course they didn't want to talk to you. There's nothing to say," he said. "There is no industrial future in this country. Manufacturing is not the future of Saudi Arabia."[12] He had been even more vehement in an earlier conversation, dismissing the entire New Economic Cities program as "a scam [that] will not happen. It's just a big real estate project and that's where it's going to end."

He cited specific planned projects that he said will not—or should not—be built because they do not make economic sense. "A refinery to be built by the Chinese in Jizan," in southwestern Saudi Arabia, across the country from the oil fields? "For what? Where are they going to get the oil? There are no pipelines, and Aramco isn't on board. Are we going to supply oil to this refinery so the Chinese can make money? And an aluminum smelter? When we are already burning 2 million barrels a day [of oil equivalent] to generate electricity? I don't think so."[13]

On the refinery, the answer to his rhetorical questions turned out to be yes. In January 2010, King Abdullah ordered Saudi Aramco to build it, without waiting any longer for foreign investment, Chinese or otherwise. That was a political decision, not an economic one. As noted in chapter 2, the Jizan region is among the poorest and most restive parts of the country, and the king has been trying to raise the level of prosperity there. Sfakianakis may have been unduly dismissive about the potential of the aluminum industry, too. According to a National Commercial Bank report, the kingdom has "massive quantities" of alumina, and planned smelters will make it a "global supplier" of aluminum by 2016—assuming, of course, that enough electricity becomes available.[14] Indeed, in December 2009, the U.S. aluminum giant Alcoa announced that it would join the Saudi state mining company, Ma'aden, in a $10.8 billion project to create an integrated aluminum complex, from mine to finished products, in northeastern Saudi Arabia. The announcement did not specify a source of electricity for this venture.[15]

REASON FOR SKEPTICISM

In conversation, if not in his written reports, Sfakianakis tends to exaggerate for dramatic effect, but it is true that despite the Alcoa announcement, there are ample reasons for skepticism not only about the New Economic Cities but also about the entire industrialization program. Already the New Economic Cities project has been scaled back from six planned cities to four. The remaining cities are reporting mixed success, and by 2011 the government had toned down the overheated rhetoric about their potential. The most advanced project is King Abdullah Economic City, on the Red Sea coast north of Jeddah, planned as a transportation hub with the region's largest container terminal. The other three still on the books are: Prince Abdulaziz bin Mousaed Economic City, a planned rail and truck hub and agribusiness center in the north near Hail; Knowledge Economic City, a high-tech center that according to SAGIA will "play a crucial role in transforming Saudi Arabia into a global force in knowledge-based industry" outside Medina; and Jizan Economic City, planned as a trade and information center that will serve much of East Africa from its location near Jizan in the southwest.

Is this initiative all pie in the sky? The worldwide economic recession undercut all four planned New Cities because their success depends on private investment. The government is providing infrastructure and incentives, but business and residential development is premised on private capital, which except at King Abdullah Economic City has been slow to materialize. Eventually the sheer power of government money is certain to attract some amount of activity and the people to participate in it, but it is an open question whether those numbers will amount to viable, livable urban entities that will offer an attractive way of life to sophisticated people. After viewing mock-ups of the planned cities Nicolai Ouroussoff, architecture critic of the *New York Times*, wrote that "architecturally they couldn't be more dreary—bloated glass towers encircled by quaint town houses and suburban villas decorated in ersatz historical style" on a "gargantuan scale" that reminded him of Brasilia, the government-created capital of Brazil. There is a reason people who live in Brasilia flee to Rio de Janeiro on weekends.[16]

There is ample reason to be skeptical about all these grand plans. Some of the lofty language is virtually identical to the words of plans adopted with great fanfare in the 1970s. Perhaps a greater cause for doubt about the entire economic vision, or at least for withholding a passing grade, is the lack of clarity about how all these programs—the industrial strategy, the New Economic Cities, the cluster industries—are going to come together in a coherent pattern of development. All three share the weakness of being top-down planning; that is, they were conceived by government officials and executives of state-owned companies, not inspired by risk-taking entrepreneurs with new ideas.

A DEARTH OF ENTREPRENEURS

At least until recently, Saudi Arabia was not set up to encourage inventors and innovators who build better mousetraps in their garages and then go in search of venture capital. Instead, in the past and on a smaller scale, government planners in multiple ministries did what they are doing now: committing the country to enormous, costly new urban and industrial agglomerations—new cities, new industrial zones, new lines of products—and then seeking private developers to carry out those plans. Sometimes these ambitious projects have been successful, when corporations found the conditions to be economically advantageous: free land, subsidized electricity, government-funded infrastructure, and availability of cheap, imported labor. (Of course, the last element subverts one of the purposes of these efforts, that is, providing jobs for Saudis.) That is what happened in the industrial port cities of Jubail and Yanbu, developed by a royal commission, and in the sprawling industrial city south of Riyadh. The vast amount of government cash available to support these projects has been a powerful incentive and a useful lubricant.

Moreover, individual Saudi investors have developed enormous personal fortunes and are looking for safe places to invest—namely, at home and insulated from the vicissitudes of the outside world.

But success in ventures of the scope of the New Economic Cities is hardly guaranteed. It is likely that some of these undertakings will turn out to be successful and economically self-sustaining. It is equally likely that billions of dollars and many years will be spent to little long-term benefit. The Saudis have the great advantage of being able to afford to make some mistakes because they have the money. The question is whether they have the time to make the economy self-sustaining and sufficiently expansive before the country is overwhelmed by its population growth.

The government's omnipresent role in economic planning arose in part from Saudi Arabia's long-standing deficit in entrepreneurial creativity. Investors have been willing to build supermarkets and hotels because there was an obvious need for them, but new products that would attract new markets have generally not emerged in the Saudi environment. By and large, the great fortunes of the country's non-royal families were built on construction and on exclusive distributorships of imported consumer products not on inventions or on manufacturing breakthroughs.

According to David Hamod, president of the National U.S.-Arab Chamber of Commerce in Washington, Saudi Arabia and the entire region are short of entrepreneurs for several reasons, including an aversion to risk. Entrepreneurship, he wrote, thrives in "an environment that celebrates not only success, but failure." This point, he wrote, "is critical, and it represents one of the main reasons why creating entrepreneurial ecosystems in the Middle East and North Africa has historically been a challenge. Many nations around the world frown on failure, but few are as tough as the Arab world."[17]

That situation is beginning to change, as evidenced by the Saudi Fast Growth 100 listings, which were developed by SAGIA, a group of Saudi banks and investors, and Professor Michael Porter of Harvard Business School to encourage and evaluate start-up companies. Hamod's organization became a partner in 2010. The group publishes an annual list of the fastest-growing start-ups in Saudi Arabia. In 2010 it included FullStop, an advertising and public relations company, with 28 employees; SecuTronic, a "high tech security" and telecommunications company, which employs 116; and Body Masters, a fitness outfit with 400 workers.[18]

As Hamod noted, "the Kingdom's business environment has not always favored start-ups. Fifteen years ago, the entrepreneurial environment here was akin to Saudi Arabia's vast Empty Quarter. Today, that start-up 'desert' is in full bloom."[19] As an example of how the culture is changing, Hamod cited a 2009 agreement between King Saud University in Riyadh and Kent State University in Ohio to establish an entrepreneurship curriculum to foster the development of small- and medium-size businesses.

"Things are changing; there's a new class of middle-level executives and managers," said Manuel Ron, an American who formed his own Riyadh investment company with Saudi partners in 2009. "The private sector is driving growth for the first time. In previous generations all business started at the top; these new guys are different, they will do these mid-level and small deals."[20] They know they can make more in business than in government jobs and that there is probably no room for them in the oil industry, so they are going out on their own.

The late Gene W. Heck, a roly-poly dynamo who lived and did business in Riyadh from 1984 until his death in 2010, was the endlessly upbeat opposite of the skeptical John Sfakianakis. In a book predicting a prosperous, full-employment future for Saudi Arabia, he listed the reasons for his rosy forecast: "An ambitious, intelligent and increasingly educated people; a modern educational infrastructure; imposing modern physical infrastructures; abundant liquid and hard-mineral resources; ample private sector liquidity and prudent public policies, focused equally upon free enterprise and industrial diversification, designed to promote economic growth." These policies, he wrote, include "a strong commitment to free market precepts, the free movement of capital, and a comprehensive package of financial and taxation incentives custom-tailored to encourage balanced private sector expansion."[21]

The government's long-term economic plan adds other positive indicators to Heck's list, including "political stability," a centuries-long tradition of trade and commerce, "world class infrastructure," and "deep-rooted and strong cultural and religious traditions." Indeed, because of all those assets, an economic boom of sorts is already under way, stimulated by oil money and expedited by vast government investment in infrastructure. The government's plans aim to encourage and expand private investment in that boom, to steer projects to regions that need them, to persuade affluent Saudis to invest at home, and to maintain what the master plan calls "strategic clarity" in choosing which opportunities to pursue.

A cross-country railway system is under construction, as are new ports on both coasts and new airports all around the country and electric power plants and transmission lines. Ma'aden, the mining company, is digging up gold at five mines, phosphates from huge deposits in the north, and bauxite to be shipped on a new rail line to the new aluminum complex it is building in partnership with Alcoa.[22]

Dow Chemical Company and Saudi Aramco, in a joint venture, are constructing a $20 billion petrochemical complex. In 2010 General Electric, which has been constructing power facilities in Saudi Arabia for seven decades, undertook a long-term commitment to research, development, training, and manufacturing in the kingdom. Akram Hamad, GE's regional vice president, declared that "by 2013, Saudi Arabia will be the manufacturing hub for GE in the Islamic bloc" of countries.[23] Cisco Systems undertook a five-year program to supply Internet-related equipment, to train technicians, and to extend Web access to lower-income communities.[24] Coca-Cola Company, Kimberly-Clark, and Colgate-Palmolive are manufacturing consumer products in joint ventures with private Saudi companies.

In May 2010, a regional business information website known as AMEinfo posted an announcement about a new venture to be developed at Knowledge Economic City:

Madinah Knowledge Economic City (KEC) signed an agreement on 23/5/10 in Jeddah with DeepCloud SA, a Saudi Arabian company, to develop, own and operate the DeepCloud Madinah Technology Center on a 30,000 sq meters land in KEC. The Technology Center will be a state of the art, next-generation cyber-technology facility anchored by the region's first carrier and vendor neutral Tier IV Internet Data Center (IDC).

It will also be the first of several independently accredited IDCs that DeepCloud will develop in the Kingdom. DeepCloud has partnered with Oracle Corporation, which will serve as the design and technology partner for the project. . . .

The Tier IV IDC at the DeepCloud Madinah Technology Center will serve industries and businesses throughout the Kingdom, the MENA region and beyond that require professionally managed, highly reliable, bandwidth-intensive physical environments within which to operate their mission-critical hardware and applications.[25]

Aside from the geek-speak, the fact that such an announcement concerned a development in Saudi Arabia is in itself evidence of how far the kingdom has already progressed.

THE WTO FACTOR

Membership in the World Trade Organization has opened up the Saudi economy in ways that create opportunities where none had existed. Before Saudi Arabia joined the WTO, the economy other than oil was controlled by powerful, rich families who dominated the construction industry and the import and distribution of the consumer goods for which oil money created a voracious market.

Getting into the WTO was not an easy matter because Saudi Arabia wanted exemptions from the organization's free trade rules to accommodate its culture. For example, it did not want to be required to import pork products or gambling equipment or to do business with Israel. Further, it did not want to be forced to abandon its policy of subsidizing necessities such as gasoline and electricity. The negotiations took twelve years to achieve accession, which occurred on December 11, 2005.

Brad Bourland, who at the time was chief economist at SAMBA (formerly the Saudi American Bank), gave this summary of what was involved:

In the process of preparing for membership, Saudi Arabia enacted 42 new trade-related laws, created nine new regulatory bodies, and signed 38 bilateral trade agreements. When the Kingdom first applied for membership in the WTO's predecessor, the General Agreement on Tariffs and Trade (GATT) in 1993, 75 percent of the Kingdom's tariffs on imported goods were at 12 percent. By 2003, 85 percent of tariffs were 5 percent or less, and the commitments made for WTO membership will now bring tariffs down further.

To become a member, Saudi Arabia made major commitments to reduce tariffs, open services sectors of the economy to greater foreign participation, and to implement all WTO rules upon membership without recourse to transition periods. This means that when Saudi Arabia became a member, it was committed immediately to an intellectual property rights environment, a foreign investment environment, transparency in trade issues, legal recourse for trade partners, and elimination of technical barriers to trade, all in compliance with WTO requirements.

Saudi Arabia also agreed to join several sectoral initiatives upon accession that lower tariffs and other trade barriers for telecommunications services, information technologies, pharmaceuticals, civilian aircraft and parts, and chemicals.

"We believe," Bourland wrote at the time, "that WTO membership furthers several primary goals of economic policy—diversification of the economy away from oil, job creation for Saudis, and attraction of foreign investment."[26]

These developments provide ample evidence that the kingdom's economic policy has been consistent and coherent for quite some time and that the expansion of Saudi Arabia's economy far beyond oil exports is already well under way. They do not provide convincing proof that the grand designs of the long-term plan, including full employment and development of the New Economic Cities into self-sustaining communities, can be achieved. John Sfakianakis and other skeptics can still find abundant entries in the negative column of the ledger book.

REALITY CHECK

Not long after the twenty-year master plan was unveiled in 2005, an engineer named Ahmed Al-Sadhan presented to an interministerial group a slide show about the plan that included the findings of an analysis by the United Nations International Development Organization (UNIDO). One slide said, "UNIDO diagnosis shows that performance is poor. MVA [manufacturing value-added] in GDP is around 9% (very low). In Malaysia and China it is around 35%; even in Egypt is 20%."

Worse yet, "manufactured exports/total exports has declined. . . We have not improved beyond 1980. We have actually moved backward from 1990-2000." His conclusion read: "We have far to go; rising oil revenues have hidden the reality of industrial stagnation."[27]

To Sfakianakis, that finding was hardly surprising. He said he does not object to the country's petrochemical-focused industrial strategy in itself, only to the idea that it will provide enough jobs to employ all the people

who will need them. Efficient industrial operations are generally not labor intensive. They tend to be similar to the Advanced Electronics Company
(AEC), a highly sophisticated outfit in Riyadh that produces defense electronic equipment, avionics, and telecommunications gear. When I visited its
plant in 2006, it had fewer than five hundred employees. In that same year,
AEC began assembling computers for the Taiwan-based computer maker
Acer. This arrangement was a breakthrough of sorts for a Saudi company,
but the computer operation added only sixty workers to the payroll.[28]

AEC is what is known in Saudi Arabia as an "offset" industry. These enterprises are established under the Economic Offset Program, which was created in 1984 as a subsidiary of the Ministry of Defense and Aviation and
was designed to bring higher-level foreign investment and technology to the
kingdom. It requires some corporations from the United States and Europe,
mostly defense contractors, to reinvest a certain percentage of their contracts'
value in high-tech joint ventures with Saudi partners. According to the U.S.–
Saudi Arabian Business Council, "Among the major American companies
involved in this program are the Boeing Company, General Dynamics
Corporation, General Electric Company, United Technologies Corporation,
and Lucent Technologies."[29]

Some of these investments have resulted in viable enterprises such as AEC,
but the employment impact has been limited. At the end of 2006, after
twenty-two years of operation and investments of 17 billion riyals, or about
$4.5 billion, Saudi government statistics showed the Offset Program had cre-
ated 3,640 jobs for Saudis.

Those numbers reinforce the skepticism of Sfakianakis and other critics
about the long-term employment impact of the industrialization campaign.
Privately owned industries in high-wage environments always seek maximum output from minimum staff. For years there has been a built-in tension
between the government's desire to find jobs for as many Saudis as possible
and profit-seeking business executives seeking to minimize labor costs.

Sfakianakis said he doubts that an automobile industry, for example, will
produce the levels of employment that Saudi planners envisioned—at least
not if the industry expects to be profitable. "Cars?" Sfakianakis said. "Auto
assembly? A modern car plant to break even has to produce a million cars a
year, and you're competing against giants." The Saudis are not competing
against only Japan and Korea. Turkey and even Iran are well ahead of Saudi

Arabia in developing domestic auto assembly industries, he said, as is Egypt. "And tires for the cars? How many tire plants can you have?"

Sfakianakis continued, "They can have factories, some industrial plants, but they aren't going to employ Saudis." Employers are in business to make money, and "labor here is not very productive or efficient."

Jadwa Investment Group's Brad Bourland agreed. "A cluster of automobile-related industries is not realistic. You don't get any comparative advantage by doing things here," he said. "Say you want to create a factory to make dashboards for Toyotas. SABIC doesn't give you any break on the resins and polymers. You pay world prices for those materials."[30]

Saudi Arabia is far from reaching critical mass that would represent a self-sustaining industry in automotive manufacturing, assembly, and parts, but there have been encouraging developments. There is a modest Daimler-Benz truck assembly plant in Jeddah, and General Motors manages a bus assembly line for a Saudi company. Abu Dhabi's Gulf Automotive Manufacturing Company is building a plant in Dammam that is expected to produce 15,000 vehicles annually. At the end of 2010, an investment firm established by King Saud University and partners from Egypt and South Korea announced a plan to begin building small cars for the Gulf market in 2012. And in early 2011 Isuzu Motors of Japan announced that it would build an assembly plant in the kingdom to produce medium-size trucks for the regional market, with an eventual target of 25,000 vehicles a year.

Industrialization, of course, is not the Saudis' only path to employment in the modernizing economy. Service industries and distributors are in the market for workers too, along with the fast-growing health care business. Businesses that sell to the public need marketers, advertisers, customer relations staffs; but all of these jobs require outgoing personalities, which many Saudis do not have, and fluency in a foreign language, usually English. Hotels need front-desk staff, and Saudis could be doing those jobs that the Pakistanis and Indians are doing now—if there were enough Saudis who spoke English and were willing to stand on their feet for hours at a time being helpful to strangers.

To raise the country to the next level, a new workforce of better-educated, technologically savvy, energetic people—including women—will have to be developed. That task is just beginning.

5

THE LABOR MARKET
AND ITS DISCONTENTS

Saudi Arabia has an estimated 400,000 to 500,000 unemployed citizens, and more join their ranks every year as the labor force expands through population growth, and more women seek jobs. Meanwhile, at least 4 million foreigners work in the country. Those foreign workers send almost $20 billion out of the kingdom to their home countries annually.[1]

This imbalance in the labor market is Saudi Arabia's greatest economic conundrum, its biggest management problem, and one of the biggest potential threats to its social stability. Every long-term plan issued by every organization in the government that has anything to do with economic matters is aimed at narrowing the gap and at putting more Saudis to work, even as more job seekers enter the labor market each year because of the growing, mostly young population. The plans for creating jobs are ambitious, the goals are lofty, but the obstacles are many.

Even if the private-sector economy grows as anticipated in all the plans, it is far from certain that the projected growth will produce the required number of jobs or that those jobs will go to Saudi workers. According to Banque Saudi Fransi researchers who analyzed government data in 2011,

> The swiftly growing pace of youth unemployment is happening despite the net addition of 673, 601 jobs by the private sector in 2009. . . . Only 9.9% of labor force employees in the private sector were Saudi nationals that year, down from 13.3% in 2008. Between 2005 and 2009, less than 9% of the more than 2.2 million jobs created in the private sector went to Saudis. . . .

105

As many young Saudis struggle to find work, 982,420 work visas for foreigners were issued to the private sector in 2009, more than double the number granted in 2005.[2]

That means the government has been unable or unwilling to rectify a problem it has recognized for thirty-five years. That is how long it has been since I first heard Saudi officials talk about the need to create more jobs outside the oil fields and to reduce dependence on imported workers. The same conversation is still going on and skepticism about real change is warranted, but it does appear that economic realities are finally forcing the Saudis to do some things differently.

The labor imbalance has many causes. It originated in modern Saudi Arabia's upside-down economic history. When serious oil money began to flow in during the late 1940s, the country was transformed from nomadic herding and subsistence farming to a wealthy, urbanized, air-conditioned society in a single generation. Rolling in cash but lacking the skills to build power plants, operate hospitals, maintain aircraft, mechanize agriculture, or operate machine tools, the Saudis naturally imported foreigners to do the work.

Except in the communities around the oil fields on the Gulf coast, the Saudis never went through a phased industrialization process in which a dirty-hands job in a mine, factory, smelter, or slaughterhouse represented a step up the economic and social ladder. The ease of importing labor instilled in a suddenly prosperous population a disdain for hard labor and blue-collar work in general. Construction workers, trash collectors, gardeners, retail clerks, hotel room cleaners, restaurant staff, hospital workers, and taxi drivers, as well as factory hands, are mostly foreigners. Saudis could do those jobs but don't want to do them. Who wants to work outdoors in Saudi Arabia's intense heat and frequent sandstorms, or in some hot, smelly restaurant kitchen, when it costs so little to import South Asian laborers?

Outside the oil patch, people ceased to admire or value hard labor and mechanical aptitude, which were necessary in the era of subsistence farming and nomadic life. People seeking husbands for their daughters wanted men from good families with university degrees, not factory managers or mine superintendents or electricians. Soft hands and good manners were preferable to calluses and gruff personalities.

Thus the Saudis today find themselves trying to persuade the next generation to move downward on the ladder of professional aspiration and into the technical and mechanical jobs that elsewhere were steps upward out of poverty. In broad terms, the Saudis have recognized that they now have more than enough people with advanced degrees in religious studies and mass communication. They need workers who know how to make things, transport them, sell them, install them, and maintain them. It is a hard transition.

When the late Ghazi Al-Gosaibi was minister of labor in 2008, he donned an apron and went to work for several hours in a fast-food restaurant in an effort to persuade young Saudis that such work was not beneath them. "There's no greater honor than starting at the bottom and finishing at the top," he declared. "It is not an accomplishment when one finds oneself already at the top."[3] That message apparently did not get through to the young Saudis. A frequent complaint of frustrated employers is that those youth looking for jobs today seek supervisory and managerial positions without ever having done any actual work.

The attitude problem compounded a genuine skills gap that existed across the employment spectrum. At least until the 1970s the country was short of people who knew how to do the indoor jobs associated with the middle class. Saudi Arabia lacked schoolteachers, doctors, nurses, accountants, travel agents, and hotel staff, so it imported them, too, in addition to foreign laborers. As the country began to industrialize, employers in the private sector often found that foreign workers brought greater industrial competence at lower wages than Saudi job applicants, who even now tend to have an exaggerated idea of their value. The cumulative result is that Saudi Arabia is, as the scholar Steffen Hertog has written, "a country without a national working class."[4]

"This is the curse of oil," said Khaled Al-Seif, one of the country's most successful businessmen. "We really spoiled people with free land for housing, free education, free medical care. We had skilled labor [in the past] but there was an erosion because they didn't need to do that work anymore."

The country's problem is not unemployment, he said, for "with all these foreigners, you can't call it unemployment." Any male university graduate who wants a job can find one, he said (although I have met male university graduates who had been unemployed for some time), but "the problem is with people who didn't get a high school diploma or are only high school graduates. In the past many of these went straight into the military. That's not possible anymore. We have to look for solutions for them."

One example is a school that Japanese automakers founded on the outskirts of Jeddah to train young Saudis to repair automobiles—a job that can be socially acceptable if done at an air-conditioned dealership instead of in an improvised sidewalk workshop. Another, Al-Seif said, was a partnership between the business community and the Ministry of Industry to train security guards. "In a four-week course, we created 60,000 jobs," he said.[5] That figure is almost certainly an exaggeration, but whatever the real number is, this example of job training only underscores the problem: A security guard who screens visitors at one of Riyadh's big banks is paid 2,000 riyals a month, or about $533, a poverty-level wage in today's Saudi Arabia. A Bangladeshi who lives in a single room with three or four others to save money and send it home to his family might work for that pay, but most Saudis will not. (In 2011 the minimum monthly wage for a civil servant was set at 3,000 riyals, so salary alone cannot account for the preference for government jobs.)

As long ago as 1986, an American scholar observed that "Saudization" had already become "a buzzword for the nation's human resource development. In theory it symbolizes the replacement of expatriate labor with similarly skilled, trained and highly educated Saudi nationals. In practice, it remains a distant goal for all but a few government agencies, public corporations, or private businesses. It is not an easily obtained objective, but political and economic pressures continue to make it a high national priority."[6]

It is still true a quarter century later. Meanwhile, the population has grown rapidly, but the engine of the country's development, the oil industry, has not. Saudi Aramco today has only about 55,000 employees, fewer than it had a decade ago.

Legal and social restrictions on the employment of women aggravate the employment problem. In the spring of 2010, according to Deputy Labor Minister Abdulwahed Al-Humaid, the unemployment rate among the relatively small number of women seeking work outside the home was 28.4 percent, and 78 percent of those unemployed women have college degrees. Matching the jobs that women are able or permitted to do with women who want them is complicated by the transportation issue. Women are not allowed to drive, and public transportation in the cities is virtually nonexistent. A respectable

Saudi woman cannot ride in the battered jitneys and minibuses that transport South Asian laborers.[7]

All of these pressures underlie the government's plans to overhaul the economy, reform the education system to produce employable graduates, promote industrial development, and encourage entire new lines of enterprise, such as tourism.

HAVEN'T BEEN THERE, HAVEN'T DONE THAT

On a murky morning in the early spring of 2010, a majestic white cruise liner, the *Crystal Serenity*, sailed into the harbor of Jeddah, Saudi Arabia's principal Red Sea port. About two hours later some five hundred passengers disembarked from the ship, boarded waiting buses, and set out to tour the city. I was among them. I had spent a week in Jeddah just a few months before and did not need the guided tour, but I wanted to see how the Saudis handled this event. We went to the neighborhood called Balad in Jeddah's old city and strolled through the Souk al-Alawi, a market similar to the souk in any Arab city, where merchants hawk clothing, small appliances, religious items, carpets, spices, and vegetables. We visited a restored 106-room house of the pre-air-conditioning Red Sea style, with the wooden shutters known as *mashrabiya*, in which King Abdul Aziz is said to have stayed after conquering the Hejaz in 1925. (Before that the Red Sea coastal region known as the Hejaz, which includes Mecca, was a separate country.)

We tourists went to see Jeddah's fish market and the mosque known as the Floating Mosque, so called because it is constructed on pylons in the sea. After lunch at a trendy restaurant on trendy Tahlia Street, we toured a quirky museum with a collection that blends art, science, history, and whimsy. Then we went back to the *Crystal Serenity* and sailed away to the next port of call.

Anywhere else this event would have been entirely routine and unremarkable. In Jeddah it was something of a landmark and drew front-page coverage in local newspapers. Tourism is still a new concept in Saudi Arabia, which ever since its founding in 1932 had discouraged foreigners from visiting unless they had specific business there.

There are of course millions of foreigners in Saudi Arabia, but they are not tourists; they work there and are isolated to a great extent from the local people. Americans and other non-Muslims were grudgingly accepted so long as their presence was necessary for the country's development, as in the oil and aviation industries. Armies of laborers from Asia clean Saudi Arabia's streets and toilets, cook its fast food, construct its buildings, and perform other tasks that Saudis disdain, but they are rarely allowed to settle in the kingdom or bring their families. The vast majority have no path to citizenship. Casual visitors and curiosity seekers were traditionally turned away, in accordance with the Wahhabi Islamic belief that infidels are to be shunned. Even Muslims from other countries who journey to Saudi Arabia for the annual pilgrimage to Mecca are usually required to leave as soon as the rites have been completed. It is a measure of Saudi Arabia's need for new sources of employment that its rulers brushed aside opposition from conservatives and the religious establishment and began to encourage tourism.

Success in this novel endeavor is far from assured. The entire concept of tourism is a hard sell in a country best known for oil wells, veiled women, its ban on alcohol, and the September 11 hijackers. After the onset of al-Qaeda terrorism inside the kingdom in 2003, the U.S. State Department discouraged Americans from going there and issued frightening warnings about threats to their safety. Contrary to the image held by most outsiders, Saudi Arabia has abundant historic sites, scenic landscapes, and broad beaches, but religious and social customs impose limitations that have long combined to discourage the type of visitors who bring real money. Archaeologists exploring sites from the biblical era have also reported conflicts with religious conservatives who oppose exhumation of any relics from the era before Islam.

Now the urgent quest for new sources of employment, combined with a new generation's desire to be part of the wider world, is driving a complete reversal of the kingdom's traditional aversion to foreigners. It is much easier for journalists and academic researchers to go there now, and the country began issuing tourist visas in 2006. The government has decided not only to accept but also to solicit and encourage tourists in the expectation that the traffic will mean jobs for Saudis in hotels, restaurants, museums, and travel agencies. As a result, the country is hosting more tourists, such as the visitors from the *Crystal Serenity*.

Because for centuries it has been the port of entry for the annual Muslim pilgrimage to Mecca, about forty miles inland, Jeddah is by far the most sophisticated and socially varied city in the kingdom. Millions of Muslims from all over the world—most of them not Arabs and most of them from societies where attitudes about behavior are considerably more relaxed than in Saudi Arabia—pass through Jeddah every year, so foreigners are not a novelty. But even in Jeddah, as the *Crystal Serenity*'s passengers discovered, the country's unique social rules present obstacles to casual tourism.

All women who took part in the tour, including my wife, were required to wear the abaya, the enveloping black coverall that all females in Saudi Arabia wear when off the ship. The cruise ship provided the abayas and brought on board an American woman who lives in Jeddah to explain how to wear and adjust them. Many of the passengers found it amusing to wear them just for the novelty—"My grandchildren will be hysterical when they see this picture"—but some women were offended. And novelty wears off quickly in the Saudi heat.

Religious rules also limited the itinerary. Non-Muslims are prohibited from going to Mecca, the country's biggest attraction, and from entering any mosque. We visitors could see the Floating Mosque only from the outside. For experienced travelers such as those on the *Crystal Serenity*, this rule invites unfavorable comparisons to Cairo, Istanbul, and Damascus, where the great mosques are landmarks of magnificence and draw large crowds of tourists.

Upon entering Saudi waters, the cruise ship was obliged to close its bars and lock up all the liquor. Passengers who had alcohol in their rooms were required to surrender it. Immigration authorities issued landing cards that bore a warning in bold red letters: Death to Drug Traffickers.

In most ports, adventurous travelers who dislike organized tours can strike off on their own, but the Saudis did not permit individual exploration of Jeddah. Permission to go ashore was granted only to those taking part in the organized tours. (As a frequent visitor to Saudi Arabia, I have a multiple-entry visa, and if I had flown in on my own, I could have gone wherever I wanted. As a cruise passenger, though, I was not permitted to leave the group.) Saudi Arabia charged each person fifty-five dollars for a one-day visa; neighboring countries charge about fifteen dollars. Passengers who chose to remain on board rather than go ashore—some stayed because they were fearful, others because they dislike Saudi Arabia's human rights record—were instructed not to go to the ship's railing in bathing attire.

Jeddah itself is not a particularly attractive or interesting city. The old town is shabby and dilapidated. The government has hired contractors for a billion-dollar restoration project, but meanwhile many of the traditional-style houses have fallen into disrepair. The souk sells mostly cheap consumer goods and lacks the appeal of the souks in Cairo and Damascus. Jeddah's traffic is heavy, and the architecture is mostly undistinguished. Untreated sewage flows on some streets. The newer neighborhoods sprawl in all directions without the sort of focal point provided by Notre Dame Cathedral in Paris or the harbor in Hong Kong (a flaw that may be remedied by a planned Ferris wheel that will rise 492 feet). The city's best-known landmark is the world's tallest fountain, which shoots water more than 1,000 feet into the air; but it was not operating on the day of our tour.

Still, the Saudis made the most of what they had for the *Crystal Serenity*'s passengers. Entry procedures were smooth and, by Saudi standards, rapid. The buses were ready. Tour guides, recruited for the day from full-time jobs in other businesses, were friendly and helpful and spoke good English. (All were men, of course.) We were asked to list our religions on our landing cards, which made some Jewish passengers nervous, and upon returning to the ship each passenger was presented with an Islamic recruitment video. Otherwise the entire subject of religion was pretty much ignored.

As an economic event, the *Crystal Serenity*'s visit was negligible, but as a symbolic event, it was important. Because Saudi Arabia has no choice but to develop new sources of employment, it must promote entire new enterprises, even if they conflict with social tradition. According to Abdullah Al-Jehani, vice president of the Saudi Commission for Tourism and Antiquities, the government agency created in 2001 to develop the industry, the tourism business was providing jobs for 445,000 Saudi citizens at the time of the *Crystal Serenity*'s visit.

On the face of it, that employment figure seems wildly inflated, but Al-Jehani and the commission have a liberal definition of "tourism." It includes the care and feeding of everyone who visits Saudi Arabia for religious pilgrimage, business conferences, and trade shows, as well as people from neighboring countries who drive into Saudi Arabia to visit relatives. Overall, that number is more than 11 million people each year. The annual Muslim pilgrimage to Mecca alone brings nearly 2 million foreign visitors to the kingdom, creating a market for accommodations, food, transportation, and other services that are provided mostly by Saudis. Categorizing the pilgrims as "tourists" might seem like a stretch, but Italy's tourism figures include people who primarily visit the Vatican.

By comparison with pilgrims and business visitors, the number who travel to Saudi Arabia simply to see the place is tiny, but that sector is most likely to grow and to cause tension between the outward-looking elements of Saudi society and the traditionalists.

"When this commission started, the word 'tourism' had a certain meaning for certain groups," Al-Jehani said. "What comes to their mind is beaches and drinking." Part of the commission's job, he said, is to broaden the definition of tourism and to convince people there will be no wave of bare-breasted women on the beaches or hard-drinking rowdies looking for sex, as in some other Arab countries.

"The type of tourist that we are aiming for is not really the regular tourist that is looking for the sun and the beach," said Al-Jehani, who studied marketing at Arizona State University. "For them Saudi Arabia is not the place. We are talking culture and heritage, people who are looking to see the history and culture of the country, and you find that those are of a certain caliber, people who work in universities and museums."

He said agents of the commission visit high schools to "tell [students] about an industry that can create jobs for them, and for the local community, what can we do to increase the economic value of your community by creating establishments and events there."

Al-Jehani's boss, the president of the Commission for Tourism and Antiquities, is Prince Sultan bin Salman, best known to Americans as a former shuttle astronaut with the U.S. National Aeronautics and Space Administration (NASA). He has set a target of 88 million "tourists" a year in Saudi Arabia by 2020, although 84 percent of them would be "local," that is, Saudis taking their holidays inside the kingdom. His projected employment figure at the time I talked to Jehani was 1.5 million. By 2011, it had grown to 2.23 million.[8]

Persuading Saudi families to spend their vacations in the kingdom instead of traveling to cooler, more congenial lands may be a more achievable goal than developing foreign tourism on a sufficient scale to be an important source of employment. On that front, the commission is struggling against Saudi Arabia's reputation as an austere desert where there is nothing to do and against a cultural climate that is hostile to infidels and discourages female and gay travelers. Nevertheless, more foreigners will visit the country and interact with the Saudi people in the future than they had in the past, demonstrating another way in which Saudi Arabia is becoming a more open, modern, international society.

In fact, the country has quite a bit to offer the tourist: Nabatean ruins that rival those of Petra; scenic mountains and lush valleys in the southwest; and excellent sites for snorkeling and spotting rare birds, as well as historic and cultural relics from ancient civilizations. In the cities, modern hotels and good restaurants are abundant. The Saudis only recently began developing an infrastructure of organization and accommodation that can match visitors to the attractions. The country now has a hotel and restaurant management school, seventy-six licensed tour operators, and, according to Al-Jehani, 115 Saudi tour guides.

Still, Al-Jehani said, only 26 percent of all people employed in this broadly defined tourism business are Saudis. (At popular chain restaurants, such as Applebee's and Ruby Tuesday, the waiters are almost all from the Philippines.) One of the commission's goals is to increase that figure by enticing more young Saudis into the business, but it will not be an easy task considering that many Saudis are averse to walking in the sun and chatting with foreigners. Working inside an air-conditioned museum or travel agency office is one thing; exploring the ruins of the old royal capital of Diriyah in the midday sun with groups of infidels that include women is quite another.

The government requires that tour guides be Saudis, but "Saudis don't like to do it, to take walking tours and talk to tourists," said Fahad Al-Safh. And he should know. A pioneer of tourism in Saudi Arabia, he started his Arabian Explorer Tours company in 1993, organizing weekend excursions for foreign diplomats and corporate employees who were in the kingdom anyway and looking for something to do on weekends. He is a true believer.

"Everybody said, 'You are crazy!'" when he started. He said his friends predicted it would cost him his other business, interior design. His travel business did come close to collapsing during the wave of domestic al-Qaeda-sponsored terrorism that beset the country in 2003–2007, he said, "but we have a big treasure for tourism, more than Egypt! This will be a very big market." According to his catalogue for 2010, "you can have walking & bus tour to see gazelle, Ibex, elephant, camels, lamas, horses, crocodiles, ostriches, rabbits, variety of birds species (big Bedouin colorful Bedouin tent & colorful Arabian coffee and tea room)." Elephants? There may be one or two in zoos, but they are not exactly native species.

Al-Safh acknowledged that he operates in an environment that presents unique difficulties and restrictions in addition to the tour guide requirement. There are no souvenirs such as mugs and statuettes, no unaccompanied female clients are allowed, and security escorts are required for trips outside Jeddah. The government, he said, "wants this to happen but is afraid. We have to work slowly. We don't want to make it like Dubai," the wide-open emirate next door.[9]

Another believer is Rita Zawaideh, a Jordanian-born Christian who operates Caravan-Serai Travel in Seattle, Washington. She also leads tours of Saudi Arabia for clients.

"We have been trying to do this for years and now thank heaven it has finally happened," she said. "As a woman, an Arab woman, a Christian, I wasn't sure how it would go, but with a lot of help from different people and the fact that we only do the Middle East and North Africa, that helped a lot. And a lot is because of my ancestry and belonging to the tribe that I did, one of those recognized by [the Prophet] Muhammad—people from our tribe helped him. Different tribal leaders treated us like royalty. That's how you do business in the Middle East."[10]

In the fall of 2009, her company offered a two-week tour of Saudi Arabia for $6,318 per person, not counting airfare. It sounds like the old joke about Philadelphia: What was second prize? Three weeks? But the itinerary might intrigue a certain type of intrepid traveler.

Days 1 and 2: Riyadh, "a modern, shining city in the middle of the desert." Tour Masmak Fort, captured by King Abdul Aziz in 1902; Diriyah, ancestral home of the Al-Saud family; the old souk and the camel market; the city's two fanciest shopping malls, which are in the city's tallest buildings; and the national museum.

Day 3: fly to Najran, in the mountainous southwest near the border with Yemen; tour a big dam; and see rock carvings and an ancient well astride the frankincense trade route.

Day 4: tour Najran City, its museums, and historic castle.

Day 5: tour Abha and the surrounding mountains; ride a cable car; visit a terraced mountainside village, where inhabitants used ropes to get from one place to another; and visit local museum and a national park.

Day 6: fly to Jeddah, then on to northwest corner of country to Al Ula, which serves as a base for visits to the ancient city of Madain Salih.

Day 7: visit Madain Salih, spectacular ruins left by the Nabateans, the same people who built Jordan's famous Petra; and see the railway station and remnants of the Hijaz Railway, blown up by guerrillas under the command of Lawrence of Arabia during World War I.

Day 8: return to see Madain Salih "in the morning light," and tour the desert by four-wheel-drive vehicle.

Day 9: travel overland to Al-Jouf, near the border with Jordan; on the way visit Taimi, part of the ancient kingdom of Midian and source of the Taimi Stone, with inscriptions in Aramaic, that is in the Louvre.

Day 10: tour Al-Jouf and the surrounding region, once home to Assyrians and Nabateans.

Day 11: travel to Hail, an agricultural city on the overland pilgrimage routes from central Asia, and see rock carvings.

Day 12: tour Hail, the crossroads of trade and pilgrimage and said to be the center of Arabic spoken "in its purest form."

Day 13: fly to Jeddah, "said to be the burial place of Eve, thus the name Jeddah, which is grandmother in Arabic." Visit quirky local museum; then dine at popular outdoor restaurant on the seafront Corniche.

Day 14: tour Jeddah's old city and its souk, and open-air sculpture museum on the Corniche.

At each stop, the scheduled activities cover pretty much all there is to see. But the novel tour could appeal to the "been there, done that," well-traveled veteran or to people of Arab descent exploring their heritage, and the hotels and restaurants are more than adequate.

Zawaideh said that through her family connections she is able to "take people into homes of people I know, the wives are there without their covering. The clients are going into homes of friends and relatives; you are going to visit someone who isn't being paid for it, enjoying their hospitality."

She said she is not much concerned about safety in Saudi Arabia. "The only thing they have to worry about is maybe the morality police if they're not dressed right," she said. "We get that with Europeans who say they're going to do their own thing" and insist on dressing as they would elsewhere.

It is not only the influx of foreign tourists that represents a seismic cultural shift for Saudi Arabia. The elevation of pre-Islamic sites such as Madain Salih to national asset with protected status is also a recent development in a society that has traditionally scorned everything that predated the Prophet Muhammad as relics of paganism.

"People have been coming to Saudi Arabia for 1,430 years," or since the first Muslim pilgrims went to Mecca, said the Tourism Commission's Al-Jehani. "But when you start talking about cultural tourism and sporting events, this is a new thing that is being developed. In Mecca, Medina, and Jeddah you find people of Pakistani origin, Indian, Turkish; they are living there. In the rest of Saudi Arabia, thinking about incoming tourism just started in the mid-1990s. Before that there was no tourism other than the pilgrimage. It will take time for people, and it will take time for Saudi Arabia to build the infrastructure, but it's a good start."

To some extent the tourism business is being developed by a few hustling entrepreneurs like Al-Sahf. Mostly, though, encouraging tourism was a top-down decision, as are most major economic initiatives in Saudi Arabia. The government created the Commission for Tourism and Antiquities and announced what kind of tourism it would welcome. It is not clear that a state-directed approach to economic planning will be successful in achieving the government's ambitious targets for industrialization, but in the case of tourism, it has the potential to open doors for small businesses because, unlike petrochemical factories, they require little capital investment.

ZERO UNEMPLOYMENT?

According to the country's master economic and industrial development plan through the year 2025, the total Saudi labor force in 2009 consisted of 4,885,960 workers. That figure is projected to grow to 11,850,180 by the end of the planning period. The Saudi workers represented less than half the total work force in 2009, but they are projected to constitute almost 80 percent of the workforce by the end of 2024 as the need for imported labor declines.

Female participation in the labor force is projected to rise from 14.16 percent in 2009 to 30 percent in 2024.[11] The overall unemployment rate, improbably given as a mere 2.84 percent in 2009, is projected to be 0 percent at the end of the planning period.

How are these feats to be accomplished, especially when the planning document calculates that the number of workers with no education or only primary schooling—exactly the type of untrained people who are the hardest to employ—will rise from 1.2 million in 2009 to nearly 1.8 million at the end of 2024? As with all aspects of economic development, the government has a plan, namely, the Saudi Employment Strategy.

Commissioned by the Ministry of Labor, it sets three overriding objectives: "realization of full employment," "maintenance of [a] durable increase in national manpower participation," and "raising Saudi labor productivity to match the standards of productivity in advanced economies." Each goal is to be achieved in stages: a two-year short term, a three- to five-year medium term, and a long term of up to twenty-five years. The plans call for a combination of government action, changes in law and regulation, training programs, and exhortation. The strategy drills down into details, such as "deepening labor offices' services to include business inspection, job search guidance, training, re-training, termination of services and job disputes"; "increasing flexibility for transfer between educational specializations"; and "granting allocations to businesses to train and qualify their employees" for higher-productivity positions.

"We believe the private sector should be a partner with government," Deputy Labor Minister Al-Humaid said. "We decided it's not very useful just to write a labor strategy and impose it. We asked a private-sector consulting company to do this for us. We talked about broad vision and ideas, building a productive society. Everyone agrees with this. Then we gave them the European Union's labor strategy and the strategies from Malaysia, from South Korea—from successful countries. Then when they were finished we asked for public comment and put it on our Web site. So we think of this as a partnership. We are not imposing it."

He said the labor strategy reflects an understanding throughout the government and the business community that the labor market is distorted by three basic, deep-rooted problems: the poor skill level of Saudi workers, the preference for government jobs, and the easy availability of cheap, imported labor. "For decades we allowed recruitment from anywhere in the world with no minimum wage," he said. "Firms want to maximize profits, so a Bangladeshi at six hundred riyals is better than a Saudi for three thousand. Saudis can't live on South Asian wages."

Like other government officials, he failed to mention another reason that the government encouraged imported labor for so many years: The foreigners are much easier to fire and easier to manage politically. Any foreign worker who makes trouble, such as trying to organize for better pay and conditions, is promptly sent home.

For Saudi citizens, he said, "government jobs are still very attractive—low pressure, shorter work hours, two full days off, good security. But we believe in small government. We shouldn't employ people just for the sake of employing them." Like many educated Saudis, he is aware of the high price Egypt paid—and is still paying—for a decades-long policy of giving a government job to every university graduate. The state's huge payroll is bloated with thousands of people who have nothing to do except gum up the bureaucracy.

The good news, Al-Humaid said, is that the "social stigma" against industrial jobs is dissipating under the pressure of necessity. "When Saudis find the right job," they work, he said. "Most important is the wage, and the work environment."[12]

DECLINING PRODUCTIVITY

Several banks in Saudi Arabia issue periodic reports on various aspects of the economy. These analyses are often more realistic, and therefore more useful, than the optimistic forecasts that government agencies generate. In January 2010, Banque Saudi Fransi issued one titled "Slow but Sure: Saudi Arabia Set for Steady 2010 Recovery" that contained two discouraging findings about the government's efforts to restructure the labor market.

One was that "after rising for most of the decade, productivity among private sector enterprises is slipping. . . . In our opinion, productivity is—in the long run—the only sustainable engine for job creation for the private sector." The productivity decline was measurable in finance, insurance, and real estate; in construction; and in agriculture, the report said.

The second finding was that "the government added 69,726 civil service employees in 2008, the biggest year-on-year climb in the workforce in more than two decades."[13] The government might have increased hiring to help offset the impact of the global recession, but that move did not bode well for its effort to wean Saudis off the public payroll.

A month later, Riyadh-based Jadwa Investment Group issued its annual assessment of the Saudi economy for 2010. It predicted that "government spending will provide the main stimulus to the economy in 2010" and "a rise in expatriate remittances stemming from the continued growth in the foreign labor force."[14] Those comments too show how difficult it is going to be for the government to shift the burden of economic growth to the private sector and to reduce its dependence on imported labor.

One way to increase private-sector employment is to sell off state-owned corporations; overnight, employees of the state become employees of investor-owned businesses. The Saudi government has been privatizing state enterprises at an accelerating rate since becoming a member of the World Trade Organization in 2005. The state telephone monopoly has been broken up, and there are now three competing companies. Parts of the national airline, including its catering service, have been sold to investors, while the water treatment and distribution network has been opened to private investors. Some infrastructure projects that provide basic public services, such as electricity and transportation, are now built and operated by private companies under what Khaled Al-Seif described as a "B-O-T [Build-Operate-Transfer] system."

"This was how the government liberated the economy," Al-Seif said. "In the old days the government owned everything."

The B-O-T system originated in the days of rock-bottom oil prices in the 1980s, he said. "The government had no capital to spend; it couldn't finance the infrastructure that was required. We in the private sector came up with B-O-T. The private sector would finance and build a power plant, let's say, or the new Haj [pilgrimage] terminal [at Jeddah airport] and operate it. It's a tender process—you build on government-owned land, you get an annual payment. It's a twenty-year contract; you get your expenses back plus a profit. Eventually the project will revert to government ownership," and the workers will go on the government payroll, but by that time presumably the private sector will have expanded to the point where it can provide other opportunities for the young and ambitious. That goal, at least, is what the long-term labor plan calls for.

Carrying out that plan will require the government to make some difficult decisions that are surely going to be unpopular with the business community. For instance, a number of young princes who have decided their future lies in investment rather than in government might prove just as resistant to workplace change as their non-royal partners are. One step the government can be expected to take will be enforcing existing rules that limit foreign laborers to the types of jobs specified on their *iqama* (work permit). The news media have reported many examples of foreigners who were admitted to the country as ordinary laborers who are working in professional or supervisory positions, or even imported housemaids working as beauticians, because employers value their loyalty—or their docility—and their willingness to work hard for less money than comparably qualified Saudis earn.

The government could establish a minimum wage that would apply to all workers, Saudi and foreign, thus diminishing the competitive appeal of the foreigners, but the business community would resist that step. Or it could simply slash the number of work permits for foreigners and insist that Saudis do the jobs instead. Indeed, the government has tried that approach several times, directing that taxi drivers and sales clerks in the gold markets and lingerie shops be only Saudi nationals; each time the government has backed down in the face of employer reluctance and the Saudis' lack of interest in taking such jobs.

At one point the Ministry of Labor set a minimum quota of 30 percent Saudi hires in several lines of business. The result was given in *A Business Guide to Saudi Arabia*:

In April 2006, in accordance with the new labor law, the Labor Ministry announced a reduction in the Saudization quota from 30 to 10 percent for jobs with a low volume of Saudi applicants. The reduction applies to positions in industries such as bakeries, tailor shops, carpentry, aluminum works, auto workshops, laundries, farms, gas stations, truck driving, pharmacies, and optical centers. Saudization quotas in health care have also been reduced to as low as 1 percent for pharmaceutical companies employing more than 50 people. In February 2008, the Ministry of Labor announced a reduction in the Saudization quota from 30 to 20 percent for industries involved with foodstuffs, beverages, textiles, readymade garments, shoes, furniture, and paper.[15]

That is, the government set arbitrary "Saudization" quotas and backed off when they turned out to be unenforceable.

Near the end of 2010, that same outcome befell even a government order that the country's corps of "Koran memorization teachers" become all Saudi. As foreigners departed, newspapers reported more than a thousand vacancies went unfilled by Saudis, and the government again relented.

As for reducing the number of foreigners in the economy as a whole, the Ministry of Labor announced in 2010 that the number of work visas issued to foreigners in 2009 had declined by 15 percent from the year before, to 1.54 million, but that reduction was attributable more to the worldwide economic recession, which brought a number of major development projects in the kingdom to a halt, than to any overall change in the system.[16]

In fact, after analyzing the results of the country's 2010 census, the economists at Jadwa Investment Group found

a far greater expatriate population than had been assumed. Since the last census, in 2004, the expatriate population has grown twice as fast as the number of Saudi nationals.

Of the 27.1 million person total population arrived at in the census, which was conducted in April, 18.7 million were Saudi nationals and 8.4 million expatriates. The previous census was held in September 2004, when the total population was 22.7 million, split between 16.5 million nationals and 6.1 million expatriates. Between the two censuses, the number of Saudi nationals rose by 19 percent, while the number of expatriates increased by 38 percent. If the population grows over the next decade at the same pace as it has since the 2004 census, by 2020 the Kingdom's population will be 37.2 million, with 22.8 million Saudi nationals and 14.4 million expatriates.

Even more alarming, the report continued, "given the high government spending planned over the next few years (expenditure of $385 billion is contained in the 2010–2014 five-year development plan) we anticipate further rapid growth in the expatriate population."[17]

These failures are not surprising. When laborers from impoverished countries are willing to work very long hours for minimal wages and live five or six people to a room to make ends meet, the appeal to employers is obvious.

If American employers could import low-cost labor at will, they would do the same thing; instead, they take factories to where the low-cost foreign workers are.

At one point in a long conversation about the Saudi economy in May 2010, the ever-blunt John Sfakianakis, chief economist at Banque Saudi Fransi, waved his hand toward the big window in his office and the busy street below, where workmen in yellow suits—foreigners all—were cleaning the pavement. "The only way for Saudi Arabia is to stop importing foreigners," he said. "Get rid of those seven Bangladeshis sweeping the street for 700 riyals a month, buy a sweeper with an air-conditioned cab and pay one Saudi 3,000 riyals a month to do it."

High-tech street cleaning is not what the government's planners envision in their aspirations for a "knowledge society" and a modern, industrial economy. To reach that goal, they will have to overcome the mismatch in capabilities between what employers will want and what young Saudi job seekers know how to do. That task has been assigned to the country's schools and universities.

6

The Education Revolution

Until recently, the public education system in Saudi Arabia was a sinkhole of irrelevant curriculum, outdated teaching methods, hateful rhetoric, poorly trained teachers and administrators, and low student performance. The people coming out of its schools could not fulfill the country's grand ambition and bold plans to convert itself into an industrialized, knowledge-based society, with a place at the table of the world's most advanced nations.

This unhappy reality was not readily apparent to Americans and other Westerners who went to Saudi Arabia on business. More often than not, the Saudis they met were urbane, well-educated English speakers, many with advanced degrees from American and European universities. It is often said that more members of the Saudi cabinet have PhD degrees from universities in the United States than do their counterparts in the American government. These sophisticated Saudis, unfortunately, are not representative of the society as a whole, as the Saudi government, spurred by King Abdullah, has finally recognized.

King Abdullah has made education reform and expansion the hallmark of his reign. Saudi Arabia is in the midst of a massive, ambitious, nationwide program to build more schools and universities, get more students into them, make the curriculum relevant to the job market and the outside world, send more young Saudis abroad for study, and develop research initiatives in partnership with American and European universities and corporations. Whether the goals are achievable, and sustainable if achieved, is open to question because the kingdom is trying to come from far behind, opposition to change is entrenched, and the degree of support for reform among potential successors to the aged king is unknown.

In earlier times a few lonely voices raised concerns about the mess in the schools, but most Saudis were in denial about the sad state of the public education system. It was understandable because by comparison with the past it appeared that the Saudis had a great deal to be proud of. When the modern kingdom was founded in 1932 there were hardly any schools for boys and none for girls. Illiteracy was prevalent among men and nearly universal among women. By 2004, illiteracy had been reduced to 12 percent among men and 24 percent among women, mostly of the older generation. In 1970 the country had only about 100 public high schools with 500 teachers; by 2005 it had 4,200 high schools with 79,800 teachers.

There was abundant anecdotal evidence that those impressive numbers masked a failing system that did not produce enough graduates who actually knew how to do, make, or invent things. The system's actual poor results could be recognized in the inability of Saudi businesses to find qualified Saudi workers.

By the time Abdullah became king, in 2005, hard data reinforced these impressionistic observations. Saudi students in 2003 participated for the first time in the worldwide Trends in International Mathematics and Science Study (TIMSS). Describing itself as "an international organization of national research institutions and governmental research agencies," the International Association for the Evaluation of Educational Achievement developed and administered the quadrennial assessment to demonstrate the math and science knowledge of pupils in the fourth and eighth grades.

Saudi Arabia withheld its fourth graders from the TIMSS evaluation; only eighth graders took part. In math, their score was 332; the international average was 466. The United States scored 504. Saudi Arabia trailed Iran, Egypt, and Bahrain, to say nothing of high-achieving Singapore, which led all countries with 605. In science, the Saudi score was 398, against an international average of 473. Here too Saudi Arabia was behind its neighbors Iran, Egypt, and Bahrain. Singapore led with 578, followed closely by Taiwan.

When this exercise was repeated four years later, the gap had widened. The Saudi science score improved marginally to 403, but the international average had gone up to 500. In math, the Saudi score actually went down to 329. Of all participating countries, only Ghana and Qatar fared worse. At the top was Taiwan, with 598.[1]

"The curriculum is awful and the teaching is awful," said Alan Kantrow, an American consultant who has made extensive studies of the Saudi system for private clients. "The scores were terrible then, and there's even more terrible data now," partly because of "a huge lack of quality textbooks that are . . . current or accurate in math or science available in the Arabic language.

"You can look at the data," he said. "The range of countries against which the TIMSS scores give you benchmarks includes not just Singapore and Switzerland but a whole range of developing countries, against which Saudi Arabia still does terribly."[2]

The country was still absorbing the bad news from TIMSS when, in January 2008, the National Competitiveness Center, a unit of the Saudi Arabian General Investment Authority, published a scathing, comprehensive assessment of the entire system that documented its many failings. SAGIA's mandate is to encourage and support foreign investment in the Saudi economy, not to educate the country's young people, but the authority's leaders recognized that the education system's deficiencies were producing a labor force that could not do the jobs foreign investors would require. On its Web site, the authority proclaims, "Education is central to the Kingdom's development agenda as nowhere else in the world."[3]

SAGIA created its own education unit, headed by an American-born woman, Kim Pringle Al-Sahhaf, who has lived in Saudi Arabia more than twenty-five years. Part of the unit's assignment is to develop new curricula for the schools that will be built in the New Economic Cities, an Investment Authority project. One goal is to work in consultation with employers to develop graduates who would be useful to them. For example, if the big money is coming from China, some students will learn Mandarin.

"We are changing everything for a sustainable, long-term effect," Ms. Pringle Al-Sahhaf said. "In the past we were in denial. Now we recognize the problem. There are still some people who don't recognize the need to make major changes, but I think we're there." King Abdullah, she said, is "very supportive" of educational innovation.[4]

In her introduction to the nationwide school assessment that her unit produced, she wrote that "education drives our economic diversification away from oil, providing the human capital to attract foreign direct investment, build an innovation-based economy, and redefine Saudi Arabia's position in the world." This often-proclaimed national objective is shared across the portfolios of several ministries, but the study her unit produced, under the bland title "The Education Sector in Saudi Arabia," exposed in blunt terms the multiple failures of the public education system.[5]

"Though the leadership's commitment to education is strong and education expenditures high, Saudi Arabia's return on investment is comparatively low," the study said. "Relative to Saudi Arabia, such developing countries as India, China, Jordan, and others spend far less per pupil but generate significantly more engineers, scientists, and knowledge-based economy workers to enhance country competitiveness."

Among the study's specific findings are:

- Saudi high school students spend 816 hours per year in school, much less than their contemporaries elsewhere. In Germany and the Netherlands, the figure is more than 1,100 hours.
- Saudi high schools have 0.6 computers for every 100 students. Industrialized, competitive economies have up to 75 times as many; for example, the figure is 37 in Denmark.
- The productivity of Saudi workers, in terms of output per unit of time, is half to two-thirds that of industrial Europe.
- In measurements of education quality compiled by the World Economic Forum, such as extent of staff training, Internet access, and quality of school management, Saudi Arabia trailed the world's most competitive economies in every one except expenditure.
- In the rankings of world universities compiled by Webometrics, a Spanish research group, as of 2006 no Saudi University was in the top 1,000. The highest-ranked, King Fahd University of Petroleum and Minerals, was number 1,128. The most influential institution, King Saud University, was at 3,108. (By 2010, after five years of King Abdullah's efforts to energize the system, these rankings had improved dramatically; King Saud University had moved up all the way to 164.)[6]
- For every 1,000 students who go through the public university system, Saudi Arabia graduates 9 engineers; in Sweden, the figure is 78. More than 90 percent of Saudi teachers are Saudi citizens, but only 20 percent of the kingdom's doctors, engineers, and research scientists are Saudis.

- In 2006 the United States granted 179.2 patents to Finnish inventors for every million residents of Finland, 123.1 for every million South Koreans, and 2.5 for every million Kuwaitis. For Saudi Arabia, the figure was 0.8.
- The "vast majority" of public school principals are "older teachers, who have received no specialized training in how to run a school, manage people or budgets, or communicate effectively."

None of these dismal findings can be attributed to a shortage of resources. Saudi Arabia has been throwing money at the school system for years, and the rate of spending has increased under Abdullah. As a percentage of national income, Saudi Arabia spends more on education than the United States or Germany and three times as much as Singapore. Expenditure per student in Saudi Arabia is higher than in most of Europe. Schools at every level from kindergarten to university are being built at a furious pace all across the country. The kingdom's Ninth Five-Year Development Plan (2010–2014), endorsed by the Council of Ministers in August 2010, allocates more than half its $385 billion in spending to "human resources," including education. "The spending plan allocates funds for 25 new colleges of technology, 28 higher technical institutes and 50 industrial training institutes, and aims to expand the capacity of public universities to 1.7 million students and primary, intermediate and secondary schools to 5.31 million students," according to the Saudi embassy in Washington.[7] The national budget for 2011 allocated $40 billion to education, representing more than a quarter of total spending.

The problem with Saudi education is not the availability of buildings and classrooms. The problem is what goes on inside them: poorly trained teachers who rely on rote learning and other obsolete techniques; religious restrictions that inhibit the exchange of ideas and learning about the world; textbooks that impart a narrow, xenophobic, and sometimes hateful view of other societies; and social attitudes that value conformity over individuality. Many Saudis seem to value education as a credential rather than as an end in itself or as a gateway to new ideas and new norms of social organization.

Other than the relatively few people in the oil region, Saudis who became rich practically overnight never went through the phased industrialization in which each generation considered it an accomplishment to be a little better educated than the one before. Once they had the resources, the Saudis wanted not only high school diplomas but also those badges of the educated, PhD degrees. The title "doctor" commanded respect, conferred status, and opened the door to a good government job, regardless of whether the subject of the doctoral studies was relevant to the work. (Conversely, many Saudis take it for granted that a person such as myself who writes books and is affiliated with a think tank must have a doctoral degree. They address me as Dr. Lippman and seem baffled when I tell them I do not have a graduate degree. I encountered the same phenomenon while living in Egypt years ago.)

Except at Saudi Aramco, where technical proficiency is a requirement, the long years spent developing the apparatus of the state encouraged Saudis to prefer jobs in government agencies and discouraged entrepreneurial risk. The Saudis failed to recognize that a proliferation of doctoral degrees should follow, not precede, economic development. One result of this attitude was a huge surplus of PhD graduates in religious subjects, such as Islamic history, who had no marketable skills except as teachers of the same material to others or as imams in the mosques. Another, more recent manifestation of this phenomenon has been the acquisition of fake doctorates from Internet-based "universities" abroad.

As the consultant Kantrow put it, "Attitudes shaped by oil revenue in the past still exist. The broad cultural thing about being educated to actually work gets in the way."

That attitude is reflected in enrollment figures. As of 2006, according to the Ministry of Education, 636,400 students were enrolled in the public universities, or ten times the number enrolled in government-run technical and vocational schools, including secretarial programs.

The National Competitiveness Center's assessment focused on the unsatisfactory outcomes of Saudi education, not on the causes of those outcomes. Being a government institution, it could hardly have done otherwise because one of the principal causes of those outcomes is religion, and it would have been politically impossible, as well as pointless, for a government entity to say so.

As a matter of Saudi tradition and law, religion's primacy in the curriculum is well established. The Basic Law of Government, which King Fahd promulgated in 1992, stipulates that "Saudi society will be based on the principle of adherence to God's command" and that "education will aim at instilling the Islamic faith in the younger generation."[8] One of the goals listed in the Education Ministry's Ten-Year Plan for 2004–2014 is "to develop syllabi that will ensure the development of the Muslim learner's personality to make him proud of his faith and to be loyal to his country in practice and conduct." Teaching the citizens that Islam requires obedience to the ruler is a crucial component of the House of Saud's long-term strategy to enhance its legitimacy and secure the public's assent to its rule. That political motive can obviously interfere with what modern education is designed to encourage, that is, the exploration of new ideas. "The Saudi curriculum is designed to homogenize the population and instill loyalty to the state," according to Eleanor Doumato of Brown University, a longtime student of Saudi education.[9]

With those imperatives and those rules, it was inevitable that the public school curriculum would devote disproportionate amounts of time to religious studies, which in such a short school year inevitably curtails students' exposure to other subjects. Nor is the condensed time the only restriction students face: Art classes avoid works in which bare flesh is depicted; there is hardly any instruction in music, other religions, or non-Islamic civilizations; and evolution is filtered through a religious prism. Social sciences such as anthropology are viewed with suspicion because they might lead to findings that are inconsistent with Islam. The conservative establishment and religious authorities have opposed plans to start English-language instruction earlier than sixth grade, where it begins now, because to them it is just another open door to foreign influence.

In those respects the school system is as much a reflection of cultural attitudes as a shaper of them. There is no free market in ideas. The nation's constraints on external cultural input are readily visible at any branch of Jarir, the biggest bookstore chain. The offerings include extensive collections of religious pronouncements, biographies of the Prophet, compilations of his sayings, and, for the benefit of the large foreign population, translations of the Koran. The stores feature plenty of popular English-language fiction, such as works by Scott Turow and James Patterson, and an extensive collection on economics. But they do not carry any history—not even art history—other than Islamic history. There are no books about music; about Zionism, of course; or about philosophy. Why would people want to read Schopenhauer or Hume or Voltaire? They were infidels. The Ministry of Information also simply bans any books that might question or conflict with Islam or that criticize the monarchy.

It is not surprising that many of the educated Saudis who work at Saudi Aramco and live in the relatively enlightened climate of the Eastern Province send their children to private schools or to schools across the causeway in neighboring Bahrain, where the educational environment is less restrictive.

According to Andrew Short, Saudi Arabia country director for the GEMS private school network, the private schools can offer the European baccalaureate curriculum, or the American, Indian, or Pakistani equivalents, but only to the children of foreigners living in the kingdom. The Ministry of Education requires Saudi students to follow the Saudi curriculum, he said, but parents send their children anyway because of "better teachers, better facilities and better discipline."

How could discipline be a problem in such a tightly controlled society? Short said the issue arises mostly with the children of the royal and the wealthy. These students get their instruction from tutors at home and "come to school to socialize in a safe environment" because there are no other opportunities to do so.

Short maintains, and there is every reason to believe him, that Saudi parents send their children to private schools because they recognize that success in life now requires an understanding of the world, engagement with other cultures, and a knowledge of English, all of which they are more likely to obtain in the private schools.[10] As in so many American cities, the private schools are perceived as meeting the aspirations of those who can afford them, while the public schools struggle to serve everyone else.

The demand for better schooling has created business opportunities. The U.S.–Saudi Arabian Business Council, which encourages American companies to invest in the kingdom, said in a 2009 report that "as the education industry in Saudi Arabia continues to grow, it offers numerous opportunities for companies to become involved and invest in the development of education in Saudi Arabia."[11] One of the most ambitious education entrepreneurs is none other that Prince Alwaleed bin Talal, a nephew of King Abdullah's who is said to be one of the world's richest men. In 2000 his Kingdom Holding Company established an education subsidiary, Kingdom Schools, to operate a private school network for the children of the affluent. In September 2010 Kingdom Schools selected Short's GEMS, a for-profit company based in Britain, as its operating partner.

THE TEXTBOOK ISSUE

Madawi Al-Rasheed teaches social anthropology at the University of London, but she grew up in Saudi Arabia and received her basic schooling there. In her view, the kingdom's school curriculum is essentially propaganda. The textbooks cherry-pick the events of world, Islamic, and Saudi history to establish that the Al-Saud are not only legitimate rulers but also the redeemers of an entire civilization, which before the Al-Sauds' rule was beset by enemies and had fallen into corruption.

"Saudis emerge from the classroom with a vision of the pre–Saudi Wahhabi past as a dark episode marked by fragmentation and disunity," she wrote. Other forms of political thought; personal allegiance, such as Arab nationalism and tribal loyalty; and other versions of Islam are depicted as corrupt and invalid.

"The historical narratives of the Saudi state," Al-Rasheed wrote, "perpetuate particular representations of the past that aim to bind rulers and ruled. These narratives are not concerned with historical accuracy or facts, but with establishing obedience to the rulers."[12]

A respected scholar, Al-Rasheed is also a severe critic of the Saudi regime and is no longer welcome in the kingdom, so she might be biased. However, others who have no personal quarrel with the Saudi system tend to agree with her.

It is difficult for outsiders to evaluate what actually happens in Saudi classrooms. Few non-Arabs have sufficient command of the language to understand the lessons. Saudi Arabia does not welcome scrutiny from others. Distribution of textbooks is limited. Female researchers are restricted from working with their male counterparts and vice versa. Those who have penetrated the system, however, have reached discouraging conclusions.

The German scholar Michaela Prokop has written that even if all the planned reforms and educational restructurings are carried out, they "will take years to take effect and will not only necessitate retraining of teachers but also the introduction of a methodology of teaching that allows for tolerance and understanding of the 'others.' The legacy of years of indoctrination, suppression of any creative and innovative spirit and the fear of change instilled into the minds of generations may prove to be the main obstacles to change."

As Prokop's comments suggest, even if Saudi Arabia is entirely sincere about modernizing and upgrading its schools, at least two generations have already come to adulthood steeped in the old ideas and molded by the old attitudes. She found:

> Approximately 30 percent of weekly hours in elementary school are dedicated to religious subjects, 24 percent in intermediate school, and in secondary school around 35 percent for students in the shari'a [Islamic law] branch and approximately 14 percent for those in the technical and natural science branch. Failure in any one of the religious subjects requires repeating the whole academic year. History classes such as history of Islamic civilisation, history of the life of the Prophet and his companions, or history of Saudi Arabia, and Arabic literature classes are also heavily influenced by Islamic teachings.

Even in the nonreligious universities, she observed, as much as 45 percent of the content in humanities and social science classes is religious material.[13] According to Eleanor Doumato,

> Since at least the 1960s, religion courses have been at the center of the curriculum, occupying more than one-third of students' weekly classroom hours in elementary and middle school and at least four hours a week in high school. For purposes of grade promotion, religion courses are given more weight than secular subjects. In practice, religious instruction occupies a great deal more of students' classroom time because books on history are almost exclusively Islamic history, and books on Arabic language, literature and rhetoric deal with religious literature, religious figures, and religious themes.[14]

Doumato's reference to the 1960s reflects a critical chapter in the history of education in Saudi Arabia. When oil first began to flow in large amounts, in the decade after World War II, Aramco conducted most of the students' schooling to develop potential future employees. As public education spread in the 1950s and 1960s, Saudi Arabia—lacking its own teachers—welcomed teachers from Egypt and Syria. Many were members of the Muslim Brotherhood, the grandfather of all contemporary Islamist movements.

Having been driven out of their home countries by secular, nationalist regimes, the teachers carried their religious outlook to Saudi Arabia. One of them was Muhammad Qutb, an Islamist teacher and theoretician whose brother, Sayid Qutb, has often been described as the intellectual inspiration of al-Qaeda.

Before September 11, 2001, most Americans had little reason to be concerned with what was taught in Saudi Arabia's schools. It had been U.S. policy since the earliest days of the bilateral relationship in the 1940s not to interfere in Saudi domestic affairs, and Americans who lived in Saudi Arabia sent their children to American schools, which were not subject to the Saudi curriculum. After 9/11, Americans began to scrutinize Saudi schools and other institutions and were alarmed at what they found.

"Schoolbooks condition students to respect authority, to confuse opinion with fact, and to see ethical questions in black and white, as if Islam were a single, stagnant body of knowledge with immutable answers to all life's questions," Doumato wrote in her extensive study. That description is the antithesis of a liberal education aimed at encouraging critical thinking and the exploration of new ideas.

She quoted from a tenth-grade Saudi textbook that says all creed and faith comes from the Koran and the Sunna, or example of the Prophet, the other chief source of doctrine; therefore, the text declares, "there is no place in it for opinion [al-ra'y] or individual reasoning [al-ijtihad]." That narrow view runs contrary to a thousand years of teaching and interpretation in other Muslim communities.

Year after year, she found, students are taught that "ideas that run counter to Salafi-Wahhabi orthodoxy are not interpretations and modes of thought to debate and consider, but are unacceptable, deviant and heretical, promulgated by people who are not real Muslims and who therefore must be denounced." (In broadest terms, salafism is a back-to-basics movement that aspires to emulate the religious practices and social behavior of those early Muslims who found favor with the Prophet Muhammad.)

Muslims are routinely depicted as victims of history who have been besieged by infidel enemies since the time of the Crusades. In the standard tenth-grade text that Doumato examined, *The Life of the Prophet and the History of the Islamic State*, Islamic history is presented as an unending struggle to defend Islam against internal and external enemies—meaning Jews, of course, and even Muslims from more flexible groups within the faith. Students also are taught to avoid contact with non-Muslims as much as possible.

In June 2009, then Representative Anthony D. Weiner, a New York Democrat, issued "Passing Hate on to the Next Generation," a study prepared by a member of his staff after examining some Saudi textbooks used in the 2008–2009 school year. The study concluded that "textbooks in Saudi Arabian schools preach hate towards Jews, Christians and other non-Muslims, expound historical inaccuracies, and propagate subjection of women."

The report offered specific quotations, in English translation, to support that conclusion. Among the examples, with the years in which they were found, are:

It is part of God's wisdom that the struggle between the Muslims and the Jews should continue until the hour [of judgment]. The good news for Muslims is that God will help them against the Jews in the end, which is one of the signs of the hour [of judgment]. Muslims will triumph because they are right. He who is right is always victorious, even if most people are against him. [*Source:* al Hadeeth wa Athiqafah (Sayings of the Prophet and Islamic Culture), *Page 148, 2008. Taught in 9th grade, age 14.*]

The punishment for homosexuality is death . . . Ibn Qudamah said, "The companions of the Prophet were unanimous on killing, although they differed in the description, that is, in the manner of killing. Some of the companions of the Prophet stated that [a homosexual] is to be burned with fire. It has also been said that he should be stoned, or thrown from a high place." [*Source:* Fiqh (Jurisprudence), *Page 100, 2009. Taught in 10th grade, age 15.*]

The blood money for a Muslim woman is half of the blood money for a male Muslim, and the blood money for an infidel woman is half of the blood money for a male infidel. [*Source:* Fiqh (Jurisprudence), *Page 65, 2009. Taught in 10th grade, age 15.*][15]

The Center for Religious Freedom of the Hudson Institute published an even harsher review of the textbooks in the 2008 version of a study titled "Saudi Arabia's Curriculum of Intolerance." It said the books reflect "Wahhabi teachings," which are "murderously intolerant toward the Shi'a,

Jews, Baha'i, Ahmadiyya, homosexuals, apostates, and 'unbelievers' of all kinds, and horribly repressive with respect to everyone else, especially women." Among other examples, the study said, the texts present as factual a notorious anti-Semitic forgery called the Protocols of the Elders of Zion and teach that the establishment of Western-affiliated universities in Muslim lands was an extension of the Crusades.[16]

When Barbara Walters asked in 2005 in one of her televised interviews whether the kingdom was amending its textbooks to expunge the hatred and calls to violence, King Abdullah responded, "Yes, we have. We have toned them down."

A year later, at a news conference with Secretary of State Condoleezza Rice, Foreign Minster Prince Saud Al-Faisal, a Princeton graduate, fielded the same question:

QUESTION: Mr. Minister, there's been criticism of your country for the way the textbooks are written, and though the country has pledged to change the language in the textbooks there are still charges that not enough changes have been made. Can you bring us up to date on that and tell us whether all language which is offensive to some religions other than Islam has been excised . . . ?

PRINCE SAUD: The education reforms in Saudi Arabia go beyond textbook rewriting. They go into teachers [*sic*] training, directions for the messages that are given to children in the formative years. And this is done for our own security and our own educational standard, the ability of our young people to compete in the marketplace with anybody else, and productivity. They have to be educated in the proper system of education. And so the whole system of education is being transformed from top to bottom. Textbooks are only one of the steps that has been taken by Saudi Arabia.

QUESTION: On the specific issue of the language that's offensive?

PRINCE SAUD: Of course it is—this is taken out.[17]

Since then, several other Saudi officials have said repeatedly that the government is committed to purging the textbooks to remove inflammatory material. This commitment is consistent with the government's overall campaign to repair the post-9/11 reputation of Islam by positioning it as a religion of moderation and tolerance. Even if the Saudis are cleaning up their act at home, which some analysts doubt, they have done little to retract the same ideas that they spread abroad under government sponsorship for more than twenty years. (See chapter 8.)

In May 2008, the Saudi Embassy in Washington issued a document titled "Political, Economic and Social Initiatives in the Kingdom of Saudi Arabia" that presented an extensive review of the purported changes and reforms in progress in education, the economy, and political organization. It said the kingdom "is in the middle of a multi-year program to update textbooks and curricula, introduce new teaching methods and provide better training for our teachers." At the same time, "the Ministry of Islamic Affairs is implementing a multi-year program to educate imams and monitor mosques and religious education to purge extremism and violence."[18]

Weiner and other critics, including several members of Congress, have said that such statements are public relations palliatives, telling Americans what they want to hear, and have not been backed up by a full revision of the textbooks and other prejudicial teaching materials. The Hudson Institute study dismissed the Saudis' changes as "reformatting."

Eleanor Doumato found that even some texts that have been revised still contain objectionable material. After September 11, 2001, for example, one text was "extensively revised to accord the other monotheistic faiths their place in the Abrahamic tradition. However, the new version emphasizes that the true Muslim believes in all the monotheistic texts, while Jews and Christians wrongly reject some of them."[19]

The U.S. Commission on International Religious Freedom, which Congress established to study issues of religious freedom around the world, said in its 2010 annual report that "official Saudi school textbooks continue to include language encouraging hatred and violence that adversely affects the interests of the United States and that the Saudi government, despite repeated requests over a period of several years, has failed to make its current textbooks available to support its claims that such language has been eliminated." It urged the White House to put pressure on Riyadh through such measures as denying visas to Saudi religious leaders.[20]

The State Department's annual report on human rights around the world, issued in March 2010, was a bit more generous in its assessment:

Since the government's multi-year project to revise textbooks, curricula, and teaching methods to promote tolerance and remove content disparaging religions other than Islam began in 2007, more than 83 school districts in 27 different regions and provinces have participated in the project. The program's goal is to supplement religious instruction with knowledge-based subjects such as science and computer literacy. In 2007 the Ministry of Education signed a five-year collaboration agreement with King Abdulaziz Center for National Dialogue to promote religious and cultural tolerance in the classroom through teacher training and seminars. The government continued to address and remove intolerant and extreme language while promoting tolerance and intercultural understanding in textbooks. For example, the government mandated the removal of controversial terms from school textbooks and the substitution of such terms with the phrase "there is no compulsion in religion." Although intolerant and extreme language was reportedly being removed from textbooks, prejudiced concepts and expressions remained. A 2007–2008 high school text contained stereotypical language, such as saying, "Jews' lives are ruled by materialism, and usury consumes them." Textbook reviews and revisions continued at year's end.[21]

A LOST GENERATION

The struggle over textbooks' content is symptomatic of the conflicting pressures on the Saudi government as it faces the future. Education must be modernized and upgraded, or the country will slide backward socially as well as economically; extremism and violence have to be purged from the lesson plans if only to protect the regime against its domestic enemies; and the religious establishment and the most conservative, closed-minded elements of the society must be placated or at least co-opted, because they are the foundation of the regime's legitimacy. It was the government itself that fostered extremism in the schools when it allowed extremists into the classrooms and lessons after the siege of the Great Mosque and other traumatic events of 1979. (See chapter 8.)

As Michaela Prokop delicately expressed it, "Concessions to conservative forces in the field of education, particularly in politically sensitive periods, forfeited the creation of a knowledge society and ultimately the future of the young generation, a trade-off that increasingly undermines the Kingdom's stability." Like other critics, she noted that the traditional emphasis on rote learning made it easier for teachers to impress the textbooks' odious lessons on the students: "Fear and obedience are further reinforced by the teaching method, which places a heavy emphasis on rote learning and repetition. By suppressing creativity and initiative, the philosophy of teaching imports passivity and dependence, an a priori respect for authority and an unquestioning attitude."[22]

"We lost a generation after 1979," said Awadh Al-Badi, director of studies at Riyadh's King Faisal Center for Research and Islamic Studies. "Now the people of that generation are in the prime of life and they are in positions of influence, defending their positions. . . . We wasted years."[23]

Now the government is trying to find a way to drain the swamp it helped to create—without throwing off, or even calling into question, the role of Islam in shaping state policy.

THE KING'S VISION

On the advice of friends at King Saud University, I sought out Dr. Fahad Altayash to help me understand what Saudi Arabia is trying to do in reforming its education system. They described him as the person with the broadest grasp of the biggest picture, and they were right. His business card says "Chairman Saudi Association for Media and Communications," but he also teaches at King Saud University in Riyadh and is a consultant on education reform to the Ministry of Education, as well as the ministry's spokesman.

"The criticisms of the education system have some validity," he said. "There were people infested with the ideas of extremism, from the school system or from other influences. Extremism came from other Arab countries, through teachers. Then there were other extremists, about Palestine, Iraq, even the war in Lebanon. And we had a method of teaching that that created a mechanism for transmitting the ideas of experience"—that is, rote learning and unquestioning acceptance of whatever doctrine the teachers dispensed.

"Education didn't value industrial competence," he said. "It could eradicate illiteracy, but it didn't produce things." At the primary school level, he said, "there is still too much religion and rote learning."

The king's education reform campaign, he said, is not only about purging extremism from the classrooms. The whole program represents an effort to balance ethics, knowledge, and skills: the ethics to avoid violence and hatred of other cultures, the knowledge to absorb information and ideas that look forward instead of back, and the skills to put that knowledge to work in building a modern, industrialized society. No longer are students to be held back by overdoses of religion and an excess of Arabic language courses. In the future, he said, "where you used to send a man with a gun, now you want to send a man with a necktie."

King Abdullah, like most of his brothers, had little formal education, but Altayash said the king's commitment to education can be traced to his formative years in Hail, a town in northern Saudi Arabia where his mother was born. Altayash said Hail was an important stop on overland routes to Mecca for pilgrims from Iran, Anatolia, and Central Asia. Abdullah's exposure to these different Muslims gave him an appreciation for other cultures. Saudis who were isolated in the central region around Riyadh known as the Nejd, including some of Abdullah's brothers and half-brothers of the Al-Saud dynasty, lack that regard for others.

Altayash described a wide-ranging, multilevel, cross-disciplinary program of education reform, with some overlapping elements, that is in various stages of implementation. He listed several components, not necessarily in order of importance:

- Introduce more Saudis to "the world system" through study abroad under the King Abdullah Scholarship Program, inaugurated in 2006, which as of late 2010 was supporting more than 100,000 male and female students in the United States, Europe, Australia, and even China. "When they get back, all of them are going to introduce change to their families," Altayash said. This program has been extended to run through 2015.
- Create the New Economic Cities to "provide jobs for them when they get back" and develop new curricula to complement the businesses and industries in those cities.
- Upgrade the entire university system by exposing the institutions to international standards of accreditation. "By who? We don't have an accreditation system, so we are opening up to outsiders to rate us by international criteria," he said.

- Oblige the religious universities to introduce general nonreligious subjects. At the biggest of these, Al-Imam Mohammed bin Saud Islamic University, students can now take courses in engineering, architecture, economics, laboratory science, and journalism in addition to the traditional religious curriculum.
- Bring in new math and science textbooks from an American publisher and train teachers in how to use them.
- Greatly increase students' access to computers and the information available through the Internet.
- Introduce elective choice of courses in high schools. "It helps the students prepare for university," Altayash said. "They have to choose."

At one point, he said, leaders of the education system were required to resolve what was essentially a confrontation between the Ministry of Education and the Ministry of Higher Education, which is responsible for the public universities. "The Ministry of Education challenged the Ministry of Higher Education to do better: 'Give us more qualified teachers,'" Altayash said. "The Ministry of Higher Education responded, 'Send us better students.' Now, each university puts new students through a year of preparatory training, with aptitude tests and a cumulative science test," which prospective university enrollees must pass. "But there is also a parallel test of university graduates: Who is fit to be a teacher and who is not? Are they flexible, competent, and free of extremism?" In 2010, he said, only 14,000 of the 30,000 graduates who applied for teaching jobs were accepted.[24]

A NEW ARABIC WORD: KAUST

The final building block in the new educational structure that Altayash described is the King Abdullah University of Science and Technology, which is King Abdullah's pet project and the most ambitious and controversial institution in the kingdom. It opened in September 2009 and had only about 400 students in its first year, so its future remains to be seen. From its first day, however, it has served as a nationwide metaphor for the entire struggle between the forces of progress in Saudi Arabia and the forces of backwardness. Its acronym, KAUST, quickly became an Arabic word and an instant argument starter in the nation's conversation with itself.

In a sense the word "university" is misleading as applied to KAUST, for it bears no resemblance to other institutions such as Princeton or UCLA. KAUST does not have any sports teams, cheerleaders, fraternities, freshman composition classes, admissions tours conducted by sophomores walking backward, or even any undergraduates. It does not charge tuition; students are paid to go there.

KAUST is a graduate-level science and research institution with an international faculty and student body and the best and newest laboratory equipment. It also has a mandate from the king to recruit world-class scientists and to form research partnerships with international corporations and universities to catapult Saudi Arabia into the new technology-based global economy.

The institution's Web site features this description of KAUST:

King Abdullah University of Science and Technology (KAUST) is an international, graduate-level research university dedicated to inspiring a new age of scientific achievement in the Kingdom that will also benefit the region and the world. KAUST is the realization of a decades-long vision of the Custodian of the Two Holy Mosques, King Abdullah bin Abdul Aziz Al Saud.

KAUST is governed by an independent, self-perpetuating Board of Trustees and supported by a multibillion-dollar endowment. The University, which is merit-based and open to men and women from around the world, adheres to these founding principles:

- Create an international community of scholars dedicated to advanced science.
- Welcome leaders in science, technology, commerce, business, and education through appointments and partnerships.
- Provide researchers the freedom to be creative and experiment.
- Embody the highest international standards of scholarship, research, education, and learning.
- Provide unfettered access to information and share knowledge, skills, and expertise to achieve economic growth and prosperity.
- Nurture and protect freedom of research, thought, and discourse relating to scholarly work.

Any university might aspire to those lofty goals, but KAUST is not any university. American consultants planned it, and Saudi Aramco, the national oil company, built it so that it would be free of the state's education bureaucracy. Its lavish campus on the Red Sea coast about forty-five miles north of Jeddah is similar to the Aramco compound on the other side of the country, an oasis of freedom from the country's social restrictions. It is fully coeducational: males and females work, study, and eat together. (The Quiznos sandwich shop on campus is a popular hangout.) All students, male and female, have access to a movie theater with foreign films, a boat basin, and even a golf course. Women are not required to wear abayas, and they are free to use the sports facilities, ride bicycles, and even drive electric cars around the thirty-six-square-mile campus. All instruction is in English. Partly because of these deviations from Saudi social rules, the campus is walled off from the surrounding towns and roads by multiple fences and security checkpoints.

The KAUST arrangements were put to a test a few weeks after the university opened when one of the country's most senior religious figures denounced coeducation and voiced suspicion about the course of study. On a television program, Sheikh Saad Al-Shethri, a member of the Council of Islamic Scholars, said allowing both sexes in classrooms was unacceptable. In a direct challenge to the institution's academic independence, he also asked that a religious committee be established to review the university's curriculum for its compatibility with Islamic law.

The king's response was swift and unequivocal. He fired Al-Shethri, extracted statements of support for KAUST from other religious leaders, and made sure that newspapers gave prominent play to these events. I was in Saudi Arabia when the king acted, and the people of Saudi Arabia clearly got the message: The university is the king's monument to himself and a cornerstone of the kind of future he wants to build. He will tolerate no interference with it.[25]

In the United States, mainstream universities are mostly full-service institutions of learning. Engineering students mingle with scholars of Renaissance literature, for example, or of agricultural economics. At KAUST, however, all programs focus on science and technology. The university offers master's and doctoral programs in eleven fields: applied mathematics and computational science, bioscience, chemical and biological engineering, chemical science, computer science, earth science and engineering, electrical engineering, environmental science and engineering, marine science, materials science and engineering, and mechanical engineering.

At least in theory, these programs are not to be self-contained; there are no separate departments, as there are in conventional universities. KAUST's programs involve interdisciplinary work that will bring together theory and engineering in fields such as solar energy, nanotechnology, and water desalination.

Even before it opened, KAUST had entered into research partnerships with the University of Texas, the University of California–Berkeley, Stanford, and the Woods Hole Oceanographic Institution on Cape Cod. Separately, KAUST formed a partnership with the University of California–San Diego to "develop and conduct joint research in visualization and virtual reality and training facilities, which will make the KAUST campus in Saudi Arabia the site of the world's most advanced visualization suite. The Geometric Modeling and Scientific Visualization Research Center (GM&SVRC) will allow researchers to transform raw data into a fully three-dimensional visual experience that will enhance research in a broad range of scientific and technological disciplines," their joint announcement said.[26] KAUST also has cooperative research agreements with at least seventeen international corporations, including IBM and Dow Chemical Company.

King Abdullah presided at a lavish opening ceremony in September 2009 that was attended by the rulers of Syria and Kuwait. Three of the king's sons are members of the board of trustees, as are the oil minister and the CEO of Saudi Aramco. The board also includes several independent members, such as Shirley Tilghman, the president of Princeton, and Elias Zerhouni, former director of the U.S. National Institutes of Health. The president is Choon Fong Shih, a professor of engineering who was formerly president of the National University of Singapore.

A SCHOLAR FROM SINGAPORE

"This university is the king's gift to Saudi Arabia and the world," President Shih said during a long conversation in his spacious office. "He sees KAUST as a continuation of the era when the adherents of Islam contributed to progress, to solving the issues facing humanity. He sees KAUST as being in a new age of scientific achievement, a new age of sharing knowledge."

He sees KAUST as having a catalytic effect. "If KAUST does well, other universities will ask, what is it that KAUST does well? What is it that made it work? What do they do that's right, that allows them to advance science and contribute to humanity?"

The American institution that KAUST aspires to emulate, he said, is the California Institute of Technology (Caltech), which he described as "a resource for society, thinking about issues a generation or two ahead of time, always questioning what they know, pushing, looking far ahead—preparing not for today but for ten years, a generation, two generations from now." That approach is a whole new way of thinking for Saudi Arabia, where life hardly changed for centuries and each generation lived pretty much the same way as the one before it.

King Abdullah's dismissal of Sheikh Al-Shethri did not put an end to all criticism, only to public criticism. In many conversations in the fall of 2009 and the spring of 2010, I heard skepticism and complaints about KAUST: It drains resources from other institutions that are struggling to improve, and limiting the curriculum to science and technology makes it a "polytechnic institute," as one scholar put it, rather than a true university. The president also makes too much money, more than the presidents of all the country's other public universities combined, a professor at another school said. Finally, because of its isolation from the rest of the kingdom, and because most of the students are not Saudis, some critics feel it will not have the intended impact on the country and that it does nothing for ordinary citizens.

President Shih emphatically rejected criticism of the curriculum as too narrow. "Science and technology are universal," he said. "There is no Chinese science or Russian science. . . . I'm saying, bring the best minds together and we find common ground in scientific research. I don't need to read Voltaire to understand the culture of Europe or the Greek philosophers to understand Greek culture. We can exchange this."

Engineers are people, he said, and "I reject a suggestion that engineers and scientists have no interest in social issues or matters affecting society. They have families, and they too hope for the best for their children."

As to whether KAUST was depriving other universities of resources without providing corresponding benefits to the country as a whole, he said, "Knowledge, science, is not a monopoly. Different universities have different missions—MIT, state universities, junior colleges. I don't think KAUST's mission is the same as the mission of a junior college in Los Angeles. . . . It is clear that Saudi Arabia will do well as a modern society by building a number of institutions with different missions that will allow young people to advance. Not everyone aspires to be a scientist."[27]

As long as Abdullah is king, KAUST will have enough money to recruit international talent and enough clout to protect itself from the hostile and the envious. If researchers affiliated with KAUST produce breakthroughs that are visibly beneficial to the community, it may be able to build support and acceptance. As an example, one university planner cited KAUST chemists' and metallurgists' effort to develop a concrete that is resistant to the salty, humid air of Saudi Arabia's coastal cities which attacks conventional concrete and takes years off the useful life of buildings. Applied science projects of that kind could establish KAUST if not as a world-class university at least as a major research center along the lines of the Sandia National Laboratory in New Mexico.

It is also possible that King Abdullah's successors will have other priorities and will be less committed to an institution that memorializes him. The university has a multibillion-dollar endowment from the king, but money cannot insulate the institution if future kings reject the principles on which it was founded.

7

WOMEN: THE COMING BREAKOUT

Other than terrorism, probably no issue has tarnished Saudi Arabia's reputation among Americans and other Westerners as much as the deplorable status of women. Even people who pay little attention to international affairs seem to be aware that Saudi women wear veils over their faces and are not allowed to drive. The country permits polygamy, tolerates forced marriages of prepubescent girls to middle-aged men, segregates the sexes in public places, and subjects women to innumerable legal and social humiliations every day. Many occupations are closed to women, and women need a male relative's permission to travel or go to college. Females are excluded from physical education in school and from competitive sports. Outside the home women are required to cover themselves with the shapeless black garment called an abaya.

But if there is one certainty about the next few decades in Saudi Arabia, it is that the rules governing female behavior will be relaxed and that women will find new opportunities in the country's workplace and in its social and economic life. These changes are already under way, propelled by the powerful forces of economic necessity and human nature and lubricated by the Internet.

To the coming generation of Saudis this is likely to be the farthest-reaching transformation of society. While the massive combined pressures of Islamic law, religion, and custom still constrain women, more and more women will enter the workforce. Compared to their predecessors, they will be better educated, marry later, and have fewer children. The range of jobs and professions open to them will expand, allowing them to assume more prominent roles in the media and public life. They will have more freedom to travel and make life decisions on their own, without their fathers' or brothers' input. They will dispel the presumption of guilt that hangs over them whenever they enter the legal system, whether in criminal or family law. And they will drive—if not in 2012, then in the next year or the year after that.

These changes will not come easily, and they will meet entrenched resistance from the religious leadership and from social conservatives, including many women who are comfortable in the existing system. If put to a vote today, they might fail. Some women will suffer violence at the hands of men who oppose these changes. But the changes will happen and are happening, because the economic and demographic forces behind them are irresistible.

In fact, as far as such matters are quantifiable, modest advances in the status of women can already be seen in the UN Development Program's "Gender Empowerment Measure" index, which assesses "the extent of women's political participation and decision-making, economic participation and decision-making power and the power exerted by women over economic resources." In 2009 Saudi Arabia ranked 59th of the 177 countries measured, up from 76th in 2006. Most of the countries that rank lower are in southern Asia and sub-Saharan Africa, where women may nominally have more political and legal rights but have less access to money, education, and health care.[1]

Saudi Arabia is coming to the collective realization that it can no longer afford to pump vast resources into educating women at enormous expense without recovering the constructive energy and economic productivity of those educated graduates. Young couples are finding it increasingly difficult to maintain a household on a single income; the wives need jobs. Many educated Saudi men are open to and even welcome employment of their wives and daughters outside the home, if for no other reason than the money they earn. And today's new generation of women, exposed to the world of knowledge and ideas through education and travel, is not content with a life of child rearing and idle shopping in the malls. More than half the graduates coming out of Saudi Arabia's proliferating universities are female, and many of them are not the sequestered, outwardly docile creatures their mothers were. Those who are employed are, by general agreement, better at their jobs than their male counterparts are.

"Many changes are taking place in Saudi society," Deputy Labor Minister Abdulwahed Al-Humaid told me in the spring of 2010. "There are more options for women. Some people mix their religion with custom—these are very conservative people. But it is changing. It is happening. Women who work can help their husbands. Men now want to marry working women. So there is more incentive for families to encourage their daughters to work. Economics is a very powerful force."

He said King Abdullah was encouraging this transition as a general proposition, but the Labor Ministry, like the country as a whole, was struggling with the question of what jobs are suitable for women, on the assumption that many are not. "Should women work in mines, or in building construction? You have some people who say that women should do all jobs that men do. I don't believe that," he said.[2]

According to an extensive study of female employment written by a Saudi woman for the consulting firm Booz & Company, Saudi Arabia has one of the world's lowest rates of female participation in the workforce, but it "has taken many positive steps aimed at promoting women's advancement in the labor market," beginning with its accession to international treaties and agreements requiring equal job treatment for men and women. A regulation issued in 2004 set up "special women's sections within the government and employment and training initiatives [and] the establishment of cross-sector training mechanisms, as well as a groundbreaking decision to eliminate the need for a woman to have a male guardian" who would have to approve her employment. "In 2006 the Saudi labor code was revised to include new gains for working women in regard to maternity and medical care leave, nursery provisions, vacation time, and pensions," the study said. The cabinet has set a goal of filling one-third of government jobs with women and has "issued a number of measures aimed at accomplishing this, in areas such as computers, librarianship, and vocational work in welfare centers and prisons."[3]

The advancement of women's rights and interests is being aided by the Saudi news media, which are ventilating issues long kept quiet: spousal abuse, child neglect, female unemployment, the poverty of divorced women and widows, reproductive health problems, the theft of working women's salaries by their fathers or husbands, and the grotesque unfairness of divorce law. Ghastly newspaper photos in 2004 of the battered face of Rania Al-Baz, a popular television newscaster whose husband beat her almost to death, galvanized public outrage about what had been a taboo subject. Lively coverage of such matters has eliminated the past pretense that Saudi Arabia is a perfect society living in accordance with the sacred rules of Islam.

Change is coming neither swiftly nor in a straight line. Social conservatism runs deep in the society, among women as well as men. The religious establishment resists every measure aimed at giving women increased independence and at widening their options. Saudi kings have made important gestures to the cause of female emancipation: Faisal created the first schools for girls in the 1960s. Abdullah created the first coeducational university and broke new ground with his 2011 decision to allow women to participate in future elections. The kings do not have entirely free hands, however, because the legitimacy of their rule is based on Islam, which can be ambiguous on the subject of women's status.

In 2000, Saudi Arabia ratified the UN Convention on the Elimination of All Forms of Discrimination against Women but reserved the right to exempt itself from any requirements it deemed incompatible with Islam. This stipulation creates endless uncertainty and argument because the kingdom's religious leaders—all men, of course—make their living quibbling over what Islam truly requires. For example, under Saudi Arabia's prevailing Hanbali school of Islamic law, "a woman may never conclude her own marriage contract; she needs a marriage guardian—normally the father—to act on her behalf," according to a study of this issue by a Muslim scholar at the University of London. "There is no set minimum age for marriage in traditional Islamic Law. A father or his appointed executor acting as guardian also possesses the right of contracting their previously unmarried wards into marriage without their consent. However, although this is the generally stated position of the Hanbali school, there is another recorded opinion that the consent of both parties is essential for a marriage contract and that there are numerous hadiths (sayings) of the Prophet in which he stated that a virgin should not be given into marriage without her consent."[4] This question could be settled by legislation, of course, but Saudi Arabia has no legislature, and the king's duty is to rule in accordance with the precepts of Islam.

The Koran stresses that Muslim women have the same religious duties as men and the same hope of being admitted to paradise. In defining the virtuous—those who are pious, chaste, truthful, humble, sincere, and charitable—the Holy Book uses the feminine as well as the masculine form of each word.[5]

But it also repeatedly belittles women. Ridiculing the pre-Islamic reverence for females as goddesses on a par with Allah, the Koran asks, "Someone who is brought up amongst trinkets, who cannot put together a clear argument?" The Holy Book teaches that men have authority over women because it is the men's money that supports the family. It also says, "Righteous wives are devout and guard what God would have them guard in their husbands' absence. If you fear high-handedness from your wives, remind them [of the teachings of God], then ignore them when you go to bed, then hit them."[6] Other translators have used "beat" in place of "hit." Muhammad A. S. Abdel Haleem, an Egyptian translator, adds in a footnote that this instruction refers to "a single slap." In the library of the King Faisal Center for Research and Islamic Studies in Riyadh, I once read a scholarly essay about this instruction that argued that the required wife beatings should not inflict pain but simply serve as a behavioral corrective, similar to swatting a child's bottom.

The Koran says nothing about driving motor vehicles, which women in all other Muslim countries are permitted to do, and does not specify that women's faces must be covered; it mandates only modesty in dress. In Saudi Arabia, the religious authorities routinely adopt the most conservative and restrictive interpretations of the faith, and they have succeeded in giving outdated social customs the force of doctrine.

From time to time the religious conservatives' pronouncements on this subject seem so far out of the global mainstream that they subject Saudi Arabia to international ridicule. For instance, in early 2010 a prominent preacher named Abdelrahman Al-Barak decreed that anyone endorsing or promoting gender integration in a workplace or classroom was an unbeliever and should be killed. This preposterous edict was greeted with derision in the Saudi press, but given that King Abdullah a few months earlier had opened a new university bearing his name where men and women study and work together, the declaration was perceived as a direct challenge to the ruler. The king responded not by locking up the sheikh but by inviting the fashionable wife of the ruler of neighboring Qatar to visit him, unveiled, in his office and allowing newspapers to photograph the event.

Silly as it sounded—especially because everyone knows that the Prophet Muhammad's first wife, Khadija, was a well-established businesswoman for whom and with whom he worked before their marriage—the sheikh's pronouncement nonetheless was emblematic of the deep divisions within Saudi

Arabia's ruling establishment over the proper place of women. Segregation of the sexes is so deeply engrained that it leads to economic absurdities, such as the development of an all-female industrial park. Even weddings are seg-regated, with men and women celebrating in separate halls. Women who speak out sometimes report death threats.

Even if the king or a cabinet minister issues new rules to give women more freedom or more protection, the rules are not self-enforcing, and some offi-cials simply refuse to follow them. The judicial system is heavily weighted against women, especially in cases involving sexual or spousal abuse. Only in 2010 did the country's few female lawyers obtain the right to represent clients in court. Women are excluded from the armed forces and from in-flight jobs on the state airline, although the airline did announce in 2010 that it would hire female ticket agents. Such is the hypocrisy of the system that Saudi Arabian Airlines hires Muslim females from other Arab countries to work as cabin attendants but will not give such jobs to Saudi women.

Saudi males and females are educated separately from their earliest days in school; even when nominally attending the same institution they are in separate classrooms. The biggest construction project in the Middle East in 2011 was an all-female university near Riyadh's airport. A few years ago, when I visited the new, privately run Prince Mohammad bin Fahd University, school officials told me proudly that the engineering department had female students. But it turned out the women did not learn chemical or electrical engineering; instead, they are taught what the school calls domestic engi-neering, or what we in the West used to call home economics.

According to the scholar Eleanor Doumato, a longtime analyst of Saudi education,

> Today [Saudi] women are educated to a level equal and arguably better than their male counterparts. Fifty-eight percent of all higher education students are women, if teachers' colleges are included, 79% of PhDs granted in the Kingdom have been awarded to women, and 40% of all physicians with Saudi nationality are women. Yet, women cannot compete in a level playing field with men when it comes to jobs. . . . Saudi Arabia has the lowest percentage of women in the workforce anywhere in the world, and 84% of women who are employed work in the country's bloated, sex-segregated education system.[7]

Every few months, the Saudi news media report some new "first woman" story: the first Saudi female pilot, the first female certified public accountant, the first woman to practice law in an actual courtroom, the first woman to hold a public signing of her book, the first female chief financial officer of a male-owned Saudi company, the first female rider to win a medal in an international equestrian competition. These breakthroughs are symbolically important, but they involve only a handful of individuals. Even women who achieve professional status in the few occupations open to them, such as medicine, are circumscribed by a potent combination of social pressure, religious tradition, and male scorn. Qanta A. Ahmed, an American-trained Muslim physician of Pakistani origin who worked at a hospital in Riyadh, recounted her experience in a book that exposed the unending mortification and discrimination to which even the best-educated women are subjected. She described her experience as a staff doctor making her rounds with a group of male and female residents:

> All Saudi female residents were entirely veiled. They would join the rounds covered from head to foot in black abayas, over which they would wear cartoonishly long white coats, tailor-made, which were always fully buttoned up to the throat and often closed with round mandarin collars rather than the standard neckline of a jacket. . . . On rounds, invariably the women would be glued to the back of the group, standing always to one side, a single invisible phalanx. Frequently I would try to move each female resident with a gentle but firm guiding hand to their draped elbow or shoulder, encouraging them to move to the fore of the group. Like a phalanx, they moved only in a cohort, afraid to stand alone, sheltering each other in a cumulative shadow of their opacity. They remained silent and respectful during acrimonious exchanges, inscrutable behind their hijabs, rarely tendering any opinion, and certainly never questioning anything that was said.

Watching one of these young doctors push back her veil to put the earbuds of a stethoscope in her ears, Ahmed observed that "it would be impossible for them to hear a soft diastolic murmur against the deafening (and now acoustically magnified) crunch of itchy polyester."

Ahmed, an acerbic observer of Saudi society—she described the women attending an extravagant wedding party as "a display of bosoms and behinds and Botox"—depicts Saudis as individually generous and welcoming but collectively as mired in hypocrisy, guilt, indolence, materialism, sexual frustration, anti-Semitism, and ignorance of the world. Having met many Saudi women and learned their secret longings, she titled one of her chapters "Desperate Housewives."[8]

The sort of humiliation she described at the hospital is institutionalized, deeply embedded in a culture that prohibits women from eating in restaurants with men unrelated to them and pays owners of restaurants to report violations. Women do not even have the same degree of control over or access to their own children that their counterparts in other countries take for granted. Unless they are accompanied by their husbands, they cannot visit the schools that their teenage sons attend, for example, because males and females are prohibited from mingling in public places. They also routinely lose custody of their children when divorced.

An outspoken woman named Fawzia Al-Bakr wrote not long ago,

> I wish any man could experience these restrictions just for a while so that he can understand what it means to be enslaved by another man who dominates him and controls his destiny, his study, his work, his children, his subsistence and his documents. . . . Women's destiny is dependent on the man's goodness and generosity; if he is good and decent, she is . . . protected, but if he is morally sick or of unsound mind, then she has no consolation.[9]

She should know. She was one of forty-five women seeking the right to drive who staged an ill-fated demonstration two decades ago that actually set back their cause. In a challenge to the authorities, they drove through the center of Riyadh in broad daylight. They magnified their offense by alerting a *New York Times* reporter, who wrote a long article about the demonstration, turning it into an international event. This protest occurred in October 1990, when American troops—including Jeep-driving women—were pouring into the country in preparation for Operation Desert Storm.

The Saudi women evidently thought that the presence of the foreign troops and hundreds of foreign journalists posed an opportunity for making a bold gesture. They were wrong. They did not comprehend that the king and senior princes, facing blistering criticism for allowing infidel armies onto the holy soil of Islam, would have to reinforce their Islamic credentials by maintaining religious and social orthodoxy. The women were arrested. They lost their jobs and their passports. They were reviled in the press. Worst of all, according to accounts from several Saudis, they forced King Fahd to back away from a decision he was reportedly ready to make that would have lifted the ban.[10]

But that was more than twenty years ago and attitudes are changing. Increasingly, Saudis recognize and are willing to say that the prohibition on women driving is not only an economic drag on the country, but is also ridiculous because it creates the very situation it was intended to prevent: Women are forced to ride alone in cars with men who are not related to them, namely, the drivers who are hired from outside the kingdom to ferry them around. Is a veiled Saudi woman safer standing on a big city street and trying to hail a taxi driven by an unknown foreign man than she would be driving her own car?

Advocates of women's right to drive were not helped by a ghastly incident in November 2010, in which a sport utility vehicle with eleven women aboard overturned. The driver and four passengers died; six others were badly hurt. As the *Arab News* noted in its account of the accident, "It is common to see Saudi women driving cars in remote areas outside Riyadh." It is one of those realities that everyone in Saudi Arabia understands but seldom talks about in a "don't ask, don't tell" environment.[11] So is the fact that many women have driver's licenses issued by other countries where they have lived. Some of these licensed female drivers staged a new right-to-drive demonstration in the early summer of 2011, but they attracted only a few dozen participants, whom the police mostly ignored.

FOLLOW THE MONEY

Women control a lot of money in Saudi Arabia and are increasingly prominent and successful in business, having seized an opportunity presented in 2006 for the first time that allowed women to obtain their own business licenses, without male partners. A regional business journal reported in 2009 that women own 20,000 small and medium-size businesses and have 50 billion riyals in their bank accounts.[12]

In the summer of 2010, the *Arab News* compiled a list of the kingdom's twenty largest companies owned or controlled by women. The firms are in a wide range of fields: industrial processing, architecture, fashion, eyewear, audio-visual production, interior design, public relations, cosmetics, and event management. The largest, Al-Sale Eastern Company in al-Khobar, is a metal-processing and salvage operation with annual revenue of 662 million riyals, or about $176.5 million.

In the spring of 2010 the Carnegie Endowment for International Peace distributed a Saudi writer's report on women's progress in business. It listed these developments:

> Taking into consideration the social and religious restrictions on women in the society, Saudi businesswomen have made major strides in the last few years toward breaking down barriers and gaining legislation that created a less restrictive business environment. For instance, in 2008 Prince Khalid Al-Faisal, Governor of Mecca, modified Article 160 of the Labor Law which prohibited men and women from interacting in a business environment. The Ministry of Labor also revised labor laws in 2008 in order to give women the choice to work. Women no longer require a male guardian's approval to get or leave a job. In the same year, the Ministry of Trade also reversed a ban on women staying in hotels alone. A new law is expected to give women the right to travel abroad without a male guardian's approval and the ability to use their national ID cards to travel to GCC states.[13]

The fact that women now have their own national identity cards is an important reform in itself. Before 2001 women were not entitled to their own ID cards; they were listed on their husbands' or male guardians' cards. Since 2005 women have theoretically been allowed to obtain ID cards without the consent of a male guardian, and another woman can vouch for the applicant's identity. Some women do not have the cards, however, because they refuse to uncover their faces for a photograph or because their husbands will not allow them to do so. As with other reforms, abundant anecdotal evidence indicates that men frequently refuse to accept women's identity cards and continue to demand male validation.[14]

The cause of female advancement also is hampered because women do not agree about what tactics to pursue to expand their free space. As in many other countries, a liberalizing trend in the big cities is not matched in provincial towns. Some women who can do pretty much what they want because they have cooperative husbands and enough money often choose to ignore the plight of their sisters and neighbors for fear of jeopardizing their own comfortable status. When an all-female hotel opened in Riyadh a few years ago, opinion among female liberals was split between those who hailed it as a sign that women are traveling and doing business in large enough numbers to require such an establishment and those who decried it as a perpetuation of a segregated system.

In general, Saudi opinion about the status and rights of women is represented by three groups. The first group, probably the largest, favors continuing the status quo either out of religious conviction or social habit. This group includes a great many women. I have met quite a few and heard about many others who find the current system a valuable insulator against unwelcome social trends and are personally comfortable with it.

The second faction, substantial but unquantifiable, understands the inevitability of change and the need for it but wants to proceed cautiously. The members of this amorphous group prefer a natural and gradual evolution rather than strong government action in the belief that to win acceptance from the public at large, change must follow rather than precede popular sentiment. A prominent representative of this school of thought is Dr. Bandar Al-Aiban, the American-educated president of the government's official Human Rights Commission. "It will work out by itself," he said. "You can't tell people to do what they don't want to do. It has to come from underneath, from the grass roots. Once there is critical mass, it will happen."[15]

The third group is the smallest in numbers, but growing, and perhaps has the greatest impact because of its members' collective skill at mobilizing media attention and using the Internet. Its members are active campaigners for change. Some are men, but most are women who are increasingly using their professional positions, social contacts, networks of colleagues, and social networking media to seek a transformation of their society. The women in this group differ in age and in tactics, but all are adept at running through whatever cracks they can find in the wall of resistance.

Many of their gains are incremental, and the Western media barely notice them. For example, the Ministry of Justice in 2010 decided that the bride's age must be listed on marriage documents in an effort to discourage marriages of underage girls. But undoubtedly the pace and scope of change are accelerating as each small piece becomes a building block for the next.

"Young women today are more aware of their strengths and capabilities," Samar Fatany, probably the country's best-known female journalist, wrote in her newspaper column. "They are no longer intimidated by the male-dominated culture that continues to marginalize their role in society. The status of women in the Kingdom is slowly changing, and women remain determined to assert their position as contributing citizens in all fields—socially, economically, and politically."[16]

Fatany practices what she preaches. The last time I ran into her, at a gender-integrated gathering in Jeddah, she was wearing an abaya decorated with bright colors, making a feminist statement that would inspire shock, and probably official reproof, in other Saudi cities.

It is much easier now than in the past for an outsider—even a non-Muslim man like myself—to meet these women and hold substantive conversations with them. Touring the country in the fall of 2009 and again the following spring, I met and interviewed more women than I had during all my previous visits combined. These Saudi women speak English and are mostly well educated and well traveled. In that sense they are not representative of the society. But in different ways all of them are changing the world into which they were born, and their impact is seeping through the country's ossified social structure. Here are some of these women.

THE UNDERWEAR CAMPAIGN

Reem Assad and her friends and supporters don't want to buy their underwear from male sales clerks, but in Saudi Arabia they have no choice. Lingerie stores do not have female sales clerks.

One of the oddest sights in Saudi Arabia can be seen at any of the country's high-end shopping malls: fully veiled women, supposedly shielded from the lascivious eyes and thoughts of men outside their immediate families, entering the Saudi equivalent of Victoria's Secret to buy panties and bras from the Indian and Pakistani men working there. A few years ago, after what she calls "an uncomfortable incident," Reem Assad decided she had had enough. It was time to boycott the shops.

"I had to start somewhere," she said. "I didn't go against the government or the religious establishment. I went against the retail industry. The retailers are the guilty parties here. They are making money out of these women's pockets."

She is not a career activist. About forty years old, she is in many ways a conventional Saudi woman of the educated upper middle class, teaching finance at Dar al-Hekma College for women and raising her children in a comfortable but not luxurious Jeddah neighborhood. When she greeted me at the door of her house, she was wearing a simple blue dress, without an abaya, and was not accompanied by any man. Her father, she said, lives in another house in the same family compound with the younger of his two wives.

She said she began her lingerie retailing campaign by approaching the Jeddah Chamber of Commerce and Industry. She sought the business establishment's support for a change in the rules of retailing but discovered "the big guys don't care." So she went on Facebook to ask women to boycott the shops. The most visible result has been the worldwide media attention she has garnered from morning television shows in New York, Swedish television, the BBC, and newspapers in several Arab capitals.

"It's really strange that Saudi Arabia is the only country where you see men selling lingerie," she said in one of her many newspaper interviews. "Women walk around covered from head to toe, and yet they have to discuss the size and material of their undergarments with strange men. Isn't this odd?"[17] Her objective, she said, was not to cause trouble but to have the government enforce a decree issued in 2006 that ordered the male sales personnel be replaced by Saudi women.

The Ministry of Labor did issue that decree and gave retailers a year to hire the required Saudi women, but in the existing Saudi system, it was unenforceable. Social conservatives and the religious establishment objected, saying that Islam prohibits women from working outside the home, that putting women in retail shops would expose them to the view of any passing stranger, and that shop windows would have to be covered if the sales clerks were female.

Besides, there was still no realistic answer to the transportation question. If women were going to work in the shops, how were they going to get there if they are prohibited from driving? Not all women come from households that can afford to employ drivers. "Don't underestimate the power of transportation in women's lives," Assad said.

Retailers also objected, arguing that no Saudi women had been trained do such work even if it were permitted. Assad and her supporters undertook efforts to overcome that objection by training women in sales and in the fundamentals of lingerie marketing.

She and Naomi McGill, a volunteer from Australia who saw the Facebook posting, put together a ten-day course at Dar al-Hekma, using bras donated by employees at Victoria's Secret stores outside the country. They developed a corps of twenty-six women who are "fully trained to do this" work and could get their husbands' permission to do it, Assad said. Nothing has happened that will allow them to work, and it is not clear that anything will happen unless malls forbid men to enter, but if the opportunity arises to work, they will be ready.

The underwear campaigners scored a victory in June 2011 when King Abdullah issued a new decree that reiterated the earlier one, requiring that female staff replace the male workers in the shops. Implementation, however, faces the same obstacles. Part of the problem, Assad said, is that "upper-class women don't care" because they travel to neighboring countries or Europe to shop. "My target audience is the middle class and the upcoming generation."

To Assad, the retail sales issue is only one aspect of a systemic ailment that is pulling down the entire country. "This country suffers from a combination of passivity and ignorance, which leads to casual acceptance of everything that's logically incorrect," she said. "Realistically, why should women here think outside the box when they've never seen the outside of the box?"

Saudis are "living in la-la land where we can afford to ignore the rest of the world," Assad continued. "But can we afford all the anger" provoked by the existing rules? Change is inevitable, she said, because "we can't afford to educate all these women without getting anything back. This is an unsustainable model. Women and men mingle in medicine, why not in the economy?"

Her campaign, and the cause of women in general, got a boost from a surprising sequence of events in August 2010. The Panda supermarket chain, known to shoppers all over the country, received permission from the Ministry of Labor to hire female checkout cashiers and announced it would do so, on an experimental basis, at one store in Jeddah. The goal was eventually to employ twenty-five hundred women, a company official told reporters.[18]

A few days later, longtime minister of labor Ghazi Al-Gosaibi died, and the king appointed the mayor of Jeddah, Adel Fakieh, to succeed him. In addition to his public position, Fakieh was the chairman of the board of Savola Group, the parent company of Panda.

"Coincidence!" Reem Assad said in an e-mail from Cairo, where she was awaiting the birth of a child. "As far as the lingerie campaign is concerned, I am planning a third round of the boycott in November/December, thereby entering the third year of one of the most pressing campaigns calling for women's employment and consumer rights. I shall not relent until something changes. And I know that one day, I am determined to become the first female minister of Labor."[19]

POETRY AND POLITICS

Nimah Ismail Nawwab's bilingual business card bears a photograph of her unveiled face and this description: "Empowerment Consultant, Young Global Leader, Int. Lecturer, Poet, Writer and Photographer."

She is indeed a poet. *The Unfurling*, a collection of her poems in English, was published in the United States in 2004. Some are about love, longing, and dreams. Some are about current events, such as the war in Iraq. One poem, "Fiery Embrace," recounts a notorious incident in which fifteen girls died in a fire at their school in Mecca. They perished because the enforcement squad known as *muttawain* refused to let them out or the firefighters in because the girls were not wearing their abayas. (The muttawain, officially the Commission for the Promotion of Virtue and Prevention of Vice, are often described as "religious police," but they are actually social police who enforce the separation of men and women and the ban on public entertainment.) Public outrage over the school fire episode, stoked by news coverage, obliged the king to remove girls' education from the control of the religious authorities and transfer it to the Ministry of Education. He also ordered retraining for the entire force of muttawain.[20]

In another poem, "The Longing," Nimah Ismail Nawwab aspires to be "a voice among the voiceless."[21] She grew up in a privileged and enlightened environment. Her father, Ismail I. Nawwab, a former professor at the University of Edinburgh and a true intellectual, was a sort of scholar in residence at Aramco. She formerly worked at what is now Saudi Aramco and still lives in the oil company's compound at Dhahran, where conditions for women have always been more relaxed than elsewhere in the country. Americans established the compound when they still ran the oil company, so it operates under a separate social system. Nawwab was one of six women

King Abdullah invited to travel with him when he visited India and China in 2006. It was a very public statement of encouragement from the center of power.

Now that her own children are adults, she spends much of her time trying to organize young people and help them find ways to develop their talents. Her work often means traveling across the country to Jeddah, where there is an active coffeehouse and art gallery culture. Jeddah even has an all-female rock band, the AccoLade.

"We have an identity crisis among our young people," she said. "I want young people to act. A big part is training, skill-building." In the absence of NGOs, which in most other countries would provide training and direction, she said, young people in Saudi Arabia "want to talk, to share ideas, but they don't know who to talk to."

She has taken it upon herself to become a catalyst, bringing together young artists—painters, sculptors, and musicians, whose ranks are expanding in a society that has never encouraged them—and people interested in social volunteering. Her weapon of choice in these culture wars is the poetry reading in a Jeddah coffee shop. "In the past five years," she said, "the media have created space for these discussions. Arabic writers are very creative now."

When we met at her home, a young, aspiring musician whom she had met in Jeddah—a man—joined us. It is against the rules for a Saudi woman whose husband or father or brother is not with her to receive unrelated male visitors, but that was Nawwab's point. To her, the rules, whether derived from Islam, from social custom, or from the whim of the monarch, no longer serve any purpose.

TESTING THE LIMITS

Wajeha Al-Huwaider also lives in the Aramco compound, in a small house she shares with a white cat, and works at the oil company, but the campaign that has made her the country's best-known social agitator has nothing to do with her day job. She is seeking to end the country's unique system of male guardianship in which women require written permission from a father, husband, or brother to travel, enroll in a university, get married, or have surgery. As more women are educated and employed, this stifling requirement, much more so than the ban on driving, has bred deep resentment.

Huwaider, in her late forties, has degrees from Indiana University and George Washington University. She sends her sons to school in the United States to insulate them from the environment of male supremacy that surrounds her. She once wore a pink abaya, simply to make a statement. She posted a video of herself driving a car on YouTube and staged a demonstration in front of a car dealership in Virginia, seeking the support of the U.S. auto industry for Saudi women's right to drive. She also started an Internet-based campaign against child marriage. Because of her public campaigning on women's issues, her husband took a second wife, which led Huwaider to seek a divorce. Being divorced only boosts her resentment at being required to have her ex-husband's permission to travel.

"I have permission," she said to me. "It is open-ended because my former husband is a nice man, but it all depends on the man. He can choose whether, when, how often, and with whom. If he's a nice man you can have a normal life, but most Saudi men are very rigid." So in the summer of 2009 she decided to do something about the situation. Every day for several weeks she went to the nearby causeway that links Saudi Arabia to the island state of Bahrain and sought to cross without showing her permission paper. Each time she was turned away, but she attracted international attention.

"I am not a dangerous person," she wrote in an article about herself in the *Washington Post*, "so why do they turn me away? Because I refuse to present a document signed by my male 'guardian,' giving his permission for me to travel. And why do I do that?

"I possess such a document, but it is humiliating to have to produce it, and I am tired of being humiliated solely because I am a woman."[22]

Her campaign to abolish the guardianship rule has not succeeded, and even women who agree with her in principle find her tactics repugnant. Her resentment is also directed against women who refuse to get involved in the issue.

"I'm trying to get women to say something, get mad," she said in a conversation over tea at her home. "I can't find what it is that would make women say, 'Yes, we can do that.'" She said she understands the passivity of cloistered women who have no way to break out and assert themselves, but she is outraged by the well-to-do, comfortable women who remain silent so as not to jeopardize their status.

"They go to Bahrain and Dubai and drink," she said scornfully. "I can sympathize with the oppressed ones. The others are selfish."

She is talking about women such as Noura Abdulrahman, an English-speaking employee of the Ministry of Education, who forcefully defended the guardianship system in a *New York Times* interview. Ms. Abdulrahman said she did not question the motives of the people she calls *liberaliyeen* (liberals), but she felt that "they're failing to understand the uniqueness of Saudi society. In Saudi culture, women have their integrity and a special life that is separate from men. As a Saudi woman, I demand to have a guardian. My work requires me to go to different regions of Saudi Arabia, and during my business trips I always bring my husband or my brother. They ask nothing in return—they only want to be with me."[23]

Don't the husband and brother have jobs of their own? Who pays for this travel? Those questions are secondary to the cultural battles, stoked by religion, over the degree to which women should be entrusted to run their own lives.

"You have to see it historically," said Thuraya Arrayed, a native of Bahrain who moved to Saudi Arabia in her youth and has long been one of Saudi Arabia's few public intellectuals. She was the first woman in the country's Eastern Province, the site of the oil fields, to hold a PhD, and after a career in Aramco's corporate planning department, she has become a popular lecturer and mentor to younger women.

"Before the discovery of oil," she said when I spoke with her, "even the British didn't want to have anything to do with us. It was the Dark Ages. It was King Abdul Aziz who unified the country. When he asked Aramco to train people, there were no schools, not for men, not for women. This society had hardly changed for a thousand years. People are scared of change. This [permission] paper only came about from trying to find a solution, a precaution, so that this opening to the rest of the world did not bring with it girls eloping or extramarital pregnancies. The paper was supposed to be a solution, not to create a problem for women but to solve the problem of the parents. Compared to the rest of the world we're not getting anything but restrictions, but if we compare ourselves to our grandmothers, we are way ahead. . . . I'm not saying we don't need people to ask for change, we do. Being quiet means you're happy with it. But when you scream and call attention, you end up with a worse situation than you had before." She was talking about Wajeha Al-Huwaider, whose confrontational tactics, she said, were counterproductive.

A PRINCE'S MONEY

Muna Abusulayman greeted me in her Riyadh office wearing a gray tunic, jeans, and a gray scarf that covered her hair but not her face. Her outfit was a measure of the self-confidence she has earned as perhaps Saudi Arabia's best-known female success story as she nears the age of forty. A popular television show host for several years, she also teaches at King Saud University, lectures frequently in Europe and the United States, markets her own clothing designs on Facebook, and is now executive director of the Alwaleed Bin Talal Foundation, the charity created by a prince who is one of the world's richest men.

The bookshelves of the reception room outside her office are lined with reprints of magazine articles about her boss, Prince Alwaleed bin Talal bin Abdul Aziz, a grandson of the founding king and nephew of the current one, and about the $20 million each he donated to Harvard and to Georgetown Universities. A magazine called *Arab Man* ranked him first on a list of the "100 Most Important Arabs." He was on the cover of *Arabian Business* for a feature about the world's richest Arabs. The headquarters of his media conglomerate, Rotana—which in 2010 formed a partnership with Rupert Murdoch's News Corporation—is known as the most gender-integrated workplace in the kingdom other than hospitals. The prince can get away with it because a prince of his stature is beyond the reach of the muttawain. His status and his attitudes are reflected in the work of his foundation's executive director.

"We are moving from the nineteenth century to the twenty-first century," Ms. Abusulayman told me. From a prominent family, she lived in Malaysia and the United States while growing up and saw more of the outside world than most Saudi women ever will. But her life has not been entirely easy: married at seventeen, she was divorced and the mother of two children before she was twenty-five. For this single mother, "the biggest issue is giving women more responsibility for their own decisions in life."

The greatest challenge confronting Saudi women, she said, is not the ban on driving. "The driving issue is a symptom, it's not the disease. I don't believe in treating symptoms." The guardianship system, she said, is a pretext, or simply "cover for taking care of women as if they can't make their own decisions. How do you give women more responsibility? If that happens the guardianship issue will be resolved."

She has been outspokenly critical of many aspects of Saudi life, but she said she is "not defensive about Saudi culture, only about attacks on it. Cultural differences should be valued and appreciated—that's why people travel, to learn about other cultures. In the States, if you answer a phone during meetings, it's rude. Here, it's rude not to answer it."

She dispenses some of the foundation's money to projects aimed at reducing poverty and disease in developing countries and some to enterprises designed to improve the quality of education and teaching in Saudi Arabia. She does not subscribe to what is now the conventional wisdom that rote learning, a fixture in Saudi education, has to go. "I don't want to abolish rote entirely; it's a useful skill," she said. "As nomads you have to have great memories. It's part of our heritage from oral literature. I'm very upset about the way education has become either-or."

Some programs are aimed at expanding the range of subjects and ideas to which Saudi students are exposed. "You need to open up new lines of inquiry," she said. "It kills me," she said, that the government funds scholarships abroad only in science, mathematics, engineering, and medicine. "There are no scholarships for the human sciences—for sociology, archaeology, political science, psychology."

One project she has funded is a study of what she calls "the translation phenomenon. Why are so few books translated into Arabic?" She said the foundation is supporting the development of a "translation dictionary" to help create uniform texts that can be read by all Arabic speakers, of whatever dialect.

A SHARP-EDGED BLOG

Eman Al-Nafjan is a much less public person than Muna Abusulayman. A young mother with two small children, she is studying for her PhD. She does not have a high-profile job. But I wanted to talk to her because as "SaudiWoman" she is a popular blogger and social critic whose commentaries are widely read.

I met her through the intervention of a female friend at the U.S. Embassy in Riyadh. Once I established contact, she was quite willing to talk to me; in fact, her driver brought her (in a yellow Hummer) to my hotel, and she took me to lunch in the public restaurant at the Four Seasons Hotel. Although a

Saudi woman alone is prohibited from meeting with a man not from her immediate family, educated women in the big cities know places where they can get away with it because the owners are princes or other powerful men who are beyond the reach of the muttawain.

"My husband says it's OK, and if he says so then it's all right," she said, in the flawless English she learned as a child in Kansas, where her father was studying for his doctorate. Her husband is from Buraidah, one of the most conservative cities in Saudi Arabia. "When we married ten years ago, he would never have permitted this [meeting with a foreigner] or an out-of-home job," she said. "Things are changing."

On her blog her favorite targets are the retrograde pronouncements of the religious hard-liners and the absurdities of the "gender apartheid" system. Here is a sample, from May 2010, aimed in part at a woman named Nora Al-Faiz. Her appointment as the kingdom's first female deputy minister was hailed as a milestone, but she objected when a newspaper printed a photo of her with her face unveiled. The blog post begins with a reference to a declaration by a well-known conservative religious figure who took an extreme position on the subject of gender integration and calls him out as a hypocrite.

Sheikh Al Najaimi who announced his support for the Al Barak fatwa [religious edict] that anyone who calls for gender desegregation should be killed was caught last month attending a women's day conference in Kuwait. The conference's attendees were mostly women and there was no segregation at all. He sat for hours with women and even had a meal with them. When he got back to Saudi Arabia, he told everyone that the majority of women were menopausal and as such it is Islamically allowed for him to socialize with them. Of course, this is not true. In the Quran, the verse is very clear that it is the woman's decision whether or not to announce that she is post-menopausal and just being menopausal is not enough, she has to have no interest in men too. However, Al Najaimi took it upon himself to make this milestone decision on behalf of all the women attending the conference. Moreover he proclaimed that those who weren't post menopause confessed to him that they were committing a sin by not covering!

And then the Deputy Minister of Girl's Education Ms. Nora Al Faiz, made it a point to appear in photos taken at official meetings in full face cover to even more discredit the photo of her face that was highly publicized when she was first appointed. I've met a few teachers since then and they keep telling me that they or other colleagues are uncomfortable with such a liberal woman!

At the same time, King Abdullah had a photograph of him and Princess Mozah, the ruler of Qatar's wife, on the first page of most major newspapers in Saudi. And then another photo of the king and Prince Sultan with a group of Saudi women, many with their faces uncovered surfaced everywhere. And this one had the names of those women published alongside it as if to show that tribal Saudi women from old families have no issue with having their pictures in newspapers.[24]

SaudiWoman often heaps scorn on the behavior enforcers of the Commission for the Promotion of Virtue and the Prevention of Vice, which she often refers to dismissively as "PVPV." "These past few weeks it seems like a day doesn't pass without a new muttawa blooper coming out," she wrote in an April 2010 posting. (*Muttawa* is the singular of muttawain, which she does not use in her English-language blog.) "I call them bloopers because the muttawas always have an excuse even if it's only an oops. These bloopers are becoming more and more frequent. It might be because of more press freedom or because average people are not putting up with it anymore. Whatever it is, muttawa bloopers are definitely not a new concept. An online Saudi newspaper recently published photos of 84 year old documents pertaining to citizens complaining about false arrests and harassment by PVPV members!"[25]

The subject that had her stirred up the day I met her was female unemployment. On her blog, she has blamed unemployment for the recently exposed problem of the recruitment of women by extremist groups and organizations linked to terrorism. She wrote, "Three factors are creating this phenomenon; the enormous percentage of unemployed women who are a product of our borderline extremist education system, their access to the internet and the fact that 83% of all Saudis are under the age of 39. Although they might not be out fighting and bombing, they are doing something just as sinister by spreading the ideology online and recruiting the men in their families."[26]

"Even when women's husbands are willing to let them work there aren't enough jobs for them," she told me. "The problem is not at the higher end but at the shopgirl level, the women who should be doing those jobs in the boutiques. There are families in South Riyadh living in serious poverty because the women don't have jobs, and couldn't get there if someone offered one." That "shopgirl" issue is the same one that Reem Assad has taken on in the lingerie stores.

FINDING JOBS FOR WOMEN

The Ministry of Labor's long-term employment strategy has a goal of expanding "employment for Saudi women who want to work." That ambition reflects official recognition that more and more women wish or need to work and that opening doors to female employment is sound economic policy. As noted earlier, foreign workers currently send an estimated $25 billion out of Saudi Arabia every year, much of which would stay in the kingdom if more Saudi women held jobs, and the kingdom spends billions more to educate Saudi women but receives no economic return on that investment.

The ministry's strategy document lists as one "mechanism of implementation" the "determination and classification of jobs that could be occupied by Saudi women." That bland language reflects the fact that many obstacles to female employment derive not from technical qualifications or physical requirements but from deep-seated social and cultural traditions—traditions that many people value even if the country can no longer afford them.

Naturally, the person responsible for implementing the employment strategy is a man, Deputy Labor Minister Abdulwahed Al-Humaid. According to him, 78 percent of the women officially listed as unemployed have college degrees. He said that his ministry's efforts to increase job opportunities for women have prompted threatening mail and angry visits from social and religious conservatives. When he receives such delegations, he said, he counters their arguments by displaying newspaper photographs of King Abdullah and Prince Nayef, the interior minister, meeting and working with unveiled women. If men of such known piety do it, he asks them, how can it be sinful?[27]

On my one of my early visits to Saudi Arabia in the 1970s, I met a Lebanese architect who was cashing in on the oil boom by designing office buildings, of which the country then had few. We toured one that was under construction. It seemed to have an inordinately large number of "utility rooms" for cleaning equipment, with sinks from which buckets could be filled.

"Some day soon," the architect said with a grin, "these will be ladies' rooms!"

His building, as with most others in that era and for years afterward, did not have any restrooms for women because women were not expected to be there. He built in the extra utility rooms on the assumption that women would be working there eventually, and it would be easy to convert the rooms to restrooms because they had plumbing. He was premature by at least a quarter century. Now women are working in increasing numbers, but the old attitudes are giving way only grudgingly. That is why fertility clinics are everywhere but there are hardly any day care centers—children are valued, and their mothers are expected to care for them at home.

In a presentation to the UN Development Program a few years ago, Muna Abusulayman listed some of the reasons why it is so difficult for Saudi women—even qualified, willing women—to find employment: Saudi society values child rearing and the family above all else and looks askance at women who are not at home with their children; there are no training programs for women whose children have grown up and no longer need care; telecommuting and working from home are discouraged; women's education does not prepare them for the workplace because "they don't learn valuable critical thinking or even technological skills that enable them to make sure of their potential"; a man who allows his wife to work is often scorned as weak or inadequate; small and medium-size companies cannot afford the separate workplaces that would be required if they employed women; and Arab television shows perpetuate stereotypes of women as weak or flighty. It is socially unthinkable for a young woman to live in an apartment by herself, which rules out job opportunities in other cities. Those obstacles compound the difficulties presented by the transportation issue and the fact that entire lines of endeavor are off-limits to women, including most physical labor such as construction work and, of course, the military.[28]

In *Girls of Riyadh*, a controversial "chick-lit" novel about young women in the Saudi capital, a central character named Gamrah wonders why her husband is so inconsiderate and demanding. "Do men sense a threat to their authority when they begin to catch on that a woman is developing some real skills in some area?" she asks herself. Are men afraid of any moves toward independent action on the part of their wives? And do they consider a woman reaching independence and working toward her own goals an illegal offense against the religious rights of leadership God had bestowed upon men?"[29]

The author, Rajaa Alsanea, would answer yes to all of these questions. When I met her, she was a graduate student in pediatric dentistry in Chicago, where she lived with a sister. Talented and promising as she was, she was also a living example of a truth about all the Saudi women I have met who have broken out of their old constrained lives: In order to do it, they had to have the encouragement of a supportive father or husband. In her case, she was raised in a family of doctors who encouraged her medical aspirations.

Her novel, written in the form of "girl talk" e-mails among four friends, is a hilarious and nasty exposé of the hypocrisy and materialism of the Saudi middle class. She wrote it in Arabic, but it was published in Lebanon because it was prohibited in Saudi Arabia. "So strong was opposition to this book," she says on her Web site, "that the author received death threats for bringing her nation's women into disrepute."

The book has since been translated into English and French and now can be found in Saudi Arabia, where its impact is debatable. Several Saudi men have told me that their wives read it, but none of the men admitted having read it himself. One prominent intellectual even told me that the author would find few families willing to entrust their children to her for dental care because her book rendered her socially unacceptable.

One reason the book was so controversial is that it dwelled at some length on the peculiar attitudes Saudi men have about sex, presumably a by-product of their upbringing. The topic is not considered appropriate for a well-bred young woman such as Rajaa Alsanea to discuss.

A century ago, young women in the United States confronted many of the same issues that young Saudi women do today. It was still news when a woman was admitted to medical or law school. Education, female suffrage, World War II, and the birth control pill wrought revolutionary changes in just a few decades. In Saudi Arabia, the pace of change will probably be neither so rapid nor so great in scope, but it is already under way. Women are demanding it, the rulers endorse it, the crustiest religious mossbacks from the old days are discredited or dying off, and economically the country has no choice.

Meanwhile, since the Mecca school fire, Saudi Arabia has trained a cadre of female firefighters; photos in newspapers showed them in their helmets and uniforms. Female journalists are proliferating, and it is no longer unusual for them to interview men. More young women are following Rajaa

Alsanea and Nimah Ismail Nawaab down the road to change through liter-ature. Family courts have been established, under the supervision of the Ministry of Social Welfare, to deal with the issue of spousal abuse, and a hotline telephone number activates a government network of protection. Women have won election to the boards of the country's influential Chambers of Commerce. Women also are learning office equipment main-tenance and photography in technical schools.

LUBNA OLAYAN'S MESSAGE

The Jeddah Economic Forum, an annual extravaganza that brings together international leaders in business, academia, diplomacy, and politics, now has female participants. Speakers have included Madeleine Albright, Hillary Rodham Clinton, Queen Rania of Jordan, and Lubna Olayan. It was a land-mark event when Ms. Olayan, the most powerful and best-connected woman in the kingdom, was invited to deliver the forum's keynote address in 2004. She was the first Saudi woman to take the lectern.

"Ladies and gentlemen," she said, "without real change there can be no progress. So if we in Saudi Arabia want to progress we have no choice but to embrace change. Not wholesale change or change simply for the sake of it—that has little value. The real value is in the changes that strengthen us and make us more competitive so that we can overcome the challenges that face us here in the kingdom and throughout the Arab world."

Ms. Olayan then laid out her "vision" of "a country with a prosperous and diversified economy in which any Saudi citizen, irrespective of gender, who is serious about finding employment, can find a job in the field for which he or she is best qualified, leading to a thriving middle class, and in which all Saudi citizens, residents or visitors to the country feel safe and can live in an atmosphere where mutual respect and tolerance exist amongst all, regardless of their social class, religion, or gender."

She did not gloss over the obstacles that inhibit fulfillment of that vision. Indeed, she dwelled on them at length: education, class, attitude, habit, in-difference, and excessive reliance on government. Building the country de-scribed in her vision will not be easy, she said, but "it is achievable."

As could have been predicted, the religious hierarchy reacted furiously—not to what she said, which they ignored, but to the fact that her head scarf slipped back as she talked, revealing her hair. Newspaper photographs of her and her hair, and of other women attending the event with hair covered but faces unveiled, inspired the Grand Mufti of Mecca to denounce "the obscene scenes of female wantonness. . . . I severely condemn this matter and warn of grave consequences. I am pained by such shameful behavior. Allowing women to mix with men is the root of every evil and catastrophe."[30]

What happened over the next few years as a result was the evolution of a typical Saudi compromise, worked out by cautious people finding their way through a social minefield. The organizers invited committees of business-women to participate in planning the forums, and King Abdullah's influen-tial daughter Princess Adela issued a statement of support.

We are happy to be part of this very important event for the Kingdom and the Arab world. Females make up half of the society and the only way we can achieve accelerated growth is by channeling all of our resources and in-volving all segments of the society. The ladies [*sic*] participation in the forum conforms to our Islamic values and principles and falls within the context of our culture and tradition. The government has taken the initia-tive to highlight the role that Saudi women play. . . . It is important for us to support qualified women by giving them the opportunity to actively par-ticipate in key social and economic activities. By providing them with op-portunities such as active participation and training, they can take on a more active and serious role in the development that the Kingdom of Saudi Arabia is witnessing today.[31]

Nevertheless, Saudi women disappeared from the forum's lineup of speak-ers. Female participants were seated in a separate section and told to cover their hair. Photography was banned. Nothing that appeared in the newspa-pers would provoke the wrath of the sheikhs. This sort of contorted com-promise—in which the old rules about women are gradually eroded but the new rules are still being written, mostly by men—is likely to continue for at least the next decade. The national tug-of-war between those pulling for-ward and those pulling backward is far from ending, but a photograph fea-tured in Saudi newspapers in December 2010 gave clues about which side is winning. It showed Ahmad Al-Ghamdi, chief of the muttawain in the Mecca region, answering questions from unveiled female journalists at a forum on women's empowerment. A few years ago there would have been no such event, and if there had been, he would not have been present, let alone allowed himself to be photographed with a group of unveiled professional women. Times change, even in Saudi Arabia.

8

ISLAM, SOCIETY, AND
THE STATE

On a balmy evening in the spring of 2011, I was a guest at the weekly open house and dinner hosted by Sheikh Turki bin Khaled Al-Sudairi, a leader of one of Saudi Arabia's most prominent families. In American terms, the Sudairis were there before the *Mayflower*.

About two dozen businessmen, government officials, academics, and journalists—all men, of course—were sitting in the sheikh's garden, munching dates, sipping cardamom coffee, and chatting when the muezzin's call rose from a nearby mosque. Except for one other non-Muslim and me, all the guests dropped to their knees alongside their host, facing Mecca, for the evening prayer. They were not in the least self-conscious about it. It's what Saudis do; the faith is in their DNA.

Americans who are reared in the tradition the separation of church and state often find it difficult to understand religion's omnipresent role in the life of Saudi Arabia. Islam as practiced in the kingdom is a ubiquitous force that influences personal affairs, government, and the economy all day every day. Whether it is a positive force or a drag on progress is a question of perspective. Saudis value their faith and the government's role in reinforcing it, but they have also been locked for decades in a struggle to reconcile Islam as it is practiced in their country with their aspirations for development, liberty, and engagement with the world.

That struggle will not end in the foreseeable future, and it is possible there will never be a definitive outcome. The country has made useful progress in purging itself of the xenophobia, hatred, and anti-intellectualism that its religious leaders have long espoused, have taught in its schools, and have spread around the world with Saudi money. Every step toward social progress and integration with the twenty-first-century world is evaluated by religious criteria and opposed by the devout.

Under Saudi law, and by Saudi tradition, the purpose of the state is to promote the faith, not to protect the rights and privileges of the individual. All Saudi citizens must be Muslims, and public practice of any other religion is prohibited. Apostasy and conversion to another faith are crimes that bring harsh punishment. Even forms of Islam other than the one decreed by the eighteenth-century Arabian preacher named Muhammad ibn Abdul Wahhab are scorned as illegitimate. (The Saudi version of Islam is known to outsiders as Wahhabism, but the Saudis have generally avoided that term because it implies reverence for a man, whereas Islam requires worship of God only. If forced to choose a label, they prefer *muwahhidin*, or "unitarians," meaning those who adhere strictly to the doctrine that there is only one God and that all forms of worship and reverence centered on humans are sinful.)[1]

The influence of religion is readily apparent to any visitor. Alcoholic beverages are prohibited, and possession and consumption of alcohol are crimes, even for foreigners. All shops, from the humblest Bangladeshi grocery to the grandest mall, close for prayer five times a day. They turn off the lights, expel customers, and lock the doors. At gasoline stations, customers sit patiently alongside the pumps with their engines idling, waiting for service to resume after prayers. Everyone knows the prayer times because newspapers print the hours of the five daily prayers along with the weather, and the resounding call to prayer rises from the minarets of the country's ubiquitous mosques. Along the highways the government has installed blue signs with brief spiritual invocations in Arabic: *Hamdullilah* [God be praised] and *Allahu akbar* [God is greatest]. A visitors guide provides the telephone numbers of volunteers who are available twenty-four hours a day to give religious information and counseling in English, Malay, French, Thai, Tamil, and Bengali. Flights of the national airline begin with a prayer broadcast over the cabin speakers. Tourists—whom the kingdom, in a radical break with tradition, is trying to attract—receive disks and pamphlets promoting Islam along with their passport stamps.

And these examples are only superficial signs of Islam's influence on Saudi life. Government, education, history, society, public behavior, family life, and even banking are deeply enmeshed in religion and regulated by the rules of Islamic law. Public discourse and the media devote endless amounts of time and space to arguments over religious minutiae and such serious theological questions as is the Koran a flexible document that must be reinterpreted for modern times, or does all innovation lead to hell? Other than oil, the country's biggest business is the annual haj, or pilgrimage to Mecca, which brings more than 2 million Muslims from all over the world to worship at the holy sites of Mecca and Medina every year during pilgrimage season. Millions more visit the sites year round for *umra*, or "lesser pilgrimage." The king's official title is Custodian of the Two Holy Mosques.

The kingdom's Basic Law of Government, issued in 1992, declares in Chapter One, Article One, that "the Kingdom of Saudi Arabia is a sovereign Arab Islamic state with Islam as its religion; God's Book [i.e., the Koran] and the Sunna [example] of His Prophet, God's prayers and peace be upon him, are its constitution." Under Article Seven, "Government in Saudi Arabia derives power from the Holy Koran and the Prophet's tradition."[2] In the country's Ninth Five-Year Development Plan, which the cabinet adopted in April 2010, the first stated goal is the preservation of Islamic teachings and values. The Ministry of Education's ten-year plan for the years 2004–2014 sets as its first "vision," or objective, "the graduation of male and female students with Islamic values and the appropriate knowledge and practice."

Saudi Arabia is unique among the world's Muslim countries in the number and variety of rules and prohibitions that are determined by religion, even when no basis for them can be found in the Koran or in the hadith, the sayings of the Prophet Muhammad that are the principal secondary source of doctrine. Passages in the holy texts validate Saudi Arabia's restrictions on alcohol and on the charging of interest, for example, but not its ban on public entertainment and the prohibition of public meetings between unrelated men and women. In the name of protecting public morality, the rulers imposed these restrictions, and the Commission for the Promotion of Virtue and the Prevention of Vice, the so-called religious police or muttawain, enforces them. The state-sponsored muttawain are responsible for monitoring public behavior and do so under the banner of the faith.

The best-known example of a Saudi rule that the muttawain enforce without any real religious justification is the prohibition on driving by women. Even government officials and senior princes of the royal family have acknowledged it has no basis in Islamic law. No other country enforces such a ban, but in Saudi Arabia the rules of the faith and the force of custom have become so conflated that the senior religious scholars and preachers, known collectively as the ulama, or learned ones, have a powerful influence on matters that in other countries would not concern them.

Saudi Arabia's unique place in Islam is a product of its history. It was the birthplace of the religion, which was a unifying and stabilizing force that brought order to the pagan, lawless Arabian Peninsula in the seventh century. The ruling Al-Saud dynasty first rose to power in an alliance with Muhammad ibn Abdul Wahhab in the eighteenth century. When Abdul Aziz Al-Saud subdued rival tribes in the first three decades of the twentieth century to create the modern Kingdom of Saudi Arabia, the instruments of his conquest were the fanatic Islamic warriors known as the Ikhwan (Brothers). In the 1950s and 1960s, secular rulers drove members of the Islamist organization known as the Ikhwan al-Muslimin, or "Muslim Brotherhood," from Egypt and Syria. They flocked to teaching and preaching jobs in Saudi Arabia and burrowed deep into its curricula and its intellectual life. Unlike other Muslim countries such as Egypt and Iran, Saudi Arabia has no history or identity as a state beyond its unity with the faith.

Europeans and many Americans take it for granted that as societies develop, the influence of religion diminishes, but such has not been the case in Saudi Arabia. The Saudis are proud of their faith and of Arabia's special position in Islamic history. A small element of the population flirted briefly with secular Arab nationalism and leftist politics in the 1960s, but there is virtually no such movement today. In recent decades, the regime's most militant critics—including Osama bin Laden—have denounced the rulers for being insufficiently religious, rather than excessively so.

It would be wrong, however, to assume that the weight given to religion in Saudi personal and public affairs is immutable. Saudis argue about it every day. In the absence of real politics, religion fills the gap; the interplay of religion and society becomes the subject of endless, and sometimes quite heated, discussion in the media. In a lengthy commentary Abdullah Al-Fawzan, one of the country's most influential columnists, dissented from a statement by the Grand Mufti, or chief religious leader, that, as in the time of Muhammad ibn Abdul Wahhab, public order and stability are best maintained through the bargain between the ulama and the rulers and to the exclusion of the people. This sort of "father knows best" view basically instructs the faithful to accept without question whatever the ulama tell them.

Al-Fawzan's remarkable attack on the Grand Mufti's self-aggrandizing orthodoxy is sometimes difficult to follow but merits quoting at length because it illustrates not only the argument itself but also the lengths to which criticism of the religious leadership is tolerated—sometimes even encouraged—by the ruling family. The House of Saud desires to maintain the appearance of sharing power with the ulama without actually doing so.

His Eminence the Mufti compared the role of the *'ulama* now to that of Sheikh Muhammad ibn Abdul Wahhab. I beg pardon of our sheikh and father His Eminence the Mufti and all his noble peers the senior *'ulama* when I say that this comparison is not valid, not for any reason having to do with them or with Sheikh Muhammad, but rather having to do with the time in question. For they, or some of them at least, might be more erudite, more studied than Sheikh Muhammad was; but compared to the reality of the age and people, not one of them could occupy the position of the Sheikh in terms of trailblazing and intellectual and cultural superiority compared to others of his society. Sheikh Muhammad was the most knowledgeable of his contemporaries in relation to the reality of his age: he was the first educated person, the first well-informed person, and the most knowledgeable and cognizant, something not true of his *'ulama* contemporaries. The reason for this was that the Sheikh's era was an extension of previous ones, in which human knowledge did not blaze forth as it does today. That is, the scientific revolution in industry, communication, and technology had not yet occurred. Sheikh Muhammad was assiduous in learning and reading, and his awareness of what previous *'ulama* and learned Muslims had left behind was sufficient to make him an intellectual pioneer with respect to the realities of his society. As for the present, it is not possible in light of such burgeoning scientific revolutions (in which Muslim scientists regrettably have little role) to be able to know everything. They might not even know anything about some great inventions, in their knowledge of what Muslim scientists bequeathed in religious and human affairs, as is the case with some if not most of our scientists. Furthermore, any religious scholar nowadays cannot stand on his own two feet, in diverse fields, without the help of others. And so, perspectives on new scientific inventions shall be left to those with creative, all-encompassing minds filled with the facts and innovations of the age. I don't mean to say that our scientists fall short in their learning and knowledge; rather, I mean that one hand whatever its strength can no longer clap by itself, as perhaps it could in the age of Sheikh Muhammad—and even two or three or ten find it difficult, for proper clapping these days can only take place in *shura* councils and representative assemblies relying in their decisions on the opinions of experts in each field.

If the venerable *'ulama* in their *fatwas* on the satellite networks and elsewhere and in their speeches broadcast to the leadership had relied on the opinions of experts in the various sciences, then perhaps the bond between *'ulama* and leadership His Eminence wants would be very useful. Yet, as we see, this has not come to pass on many an issue. For example, the *'ulama* issue fatwas and request from the leadership the prohibition of some new inventions that could bring about good if used for good, and ill if used for ill—but instead of the religious establishment playing a constructive role in eliminating evil and encouraging good, they demand shutting the door once and for all against all argument. And despite it being assumed that the leadership asks of the religious establishment that it undertake its creative role so that citizens may benefit from new tools, instead of that and indeed perhaps because of that the relationship complies with its demand to shut the door and forbid citizens from the benefits of such tools, the result being that the Kingdom of Saudi Arabia remains the only country in the world, or just about the only country, where some or all of its citizens do not benefit from these tools despite that being among their rights.[3]

This passage is tedious and narrow but, in the Saudi context, the question is crucial: To what extent can religion veto modernization or any other policy set by a government? The argument has been going on since the time of Ahmad Ibn Taymiya, a thirteenth-century theologian who taught that the ulama should rank above the ruler as the people's moral steward. The influence of the religious hierarchy in Saudi Arabia today is already less than it was in the past—innovations such as television and education for girls were introduced over the religious authorities' objections—and it continues to change as education, travel, and the Internet expand the population's awareness of other ways of life and as urbanization erodes bedouin and oasis traditions. On their satellite televisions, Saudis can see other Islamic societies where the faith, while widely embraced, is much less intrusive in the lives of individuals.

One way to understand what is happening is to envision a gauge or graph that represents the degree of religious enforcement in every country where Muslims are a majority. At the most restrictive end would be Afghanistan under the rule of the Taliban, who closed schools for girls, forced women to wear the all-enveloping burqa, prohibited barbers from trimming beards (because the Prophet Muhammad was unshaven), and banned all forms of public amusement. The Somali militia known as al-Shabab imposes similar restrictions in areas under its control. At the other end is Turkey, a secular state whose Muslim citizens are fairly free to do whatever they want. Many in cosmopolitan Istanbul even eat and drink publicly during Ramadan, the holy month of fasting. Saudi Arabia is closer to the Taliban state than it is to Turkey on this gauge, but the needle has been moving—slowly, haltingly, back and forth at times, but still moving—for eighty years.

The great open question is where that needle will or should come to rest. There is little if any evidence that any measurable element of Saudi society would embrace the secular model represented by Turkey. Yet abundant evidence shows that attitudes and aspirations are changing under the powerful influences of education, globalization, mass communication, and economic necessity. In a way, the wave of violent extremism that has washed over Islam in the past thirty years or so, for which the Saudi rulers bear as much responsibility as anyone, has been a positive force for change in the kingdom. It has forced Saudi Arabia to scrutinize its ways, to recognize its failings, and to abandon the religious smugness that disdained new ideas and scorned Muslims of other societies who did not follow the Saudi path.

It remains a fact of life, however, that religion and arguments about religion are fundamental determinants of social and intellectual life in Saudi Arabia, to a great extent because the country has no political life. In the absence of political parties, elections, trade unions, independent research groups, and nongovernmental public interest organizations, Islam provides a safe, acceptable forum for what are really political arguments. Islam can provide a path to wealth and power for people who otherwise would have neither, and once they achieve prominence, they tend to dig in to defend the status quo.

A friend who holds a prominent position in one of the Saudi cabinet departments told me the "religious element" of the population falls into four groups: the "radicals, the violent ones"; the merely pious "who don't care about anything but prayer and study"; the ulama and other religious authorities, or "creatures of the state," for whom religion is a career; and "people whose livelihood depends on this and don't want anything to change," such as publishers of religious books and teachers at religious universities. That element adds up to a great many Saudis. Given their influence and the fact that the king and princes of the Al-Saud family base their legitimacy on their self-assigned role as upholders of the true Islam, the role of religion in national life is unlikely to diminish. What is changing is how that role is defined and the amount of room it gives individuals to maneuver.

Three landmark events in the last quarter of the twentieth century stoked a deep fire of zealotry, extremism, and bigotry in Saudi Arabia. These forces led to the country's association with terrorism after September 11, 2001.

The first was the takeover of the Great Mosque in Mecca on November 20, 1979, by an armed group of religious fanatics who deemed the regime too liberal and insufficiently rigorous in imposing Islamic law. After a long siege the attackers were subdued and executed, but a traumatized government nevertheless yielded to many of their demands. Already under attack by the leaders of revolutionary Iran, just across the Persian Gulf, for being "tools" of the United States, the Saudi rulers felt they needed to burnish their religious credentials. They halted the liberalizing social trends of the 1970s that had tolerated such daring innovations as allowing unveiled women to read the news on television. They unleashed the muttawain for a new campaign of social repression. They reduced the number of males going abroad for university studies and stopped sending female students. They expanded the religious universities, churning out students steeped in the most rigid form of Islam but devoid of skills relevant to the job market. And they turned over classrooms and mosques to teachers and imams who preached a fire-and-brimstone form of the faith that emphasized shunning infidels. Outside Saudi Arabia, the House of Saud committed billions of oil dollars to the construction of mosques and religious schools that would spread the same doctrine, a program that remains an issue in U.S.-Saudi relations.[4]

The second event was the Soviet invasion of Afghanistan in the last week of 1979. In the long war that followed, Saudi Arabia—in partnership with the Central Intelligence Agency (CIA)—supported the Afghan insurgents known as mujahedeen (warriors of jihad). With the government's approval and inspired by the cause of defending Islam against atheistic invaders, young

Saudi men went to Afghanistan to fight. Osama bin Laden became their leader as they learned how to use bombs and firearms. Although the Saudi government revoked bin Laden's citizenship and barred him from the country in 1994, the young fighters who returned to the kingdom after the war as committed jihadists still embraced his goals and followed his instructions.

The third event was Operation Desert Storm, the 1991 military campaign by the United States and its allies to drive Saddam Hussein's Iraqi troops out of Kuwait, which Iraq had invaded the year before. After American officials convinced King Fahd ibn Abdul Aziz and his brothers that they might be next on Saddam Hussein's target list, the Saudis allowed more than half a million foreign troops—mostly American, including women and Jews—into the kingdom to defend it and prepare for a strike into Kuwait. In doing so, they spurned an offer from bin Laden to rally his returned fighters in defense of Islam's homeland. The rulers' decision to rebuff him and to accept assistance from a vast army of infidels instead further stoked the determination of bin Laden and his associates, known as al-Qaeda, to bring them down. It also sparked outrage among ordinary Saudis because it demonstrated that the country could not defend itself despite the billions of dollars the rulers had spent on military equipment and facilities while enriching themselves in the process.

Desert Storm shattered an important component of the unwritten social compact between the rulers and the ruled. King Abdul Aziz and his successors had persuaded a reluctant and sometimes hostile populace to accept the presence of foreigners because the kingdom needed their capital, technology, expertise, and even grunt labor to develop. Before the Americans found oil, hardly anybody in the kingdom knew how to drive a truck, fix a motor, fly an airplane, mix concrete, install electric lines, or perform surgery; thus foreigners were a necessary evil.

There was no way, however, to pretend that the infidel troops of Desert Storm were present to develop the kingdom. They were in Saudi Arabia to wage war against Muslim Arabs in a neighboring country. The king promised that the troops would leave Saudi Arabia after the war, but not all of them did. Substantial contingents remained to conduct air operations over Iraq and enforce international restrictions against Iraqi military flights. Their presence became a casus belli for bin Laden and al-Qaeda.

King Fahd and his brothers had bullied the ulama into issuing a declaration that the presence of infidel troops in the kingdom was necessary during the emergency, but dissident religious thinkers were not persuaded. In Saudi Arabia, as in most Sunni Muslim countries, the ulama are employees of the state; if they cross the ruler they can lose their jobs and privileges. For that reason, believers can discount the ulama's pronouncements. After Desert Storm, dissident religious scholars such as Safar Al-Hawali went public with their criticisms and rejected the position taken by the official establishment. Conversely, liberals and reformers argue that the rulers are dissembling when they hold back on political or social reform on the grounds that the religious leadership would not accept it. Desert Storm showed that the ulama would accept what the king ordered them to accept.

All these pressures, and the regime's misguided responses to them, blew up in the rulers' faces on May 12, 2003. Three bands of armed terrorists opened fire on housing compounds in Riyadh occupied mostly by Westerners, drove bomb-laden trucks inside, and blew them up. The attacks killed thirty-six people in addition to the terrorists.[5]

That assault was the opening salvo of an uprising by a clandestine band of extremist desperadoes known as al-Qaeda in the Arabian Peninsula. For the next three years they attacked or tried to attack government installations, oil industry facilities, foreigners' housing compounds, and individual foreigners. They kidnapped an American engineer, Paul Johnson, and beheaded him. They gunned down a BBC television crew, killing the cameraman. They claimed to be fighting for Islam, but their aims were political: destroy the Al-Saud regime and expel all infidels from Saudi Arabia. Recruiting with some initial success through the Internet, they presented the greatest threat to the regime since the mosque takeover twenty-four years earlier.

After the attacks on New York and the Pentagon on September 11, 2001, when it was revealed that fifteen of the nineteen hijackers involved had been Saudis, King Fahd and Crown Prince Abdullah issued statements deploring the mass killings and condemning terrorism. But inside the kingdom nothing much happened, partly because Fahd was incapacitated by a stroke and partly because the rulers did not appear to face any problem inside Saudi Arabia itself. Bin Laden was in exile in Afghanistan, al-Qaeda was operating elsewhere, and many Saudis were simply in denial about what had happened in the United States. The Riyadh compound bombings awakened Saudi Arabia as 9/11 had awakened Americans.

Starting with the housing compound attacks, al-Qaeda's violence made the first decade of the twenty-first century a dark time in Saudi Arabia. Police and security forces engaged in armed street battles with extremists. Raids on houses all over the country turned up arms caches and cells of conspirators. Barbed wire and reinforced barricades appeared outside hotels and shopping malls. Thousands of foreigners fled. The U.S. government ordered the dependents of its diplomats to come home and shortened tours of duty at the embassy because Saudi Arabia was considered a hardship post. The State Department issued frightening travel warnings telling Americans not to go there.

The kingdom's relations with the United States frayed as Washington demanded greater and more comprehensive action to confront the worldwide jihadist phenomenon, of which many Americans regarded Saudi Arabia as the sponsor.[6]

The al-Qaeda uprising in Saudi Arabia failed. It failed partly because the security forces responded with increasing vigor and competence and won those gun battles. It also failed because the Saudi people did not support the extremists and were horrified by their commitment to violence, which killed more Muslims than it did infidels. Many Saudis supported al-Qaeda's utopian vision of a pure Islamic state and restoration of the caliphate, with rule over all Muslims by a religiously inspired *khalifah*, or successor to Muhammad; but they understood that the armed rebels had no practical program. The terrorists offered them nothing except more violence and unfulfillable aspiration. When ordinary citizens encountered men who they suspected were part of the rebellion, instead of supporting them, they called the cops. Within eighteen months of the first bombing, twenty of the twenty-six men on the kingdom's "Most Wanted" list had been killed or captured. The others had fled or were in hiding.

By the late winter of 2010, when the Combating Terrorism Center at West Point published Norwegian scholar Thomas Hegghammer's assessment of the uprising, he titled it "The Failure of Jihad in Saudi Arabia." The campaign of violence, Hegghammer wrote, "ended in failure and defeat. . . . It took al-Qa'ida seven years to mount a decent fighting force in the Kingdom, only to see it crushed by the state just a couple of years after launching its offensive in 2003."

Nor was the government's response limited to armed force, Hegghammer wrote:

Saudi authorities also conducted a sophisticated campaign for the hearts and minds of the population in general and the Islamist community in particular. The state used all available outlets—including the mass media, the official religious authorities and the education system—to convey one overarching message: the militants were confused rebels bent on creating disorder and killing Muslims. They key to the success of this information strategy was that it portrayed the militants as revolutionaries, thereby exploiting the taboo against domestic rebellion in Saudi political culture to delegitimize the militants in the eyes of the population. The government propaganda campaign exacerbated a crucial latent problem facing [al-Qaeda in the Arabian Peninsula], namely the lack of public support—even in the Islamist community—for a violent campaign on Saudi soil.[7]

So effective was the campaign to discredit the extremists that even the influential religious scholar Salman Al-Audah, no liberal and no friend of the regime, delivered a public denunciation of al-Qaeda's tactics and of bin Laden. In 2007 Al-Audah posted a message to bin Laden in English on his "Islamtoday.net" Web site: "Brother Osama, how much blood has been spilled? How many innocent children, women, and old people have been killed, maimed, and expelled from their homes in the name of 'Al-Qaeda? Are you happy to meet with Allah with this heavy burden on your shoulders? . . . This religion of ours comes to the defense of the life of a sparrow. It can never accept the murder of innocent people, regardless of what supposed justification is given for it." Bin Laden and his campaign, he wrote, had tarnished the image of Islam all over the world and to no one's benefit. "What have all these long years of suffering, tragedy, tears and sacrifice actually achieved?" he asked.

Bin Laden's tactics, he said, were responsible for the oppression of Muslims everywhere, for the destruction of well-intentioned Muslim charities by governments acting in self-defense, and for the desolation of Muslim widows and orphans. People who had long heard bin Laden and other extremists claim that the misfortunes of Muslims are the work of "crusaders" and "Zionists" found Al-Audah's words astonishing. Cynics noted that Al-Audah issued this denunciation after he had spent some time in jail, but in truth his words accurately reflected popular revulsion against violence among conservative and devout Saudis as well.[8]

Even Yusuf Al-Qaradawi, often described as the Arab world's most influential Sunni Islamist, denounced al-Qaeda's manifestoes. He described them as "a mad declaration of war on the entire world" with no basis in Islamic jurisprudence.[9]

In retrospect, the armed violence that gripped the country beginning in 2003 was doomed to fail because it was an anomaly in Saudi Arabia, not a manifestation of the national character. In a failed state such as Somalia, an uprising of that violent nature might appeal to young men with no jobs, no social structure, and nothing else to believe in, but Saudi Arabia is well organized and pervaded by a well-understood code of behavior. As Hegghammer wrote, Saudi Arabia "has never been home to a strong socio-revolutionary Islamist community." The violence "was the result not of structural political or economic strain inside the Kingdom, but rather of a momentary conjunction between high operational capability on the part of the local Al-Qaeda network, boosted in numbers and skills by post-2001 returnees from Afghanistan, and a weak Saudi security apparatus. That gap in capability has now closed, and the [al-Qaeda] campaign has petered out. The Saudi regime is currently stronger—but also less inclined to political reform—than it has been for several years."[10]

ABDULLAH REACHES OUT

The campaign to rescue Islam from the disrepute into which al-Qaeda and 9/11 had dragged it, to persuade the Saudi public that extremism and violence were sinful, and—not the least important consideration—to restore the religious primacy of the Al-Saud regime and its appointed religious authorities was aided in 2005 when the incapacitated King Fahd died. Upon assuming full powers as king, Abdullah left his half brother, Interior Minister Prince Nayef, free to continue the armed crackdown on al-Qaeda cadres and sympathizers, while the king embarked on initiatives that could be described, in a favorable way, as public relations. He ordered three prominent dissidents released from jail. He initiated an "Interfaith Dialogue," reaching out to other religions. He even allowed Saudi newspapers to print a photograph of himself with Pope Benedict XVI. In 2007, the Saudi delegation to the International Islamic Conference signed on to a declaration that validated all groupings and schools of law in Islam, even Shiites, long a reviled and shunned minority in Saudi Arabia. All who accept the basic tenets of the faith are Muslims, the declaration said, and it is not permissible to brand them apostates, as the Sunni authorities in Saudi Arabia had long done with the Shiites.

Abdullah removed the governor of a remote province whom the local people, mostly Shiites of the Ismaili sect, accused of repressing them. He dismissed imams and religious judges whose public remarks and Internet postings he deemed extreme or conducive to violence, and preachers delivering sermons in mosques were required to carry identity cards showing that they had been vetted by the government. Abdullah committed the government to purging textbooks of hatred and anti-Semitism, with mixed results. (See chapter 6.) And perhaps most of important of all from the perspective of ordinary Saudis, he undertook a modest but symbolic reform of the muttawain.

This peculiar law enforcement force had long inspired terror and loathing, as well as contempt, because of its crude tactics. The members are often described as vigilantes, but they are not self-appointed; the government organizes, trains, and deploys them. Their responsibility is to enforce the moral code: no gender-integrated social gatherings or workplaces, no overt practice of other religions, no alcohol, no revealing clothing, no staying open for business during prayer time, no unauthorized contact with the opposite sex, no witchcraft or "sorcery." They are not uniformed but they are easy to spot because—in imitation of the Prophet—their beards are untrimmed, their *thobes* (gowns) are worn above the ankle, and they shun the *aqal*, the black circular band that most Saudi men wear over their head scarves. Opinion surveys, always of dubious reliability in a closed society like Saudi Arabia's, indicated that many Saudis supported the muttawa mission but resented the members' intimidating tactics.

King Abdullah installed a new chief of this organization, Abdul Aziz Al-Humain, who ordered the force retrained on the proper way to deal with people, including tourists, and who met with human rights advocates. Now a regular police officer must accompany muttawa units on the street, and only the police officer is allowed to make arrests. The king permitted the prosecution of a few muttawain who had clearly abused their authority. Members of the force are now required to study English, the lingua franca of the millions of foreigners who live in Saudi Arabia.

The result is that by 2010 the muttawain were a more professional force and were devoting more of their energy to enforcing laws such as the ban on alcohol and rooting out drug smugglers and less to harassing individual citizens who are trying to enjoy what few pleasures are available to them. They remain a feared force, especially among social liberals and young people looking for entertainment, but their writ is no longer limitless.

Before the wave of jihadist terrorism obliged the Saudi rulers to take stock of the system, said Jamal Abahussein, a prominent Riyadh businessman, "this was a closed society. You had to go in one direction and live a certain style of life. You couldn't deviate. When you were dining out, these people [the muttawain] would question you—'Is this your wife?' It was unbearable. You don't dictate a style of life to a human being."

No "civilized person" would attempt to justify the 9/11 attacks and the global terrorism that followed, he said, but "it resulted in a huge benefit to Saudi society. . . . Society is far more flexible now. The radical groups and their power are shrinking because the government told them, 'Stay away from people's lives, don't tell people what to do.' They still have some power but now they are educated, trained, systematized. They have an ethics code. Before, they could do anything. Now their work is defined, the employees are screened, they get very high-caliber training." He is no longer afraid to take his wife out to dinner at a popular restaurant, he said.

Reflecting what seems to be a widespread view, Abahussein said that "it wouldn't be right to eliminate them. They help a lot in eliminating crime. They stop teenagers from provoking girls. In this they are effective and welcome. Not in personal life; it's nobody's business if you are married or not."[11]

I met many other Saudis who would agree, more or less, with Abahussein's assessment. As the scholar Awadh Al-Badi put it, "On that scale measuring from the Taliban to Istanbul, it is at different points depending on what you are talking about. On some we are still close to the Taliban. On others we have moved maybe halfway." But Abahussein and Al-Badi are men; women, who face far greater social restrictions, tend to take a less benign view of the enforcers, who pursue them through public spaces in search of infractions of their rigid code of attire and behavior.

In the fall of 2010, the newspaper *Asharq al-Awsat* (*The Middle East*) reported that the muttawain had submitted their annual report on their operations to the Consultative Assembly. It said that the number of cases in which the group had acted had declined by 20 percent from the year before, attributing the decline to "fear of the consequences of negative media reports on its operations." Nevertheless, the total number of cases was 55,000, of which 16,650 involved Saudi citizens, who mostly were detained over "belief and worship issues."[12]

WHAT ARE THE RULES?

A cartoon published in the newspaper *al-Riyadh* showed a man and his veiled wife together at a shopping mall, the very picture of respectability, in an encounter with two long-bearded members of the vice squad who were peppering them with hostile questions. The cartoon was labeled "A Suspicious Situation," when common sense would say there was no cause for suspicion. But if the religious police are so arbitrary and ridiculous, why do people fear them so much? One answer is that Saudis who engage in any but the most traditional family-centered activities or wear anything but the most traditional clothing still face a chronic problem in that the rules of behavior and appearance are not fully codified. People are frightened by the prospect of a nasty interrogation and perhaps even time in jail if they transgress, and often the only way to find out that a particular statement, gathering, or garment is proscribed is the hard way. Is it permitted for a woman to wear jeans beneath her abaya and let them show, or are groups of young men free to ogle female shoppers in the malls? How long does a man's hair have to be before it is too long? Why does religion have anything to do with these questions in the first place?

It is tempting to think that the answers will come not from the hard-eyed enforcers of the past but from a new generation of flexible Muslims like Ahmad Al-Shugairi, a charismatic television host who appeals to young people with the message that they can be good Muslims and still enjoy life. He established a popular coffee shop in Jeddah where young people hang out together. Having formerly lived for years in California, he aims his message of moderate, tolerant Islam at what he calls "the MTV generation."

That message is that there are good people everywhere—not just Muslims and not just in Saudi Arabia—and a virtuous life is a life that accommodates differences and appreciates other cultures. He did a series of shows from Japan, for example, to demonstrate that although Islam preaches cleanliness, the streets in Arab countries are filthy while those in non-Muslim Japan are spotless. Even in the United States, he told an American interviewer, he often found people followed the teachings of the Prophet more closely than some Muslims did.[13]

That kind of talk can still be dangerous in Saudi Arabia, and it is far from clear whether people such as Al-Shugairi are close to approaching critical mass in what remains a conservative society, where all public discourse is filtered through the lens of religion. The higher the tide of modernization, the more furiously the old guard digs in against it. This struggle is waged in many arenas and perhaps most visibly in the religious authorities' endless condemnation of satellite television entertainment, particularly a wildly popular and slightly sexy Turkish soap opera. This clash is more than a culture war as members of the Saudi royal family own some of the most influential satellite networks and have become indirect targets of the sheikhs' rants against the programming.

By 2010, Abdullah had evidently had enough of the radical preachers and religious scholars who had been using the pulpit, the television screen, and the Internet to oppose his initiatives, to denounce every form of progressive innovation, and even to call for the death of people who introduced alien ideas into Saudi culture. Their pronouncements often were presented as fatwas, or religious edicts.

After "jihad," "fatwa" is probably the Arabic word that has most inserted itself into the vocabulary of English speakers over the past few decades. It means a religious ruling or pronouncement upon a religious subject, issued by a person of sufficient religious credentials to be credible. Because Islam has no ordained clergy and no central doctrinal authority—there is no Islamic Vatican—it is never clear who exactly is authorized to issue such a statement; for the same reason, the individual believer is not bound by it. A fatwa carries only as much authority as the believers accord to its issuer.

Since the advent of the Internet and satellite television, fatwas that criticize official policy, that deviate from the line of the established religious authorities, or—in the case of Saudi Arabia especially—that embarrass the regime with ridiculous pronouncements on social matters have plagued governments in majority-Muslim countries. Because Islam is the only channel of discourse that is never closed even in the most authoritarian countries, it cannot be shut down as one would an offending newspaper.

The proliferation of fatwas from people of questionable motives or dubious credentials reached such proportions that the entire fifty-six-nation Organization of the Islamic Conference addressed the issue at an Islamic summit conference in Mecca in 2005. The delegates said they "condemn the audacity of those who are not qualified in issuing religious rulings (*fatwa*), thereby flouting the tenets and pillars of the religion and the well-established schools of jurisprudence."[14] Undeterred, Saudi critics of Abdullah's social initiatives, such as coeducation at the university that bears his name and the opening of more employment fields to women, kept issuing fatwas, often to the fury of the king and embarrassment of the government. In August 2010, during the holy month of Ramadan, the king issued a decree banning the issuance of unauthorized or unofficial fatwas.

"As part of our religious and national duty we want you to ensure that *fatwas* are only issued by members of the Council of Senior Religious Scholars and other permitted people," the king's decree instructed the country's highest religious official, Grand Mufti Sheikh Abdul Aziz Al-Asheikh. "We have observed the fallout from unqualified people issuing *fatwas*. It is our religious duty to stop them in order to preserve our religion, which is our dearest possession, and cut off an evil which, if we do not tackle now, will return with added force." The king also instructed the Grand Mufti to compile a list of those authorized to issue fatwas.[15]

This episode was a clear example of how the Saudi regime uses the power of religion, and manipulates the long-standing partnership of throne and pulpit, to reinforce its own authority. The Grand Mufti and other senior religious figures are employees of the state who are appointed by the king and his advisers. They live very well because of the positions they hold and are thus reluctant to incur the king's displeasure by challenging his policies. A royal affirmation of their authority, as in the fatwas decree, only reinforces their loyalty to the monarch. Whenever the regime faces a serious challenge that claims religious motivation, as in the Great Mosque takeover of 1979 or the al-Qaeda uprising of 2003, the ulama come to the defense of their partners, the Al-Saud, thus reinforcing the king's position and undercutting the opposition's religious claims. It is a powerful weapon in the House of Al-Saud's arsenal of self-defense. The ulama do what they are told, but it is not in the king's interest to alienate them with radical social or political moves that are too far outside their comfort zone to be tolerated.

This intricate dynamic was displayed once again in the package of royal decrees issued in the winter of 2011, when the kingdom's neighbors were undergoing the mass political changes of the so-called Arab Spring. Most of the decrees dealt with economic and labor matters, but they included ample sweeteners for the religious establishment. The king allocated more than $350 million to establish new religious study centers, to promote memorization of the Koran, to create three hundred jobs in new centers of religious research, and to enable the muttawain to establish regional bureaus. He also prohibited the news media from "defaming or criticizing the Grand Mufti and Senior *Ulama* Commission's members." Two weeks earlier, the country's senior religious leaders had issued a proclamation forbidding demonstrations and public protests against the regime on the ground that the king and his partners embody the rules of the faith as set down in Islamic scripture. In effect, they said, to demonstrate against the regime is to demonstrate against Islam itself: "Reform cannot be achieved through demonstrations and means that incite discord in the Muslim community."[16]

SPREADING THE IDEOLOGY

The events of the first decade of this century rattled Saudi Arabia to its spiritual foundations and forced open some long-sealed windows, but the struggle against extremism has not ended. In particular, the government has not entirely succeeded in stopping Saudi individuals from making donations to organizations abroad that promote or endorse terrorism in the name of religion, some of which Saudi Arabia sponsored to begin with. This funding was a point of contention between Riyadh and Washington for several years after 9/11, and to some extent it still is, even though the Saudi government has restricted Saudi-based charities from exporting cash and has cooperated with American investigators.

This subject was difficult for the Saudi rulers because charity is a moral obligation in Islam and many Saudis take pride in their generosity to their poorer brethren in other countries. Many charitable donors were no doubt well intentioned, and if the recipient groups used some of the money to purchase weapons and train terrorist cadres, the donors either did not know or did not want to know. Some Saudis offered an analogy to Irish Americans who contributed to the Irish Republican Army, supporting the cause while overlooking the tactics.

That argument was at best disingenuous. It ignores the fact that beginning in the early 1980s the Saudi government spent billions to promote the intolerant Saudi brand of Islam all over the world and even in the United States. The government built the world's largest religious printing press at Medina and used it as a base for disseminating not just the Koran but also instructional materials, in many languages, that repeated the same hate-filled lessons that were being taught in the kingdom's schools. Saudi-financed organizations such as the World Assembly of Muslim Youth and the Muslim World League took on the same proselytizing mission. Their message that other religions and even other versions of Islam were invalid, that Muslims should be aggressive in spreading their faith, and that no differing views could be tolerated penetrated classrooms and pulpits from South Asia to West Africa. Even if the materials these Saudis disseminated and the teachers and preachers they sponsored did not preach violence, they spread ideas to which violence was sometimes a logical conclusion.

The full extent of Saudi resources that supported the dissemination of ideology and materials in other countries is difficult to quantify because it came from many sources, including private individuals, and was disbursed through many channels, some overt, some clandestine. It is however clear that the flow of money, preachers, textbooks, and recruiting materials was massive and continued for many years because it suited the Saudi regime's purposes. It burnished the Al-Saud rulers' credentials as upholders and defenders of the only true faith, it appealed to their subjects' charitable instincts, and in some places, such as Bosnia and Afghanistan, it reinforced the objectives of Saudi foreign policy. During the Cold War, disseminating Saudi-style doctrine was a weapon against communism; after the Iranian revolution, it was a weapon against Shiism. This genie will be very difficult to put back in the bottle, even if the rulers in Riyadh are so inclined.

A Library of Congress researcher with some access to classified information reported in 2010 that

> the pan-Islamic solidarity movement that drove Saudi involvement in Afghanistan during the 1980s continued to inspire international activism among Saudis [after the 1991 Gulf War] as private Saudi citizens, Saudi government charitable committees and international Islamic charity organizations based in the Kingdom funneled financial and material support

to a range of Muslim groups around the world. This included support for entities and individuals engaged in or victimized by nationalist conflicts in Chechnya, Afghanistan, Bosnia, Kashmir, Kosovo, and the West Bank and Gaza. At times this support complicated U.S. policy and peacemaking efforts in those regions and, whether directly or indirectly, contributed to the development and sustainment of a transnational network of violent activists, some of whom were affiliated with Al Qaeda.[17]

Researchers at the Combating Terrorism Center at West Point have established that the rigid, xenophobic form of Islam that Saudi Arabia promoted around the world was not the intellectual foundation of violence-prone extremist groups such as al-Qaeda. To the extent that these groups found rationalization for violence in Muslim doctrine, their ideas derived more from well-established, non-Saudi thinkers such as Sayid Qutb and from Deobandi theologians based in South Asia.[18] The Saudi money and materials contributed to a culture in which those ideas could take root. The Riyadh government took years to grasp the blowback potential of these financial and ideological campaigns, and, as exposed in secret diplomatic correspondence made public by the underground Internet organization WikiLeaks, it was still struggling to bring them under control in 2010.[19]

In January 2010, for example, Howard Mendelsohn of the U.S. Treasury Department met with representatives of the Saudi Mabahith (secret police) to discuss the fund-raising activities of three Taliban officials inside Saudi Arabia and one of their well-heeled Saudi supporters. The police officials in the meeting professed to know nothing about these individuals, whereupon the Americans provided key information about them.

U.S. ambassador James Smith reported:

Treasury analysts provided information on [names redacted], three senior Taliban officials who have made multiple fundraising visits to Saudi Arabia, according to U.S. intelligence, (NOTE: Information available to the USG [U.S. government] and shared for this exchange included telephone numbers, e-mail addresses, and passport information for cross-checking against Saudi customs databases. END NOTE.) Mabahith was not familiar with the individuals and pledged to follow up on the identifying information provided by GRPO and Treasury. GRPO and Treasury analysts also shared names and phone numbers of multiple Taliban and Haqqani associates known either to reside in or travel to the Saudi Arabia.

Reviewing a list of several full or partial names of suspected Taliban donors in the Kingdom, Mabahith recognized [name redacted], a prominent Saudi who reportedly gave [redacted] $30,000 in September 2008. Mabahith had no information regarding [redacted's] financial contributions to the Taliban, but speculated that the money could have come from a trust or a charity that was associated with [redacted], rather than from [redacted] himself. Mabahith pledged to investigate [redacted] and stated that it would not hesitate to "press him" regardless of his social status.[20]

This conversation reflected the fact that despite years of pressure from Washington the Saudi authorities have not arrested or charged or even publicly identified any prominent government official or anyone with ties to the ruling family for supporting violent movements abroad.

Senior officials of the Bush and Obama administrations testified repeatedly before Congress that the Saudi government was making serious, if not "fully successful," efforts to stop cash from flowing directly to known terrorist groups but that the Saudis were less diligent about softening the ideology that was rationalizing violence around the world. In May 2005, for example, Stuart Levey, the treasury undersecretary who was the point man on this issue, said, "In addition to the export of terrorist funds from Saudi Arabia, we are extremely concerned with the export of terrorist ideologies that promote war and killing in the name of religion. These distorted ideologies are just as indispensable to terrorists as money, and possibly even more pernicious."[21] As recently as February 2009, Director of National Intelligence Dennis Blair reported to Congress that "Saudi Arabia aggressively targets al-Qaida-associated financial facilitators, but has historically taken little action against supporters of other groups that play into Riyadh's domestic and foreign policy considerations, and do not pose a direct threat to the Kingdom."[22] That is to say, the Saudis went after groups that presented a direct threat to the regime, and after their financial supporters, but did not pursue those operating in other countries, because the Saudis sometimes found them useful as a counterweight to Iran's influence and for other reasons.

The U.S. Commission on International Religious Freedom also acknowledged the problem. It said in its 2010 annual report that "the [Saudi] government continues to be involved in supporting activities globally that promote an extremist ideology and, in some cases violence toward non-Muslims and disfavored Muslims."

Watching Saudi activities on this front since about 2005, U.S. officials of both the Bush and Obama administrations repeatedly stated that despite lingering differences over the financing issue, they believed the Saudi government was part of the solution and no longer part of the problem. At an antiterrorism conference in Riyadh, Frances Fragos Townsend, President Bush's chief adviser on this subject, went so far as to say that "we stand with the Saudis in [this] fight and this conference is a testament to their commitment—to their dedication to combating terrorism."[23] As a trouble point in the bilateral relationship, the financing issue was taken off the table when the United States successfully sponsored the kingdom's admission into the Egmont Group. A sort of economic Interpol, it is an association of 116 nations that have established effective financial crimes units and auditing systems designed to curb money laundering and terrorist financing and have agreed to share information and enforcement efforts. The U.S. effort to win Saudi admission to this group began under Bush and was completed under Obama.

Behind the scenes, however, senior officials of the Obama administration still harbored doubts. Documents in the WikiLeaks files showed high-level concern that while Saudi Arabia had been effective in cutting off funds to al-Qaeda, which presented a direct threat to the regime, it had been much less effective in stopping the flow of money from Saudi individuals to violence-prone groups outside the kingdom such as the Taliban and Lashkar-e-Taiba in Pakistan. The diplomatic cables said the agents of such groups used the annual pilgrimage to Mecca as a cover to travel to Saudi Arabia unquestioned and collect cash from sympathetic Saudi donors.

In a message dated December 30, 2009, urging all U.S. diplomatic missions in the Middle East to press their host countries for tougher action on this problem, Secretary of State Hillary Rodham Clinton said that "donors in Saudi Arabia constitute the most significant source of funding to Sunni terrorist groups worldwide." The diplomatic messages suggested that the Saudis still failed to grasp the extent to which groups such as the Taliban are allied with al-Qaeda and thus present a threat to Saudi security from abroad.

A few months later, in the spring of 2010, the Council of Senior Ulama, the kingdom's senior religious authority, issued an unequivocal condemnation of terrorism and those who encourage it by giving money to extremists. Terrorism, it said, "is a crime aiming at destabilizing security, and constitutes a grave offense against innocent lives as well as against properties whether public or private, such as blowing up of dwellings, schools, hospitals, factories, bridges; airplanes (including hijacking), oil and pipelines, or any similar acts of destruction or subversion outlawed by the Islamic Shariah [law]." The council "also regards the financing of such terrorist acts as a form of complicity to these acts that leads only to [being an] accessory to them, and to [being] a conduit for sustaining and spreading such evil acts."

Citing passages from the Koran, the council said it "rules that the financing of terrorism; the inception, help or attempt to commit a terrorist act of whatever kind or dimension is forbidden by Islamic Shariah and constitutes a punishable crime thereby; this includes gathering or providing of finance for that end, or providing help or participating in it in any form or manner including financial or non-financial interests."[24]

Leaving aside the question of why it took the ulama almost nine years after 9/11 to issue that statement, the document reflects the Saudi regime's entire approach to heading off future incidents. It decreed that terrorism is evil, sinful, and prohibited not because civil authorities say so but because God says so. By 2010, the king and senior princes, the official religious authorities, and even nonviolent religious dissidents were consistently on message: Terrorism and extremism do not promote Islam, they contravene it. Islam is peaceful, the message says, and terrorists are "deviants."

A WAR OF IDEAS

Containing internal violence in Saudi Arabia and strengthening the government's antiterror commitment and capability do not mean the problem has disappeared or that the ideas the Saudis disseminated globally have receded in other countries. Provocative radical thinkers such as Abu Bakr Naji, who espouses nonlethal attacks on oil installations to drive up the price and undercut the economic security of West, are still at large and still prolific. In 2009 a suspected terrorist feigning repentance came within inches of blowing up Prince Muhammad bin Nayef, son of the interior minister, who was the leader of the security crackdown on al-Qaeda. Every few months the Ministry of Interior reports a roundup of suspected terrorists. The umbrella organization known as al-Qaeda in the Arabian Peninsula has regrouped in Yemen, Saudi Arabia's weak, unstable neighbor, and still has the House of Saud on its target list. The kingdom has legions of bored, poorly educated young men who are easy targets for recruitment through the Internet. The myth that bin Laden and his "holy warriors" perpetrated—that is, they defeated one anti-Islamic superpower in Afghanistan and could do so again—has a strong grip on the imaginations of some young Saudis, including women. To head off these young Saudis' possible embrace of violence, the government has set up an ambitious "reeducation" program that uses the teachings of Islam and the pressures of family disapproval—two of the most powerful forces in Saudi society—to convince terrorism suspects and potential terrorists that the path of violence is the wrong path. According to the Ministry of Interior, by using this approach when Saudis who go astray are apprehended, their "deviant ideologies shall be confronted by way of various programs aiming to strip bare these ideologies and expose the superstitions behind which the rabble-rousers and corrupt ones hide, clarifying the truth for those led astray, helping them correct their life path, and rehabilitating them to become positive building blocks in society."[25]

The U.S. State Department described this program in the annual report on international terrorism issued in April 2009:

> The program was designed to reintegrate individuals into society and includes educational, social, and religious components to undermine extremist messages and foster a more tolerant attitude. The program builds on family and tribal relations to reinforce the message and speed the reintegration process. Those who complete the program and show evidence of having been rehabilitated are eligible for consideration for release from custody, though not before they have served any prison sentence for their previous crimes. Employment, coupled with tribal and family reintegration, including marriage, in some cases, are important components of the post-release program, as are monitoring and follow-up by both extended families and the Saudi government.

Abandon violence and return to the true, peaceful path of Islam, the participants are taught, and the benefits will include a job and a wife, and the embrace of the family you have shamed by your behavior.

Christopher Boucek of the Carnegie Endowment for International Peace has studied the rehabilitation program closely since its inception. He describes it this way:

> The Counseling Program is based upon a presumption of benevolence, and not vengeance or retribution. It presumes that the suspects were abused, lied to and misled by extremists into straying away from "true Islam," and that the state wants to help security prisoners return to the correct path. The vast majority of prisoners who have participated in the program, according to research conducted by the Advisory Committee, have been found to not have had a religious education during their childhood. Most of the prisoners have been found by the committee to have an incomplete understanding of Islam, and the majority have been radicalized through extremist books, tapes, videos and, more recently, the internet. The Counseling Program, therefore, seeks to "correct" this misunderstanding by reinforcing the official state version of Islam.

Boucek found that social services, financial aid to the participants' families, and a post-program aid package, which may include a job and an apartment, reinforce the message.[26]

Does it work? Boucek concluded that it mostly does, but it has also encountered opposition inside Saudi Arabia. Some conservatives have argued that a few well-publicized beheadings would produce the same positive outcome at less cost; others have expressed resentment at what they consider rewards for bad behavior.

Boucek said those criticisms are unfounded. The idea that young men enter the rehabilitation program to reap the benefits is incorrect, he said, because the suspects go to prison first. "You don't want to spend time in a Saudi prison to get this other stuff," he said. "What happens is that when you put people in a bad position long enough—prison, bad cop—and a good cop comes along and offers a way out, you are really excited to accept it." The government's objective, he said, is to "criminalize the violence but not criminalize the ideological framework," which teaches that jihad in some form is fundamental to the faith.[27] Arguments about whether jihad—often translated as "holy war" but better understood as "righteous struggle"—permits or even requires violence consume huge amounts of newsprint and airtime in Saudi Arabia. A separate, government-supported program known as the Sakinah Campaign seeks to counter extremist messages promoting violent jihad that are delivered through the Internet.

Other critics of the rehabilitation program have argued that those who are taken into custody will say anything to gain their release and the promised benefits and then will revert to their old ways when they have an opportunity. Saudi authorities have reported a low rate of recidivism among some two thousand participants, but the program's reputation suffered a blow in the summer of 2010 from news reports that twenty-five former U.S. detainees from Guantánamo Bay had returned to advocating violence after completing the rehabilitation program. Some had been rearrested, but others had fled to Yemen to join al-Qaeda in the Arabian Peninsula there.

"A CONVERSATION WITH A SIMPLETON"

Saudis were shocked when, in March 2010, a forty-five-year-old woman, Haila Al-Qasir, was arrested on charges of recruiting youths for suicide bomb squads, harboring terrorism suspects, sending money to al-Qaeda in Yemen, and enlisting women into violent jihad. It was not the alleged activities that the Saudis found shocking but the fact that the suspect was a woman.

A few months later, a member of the counseling committee that deals with terrorism suspects appeared on a television show and said that he had spent some time with the woman. He had found her "rational" and not motivated by evil intent but by "a certain stress and vindictiveness" after the murder of her husband, for which she blamed government security forces. This gentleman, Abdullah Al-Suwailam, said he and his colleagues explained to her the consequences of her actions, with startling results: "Many of her ideas changed completely after this counseling," and she had repented and "felt grief" over what she had done.

That claim prompted a disbelieving commentary from a columnist in *al-Watan*, the kingdom's most influential newspaper. "This whole radical transformation of her terrorist ideas took place in an hour and half!? This is no counseling program but potent sorcery! It's closer to a conversation with a simpleton, not a degree-holding graduate," wrote the columnist, Hissa Muhammad Al-Asheikh.[28] The point was well taken. Simplistic explanations and overblown claims only mask the extent to which dangerous views have taken root among the people.

The task of eliminating violence is unlikely ever to be complete, absent an unlikely secular revolution, because of the circumstances in which young people grow up in Saudi Arabia. Their history and mythology are steeped in tales in which armed conflict was the instrument of righteousness, from the rise of Islam itself, to the Crusades, to King Abdul Aziz's conquest of his rivals, to the wars in Afghanistan. The absence of other channels of permitted political discourse or dissent elevates the role of religion as an instrument of reform and advocacy. The lack of entertainment and the unavailability of sex also breed frustration. While jobs are scarce in the kingdom, some foot soldiers in the global jihadist network are better paid and more respected than they would be at home. The Internet provides messages of inspiration and zeal and promises of social justice to come after the triumph of a pure Islamic state. And until recently, all schoolchildren were raised in a curriculum that put Islam—specifically, the uniquely restrictive and xenophobic Saudi Islam—at the center of learning. Until recently Saudi Arabia was, and to a great extent still is, not a world of ideas, it is a world of anti-ideas where religion is true and ideas are dangerous. That approach is beginning to change, but reform has only just begun. While people may have rejected violence, it does not mean they have embraced enlightenment. The struggle to limit religiously motivated violence in Saudi Arabia can be expected to continue for years. In the best case the violence will be limited and the influence of extremist ideology minimized so that the regime can press ahead with its modernizing agenda in economic and educational matters.

THE SHIA MINORITY

None of Saudi Arabia's modernizing developments resolves the question of the rights and status of Saudi Arabia's only significant religious minority, the Shiite Muslims, who constitute an estimated 10–15 percent of the population. While many are economically successful, they are at best second-class citizens, restricted in worship and excluded from the armed forces and from prominent government office. Despite some conciliatory gestures by King

Abdullah, the Shiites are generally scorned as apostates and suspected as possible agents of their coreligionists in Iran. This issue is almost as old as the faith itself.

By the time the Prophet Muhammad died in AD 632, he had become not only the founder of a new religion but also the temporal ruler of that religion's adherents. Within a few years his followers turned against each other in a split over how to choose his successors in that leadership position. In simple terms, some of them believed the successor, or caliph, should be chosen on merit, by consensus of the community. These became the Sunni Muslims, followers of the sunnah (the path or way) of the prophet. The others believed the succession should pass to Muhammad's descendants. The Prophet left no male heir, so his followers chose his son-in-law, Ali. Thus they were Shiat Ali (partisans of Ali), or the Shiites. This schism has divided Islam ever since.

In the contemporary world, Sunnis represent the great majority of the world's Muslims, perhaps 85 percent. Most of the others are Shiites of one school or another. Shiites are in the majority in Iran, Iraq, Bahrain, and a few other countries.

Shiites, like all Muslims, believe in the Prophet, the Koran, and the authority of sharia law. They participate in the annual pilgrimage to Mecca, and to non-Muslims their mosques look similar to the Sunnis' mosques. But Shiism has unique characteristics that affect the political as well as the religious behavior of its adherents. Their devotion to martyrdom in emulation of Ali, who was assassinated, and of Ali's son Hussein, who was slain in battle; their belief in saints; their worship at the tombs of holy men; and their mystical faith in the eventual return of their leader combine to instill in Shiites a tendency to physical exhibitions of spiritual devotion that sets them apart. They pray at graves, perform passion plays, and during holy season take part in mass processions and demonstrations of penitence and mourning that are unknown to Sunnis. These Shiite events are sometimes marked by rites of self-flagellation. To rigorously traditional Sunni Muslims such as the Saudis, these rituals reek of polytheism, the ultimate sin in Islam.

For centuries this schism played out in uneasy coexistence, but the Iranian revolution of 1979 changed the balance. It brought to power a self-confident Shiite theocracy that took up the cause of scorned Shiites in other countries. When Saddam Hussein's Iraq—a Shia-majority country ruled by secular

Sunnis—invaded Iran, the schism became the fundamental political division in the Muslim Middle East and was marked by violence in Lebanon, Bahrain, and occasionally in Saudi Arabia. In its proclaimed role as the birthplace, repository, and defender of the "true faith," Saudi Arabia felt a direct threat from the Iran of Ayatollah Khomeini. One reason the Saudis opposed the U.S. invasion of Iraq was that they feared, correctly, that it would lead to a rise of an Iranian-influenced Shiite government on their border.

The Iranian-born scholar Vali Nasr wrote in a seminal study:

> In the coming years Shias and Sunnis will compete over power, first in Iraq but ultimately across the entire region. Beyond Iraq, other countries will (even as they embrace reform) have to cope with intensifying rivalries between Shias and Sunnis. The overall Sunni-Shia conflict will pay a large role in defining the Middle East as a whole and shaping its relations with the outside world. Sectarian conflict will make Sunni extremists more extreme and will likely rekindle revolutionary zeal among the Shia. At times the conflict will be bloody as it strengthens the extremists, swelling their ranks, popularizing their causes, and amplifying their voices in politics, thus complicating the broader effort to contain Islamic radicalism.[29]

Thus for the Saudi regime the contest between the Sunnis and the Shia is not only religious but also political and strategic, especially because most Saudi Shiites live in the part of the country where the oil industry is based— the part closest to Iran.[30] Riyadh does not want to see Vali Nasr's scenario become reality.

It almost did during the traumatic year 1979 when Shiite rioting erupted across Saudi Arabia's Eastern Province. The new leaders of Iran stoked the riots with broadcasts saying that the radicals' takeover of the Great Mosque in Mecca was part of a larger uprising against the Al-Saud. The Saudi Arabian National Guard rushed reinforcements to Qatif, the center of Saudi Shiism, and in three days of conflict seventeen people were killed and some oil installations sabotaged.[31] That clash ushered in a period of sustained tension, during which leaders of the Shiite community "mobilized youth around a message that directly challenged the regime, resonated with feelings of religious and community oppression, and triggered significant mass civil disobedience," according to an International Crisis Group assessment.[32]

King Fahd ended that unhappy period by meeting with leaders of the Shiite community in 1993 and promising to relax restrictions in exchange for an end to active opposition. There has been little violence since, despite occasional outbursts of vituperative rhetoric from Sunni religious figures, who scorn Shiites as infidels and polytheists, and lingering resentment in the Shia community. The regime, which prizes stability, and Shia community leaders, who have been seeking incremental improvements in their status rather than confrontation, have also had to deal with the radical pronouncements of a Shiite preacher named Nimr Al-Nimr. In 2009 he spoke openly of "justice and equality in the distribution of oil wealth," which comes mostly from the parts of the country where the Shia are concentrated, and even of secession from the kingdom. The Shiites feared that Al-Nimr's incendiary remarks would reinforce the majority's suspicion that they are not loyal Saudi citizens.[33]

Abdullah, who has preached inclusion and nonviolence throughout his reign, has made conciliatory gestures to the Shiites. He fired the governor of a southern province whom Shiites accused of persecuting them. He invited Shiite imams to participate in sessions of his Interfaith Dialogue. A Shiite carried the Saudi flag at the opening ceremony of the 2008 Olympic Games. The king also allowed the Saudi delegate to an International Islamic Conference meeting to sign off on a communiqué stating that Shiites and members of other non-Sunni groups are legitimate Muslims. "Whoever is an adherent of one of the four Sunni Schools of Jurisprudence (Hanafi, Maliki, Shafi'i and Hanbali), the Ja'fari (Shi'i) School of Jurisprudence, the Ibadi School of Jurisprudence, or the Thahiri School of Jurisprudence is a Muslim," the document said. "Declaring that person an apostate is impossible. . . . There exists more in common between the various Schools of Jurisprudence than there is difference."[34]

In a troubled world, King Abdullah said at the opening session of the Consultative Assembly in March 2009, "the Arab peoples perceive that their destiny is threatened by the Other, and feel that their hopes are scattered and their future grim. But the faithful *umma* [i.e., all Muslims] shall not give up hope in the spirit of God. For in the depths of suffering and injury they recall their history replete with victories: they conquered despair, they kept moving on the bitter mountain slope to surmount the challenge, surpassing even themselves, seeking a reunion, a unification of word and deed. And we will persist, God willing, until all differences are cleared."[35] In that flowery language was the message that Abdullah has stressed throughout his reign: It is the aspiration and the duty of Arabs and Muslims to put their common interests ahead of their differences.

These small steps, while welcomed by the Shia community, have not ended the systematic discrimination against the Shiites that Saudi Arabia has practiced and taught in schools for decades. Moreover, Abdullah has not done as much as he could. The government took no action, for example, against twenty-two Sunni clerics who in 2008 proclaimed Shiites to be "an evil among the sects of the Islamic nation, and the greatest enemy and deceivers of the Sunni people." Human Rights Watch reported in 2010 that eleven of the signatories were on the government payroll.[36]

I have met many Saudi Shiites who insisted that they are dutiful Arab citizens, not agents of Iran, and that they do not make common cause with their Shiite counterparts in Iraq. Still, their loyalty is widely doubted. That doubt is reflected in the absence of Shiites from the military officer corps. The Saudi religious authorities also routinely disrupt Shiites' attempts to pray at the graves of saints and ancestors, a practice the Saudi Sunnis regard as polytheism.

"Despite King Abdullah undertaking some limited reform measures and promoting inter-religious dialogue in international fora," the U.S. Commission on International Religious Freedom reported in 2010, "the Saudi government persists in banning all forms of public religious expression other than that of the government's own interpretation of one school of Sunni Islam . . . there is an ongoing crackdown on Shi'a Muslim dissidents, which has resulted in numerous arrests and detentions."[37]

At the suggestion of Saudi friends, in 2009 I traveled to Qatif, the city in eastern Saudi Arabia that is the center of Shia life and politics, to talk with Dr. Tawfiq Al-Saif. He is not a radical agitator like Sheikh Al-Nimr. He is a successful businessman—his company sells tracking systems for fleet vehicles—a writer, and a public intellectual who is widely recognized as a thoughtful voice in the Shiite community. We met in his spacious new house, a few yards from a handsome, new, blue-domed Shiite mosque.

The Shiites of Saudi Arabia, he said, want to be good citizens of Saudi Arabia. (I had heard similar declarations from a group of two dozen or so Shiites with whom I had spent an evening two years earlier.) Whatever sentiment might have linked the Shiites to the regime in Iran, he said, was "undermined by the events there," a reference to Iran's contested presidential election of 2009 and the violence that followed. But that shift did not ameliorate the discrimination against his community inside Saudi Arabia.

"Everyone in Saudi Arabia is less hopeful than before," he said. "We really thought that Abdullah was going to do something with respect to political reform, but it seems he is not in a hurry. . . . We want at least the ability to pressure the government at a marginal level to be accountable, but even this has not happened." The Shia "are subject to discrimination that's not acceptable," he continued, and people will eventually take to the streets. "As long as the government has the upper hand in everything, nothing will really change. Real change comes from the people."[38]

His gloomy assessment was borne out in the Arab Spring of 2011, when some Shiites in eastern Saudi Arabia staged demonstrations and protested Saudi Arabia's intervention to put down a Shia uprising in neighboring Bahrain. The Saudi government's response was to arrest the instigators.

9

SOCIAL UPHEAVAL, SOCIAL WELFARE

A handsome coffee-table book titled *A Land Transformed: The Arabian Peninsula, Saudi Arabia and Saudi Aramco* was published by the Saudi state oil company's indefatigable public relations department in 2006. Similar to other volumes from earlier decades when American oil companies still owned the organization, it painted an entirely positive picture of the changes that have swept Saudi Arabia since the big oil money began to flow in the late 1940s. Other than a brief reference to the oil company's efforts to stamp out malaria, disease is never mentioned; neither is crime, drug abuse, or any other social problem brought about by urbanization, easy money, and the rapid growth of a population largely uprooted from its traditional sources of authority.

The oil company's executives are living in an idealized past that is no longer recognizable to the citizenry. Any casual reader of Saudi newspapers can see that the country has abandoned its collective pretense that the kingdom is some special, orderly society living in harmonious accord with God's word. Saudi Arabia is now an urban, industrializing society that despite its religious rigidity and restrictions on personal behavior is facing many of the same social and public health problems that other countries confront: crime, drug addiction, poverty, AIDS, chaos on the roads, illegal immigration, a high divorce rate, and a growing disdain for tradition among bored, restless, and socially frustrated young people.

If a willingness to recognize and discuss society's problems is the first step toward solutions, Saudi Arabia is making progress. Once-taboo subjects— including even wife beating, incest, and sexual dysfunction—are routinely aired in the media and deliberated in public forums. In one memorable example, in 2008, the feminist author Samar Fatany wrote that family traditions were disintegrating because bored young people, out of the control of indifferent parents, were turning to drugs, crime, and violence under the influence of "inappropriate" material on the Internet. "Rigid interpretations of Islam far removed from reality and contradicting social values cause the moral degradation of our youth," she wrote in an article that was, by Saudi standards, daring. "The ignorance and negligence of parents have caused the spread of violence, blackmail, sexual disorders and drug and alcohol addiction over the past few years."[1]

The kingdom brings many tools and assets to its confrontation with these problems: money, shared values among most of the people, a growing pool of educated and trained talent, a young generation of volunteers looking for causes, and some receptiveness to new ideas and outside help. But it also has systemic weaknesses that reduce the prospects for success: a social "safety net" that is thin to nonexistent, a lack of effective nongovernmental organizations, a complete absence of accountability in government, and a deep-rooted aversion to people who are disabled or otherwise different. The population is still growing faster than the capacity of the system to care for it, and traditional and religious restrictions on assembly and public entertainment severely constrain any outreach to young people.

The kingdom's 2010 census calculated the population at 27.1 million. The Population Reference Bureau, a standard source of demographic data, put the population at 28.1 million in mid-2008, including foreigners, and projected it to grow to 35.7 million by 2025 and 49.8 million by 2050. The same agency calculated that 81 percent of those people live in urban areas and that life expectancy was seventy-four years for men and seventy-eight years for women.[2] Other organizations give slightly different figures, but the variations are minor.

For all its wealth, Saudi Arabia is less rich than its Gulf neighbors and the countries of Western Europe because of its growing population. In 2009, the International Monetary Fund put its per capita GDP at $23,221, or thirty-eighth in the world, while the CIA's *World Factbook* put it at $20,400, or forty-sixth in the world. This key economic indicator looked even worse a year later, after the 2010 census yielded new population numbers, and economic analysts at Riyadh's Jadwa Investment Group calculated a per capita

GDP figure of $15,734. (In the United States, the figure was a little more than $46,000.)[3]

In fact, spectacular inequalities in wealth are an easily visible feature of Saudi life, and Saudi Arabia has a spreading poverty problem. Beggars can be seen on street corners. Many families lack electricity. The Population Reference Bureau calculates 20 percent of the people live in slums—one-fifth of the population. Many of the poor are widows and divorced women who are unable to support themselves. At least 2 million and perhaps as many as 3 million people (no official figures are available) have no income other than direct cash handouts from the government. In parts of Jeddah and Riyadh, it is easy to spot the ragged clothing and neglected teeth characteristic of poor folk everywhere. John R. Bradley, a British journalist who lived in Saudi Arabia for two years and developed a dim view of it, described entire neighborhoods of "narrow lanes, pot-holed roads, open sewers and . . . frequent power and water outages." Some of these urban areas are so dangerous that the police will not enter them, Bradley reported.[4]

In 2002, Crown Prince (now king) Abdullah startled the country when he visited one of these neighborhoods. Accompanied by reporters, the prince acknowledged the problem and promised to address it. As king he has ordered a transformation of the national economy in an effort to increase opportunities for his people, but the results are not guaranteed. Meanwhile, the neighborhoods Bradley described are mostly unchanged.

FAMILY PLANNING?

Birth control pills and devices are legal in Saudi Arabia, but most religious authorities, who teach that children are gifts from God, discourage their use. Family sizes will probably decrease in the coming generation because women are staying in school longer and young families today cannot afford as many children as the traditional family produced. But there is a certain inevitability in the numbers of people who have already been born, 38 percent of whom are fifteen years of age or younger.

As an example of what the population numbers portend, former minister of social welfare Abdelmohsen Al-Akkas told me that while the median age of the entire population is only about twenty-one, Saudi Arabia will soon have a growing population of elderly people who will need care outside the traditional source of such assistance, the family. Because of urbanization, he said, many Saudis now live far from their closest relatives and in housing units that are too small to accommodate elderly dependents. But retirement homes and assisted living facilities are virtually nonexistent in Saudi Arabia, he said, and traditionalists oppose the entire concept.[5]

A study by HSBC Insurance, a unit of the international bank, concluded in 2010 that "by 2050 the number of dependent adults in Saudi Arabia will equal the number of dependent children for the first time." Opinion surveys found that people are woefully unprepared for retirement, the study said, because they do not save enough and are poorly educated about financial matters. Not surprising, the report proposed a combination of insurance and financial services, which are HSBC's business, to address this issue.[6] That may be turn out to be the answer, but at the moment there is none, and it is not clear who in Saudi Arabia is responsible for devising one.

Another consequence of the population growth is an intractable nationwide housing shortage. There are plenty of spacious villas for the prosperous, but the middle and lower classes face increasing difficulties trying to find a place to live. Many young people have to postpone marriage because they cannot find housing. Saudi newspapers reported during 2010 that a growing number of people have given up hope of acquiring the handsome villa of their dreams and have bought apartments instead—a distressing step downward in expectations for a society that values privacy and large enough residences for the extended family. The overall homeownership rate among the Saudi population is about 35 percent, or a little more than half what it is in the United States.[7]

According to several studies by banks, real estate companies, and financial journals, Saudi Arabia is already short at least 1 million housing units, whether owned or rented, and will need at least 200,000 new units every year for the next decade. So great is the need that it has attracted the attention of the International Finance Corporation, the private-sector funding unit of the World Bank. It seems counterintuitive that the World Bank should be providing any form of assistance to the world's greatest oil power, but Michael Essex, formerly the IFC's regional director for the Middle East and North Africa, said the help is needed because the kingdom has few sources of financing for housing other than at the high end.

"Saudi Arabia is not a society made up entirely of rich people," Essex told me. "There are a lot of low-income people, and they have large families jammed into small spaces. They don't have four bedrooms and multiple bathrooms. The population density per household is 6.4 people. In India, it's 5.5. There is a huge deficit of housing in the country."[8]

Providing housing for the less-than-rich is complicated by the rules of shariah law, which prohibit charging interest and thus discourage lending. The International Finance Corporation announced in 2007 that it would form a partnership with three Saudi companies "to create the first independent, specialized Shariah-compliant housing finance institution in Saudi Arabia. The new Saudi Home Loans Company will promote home ownership by making housing more available and affordable for the country's middle- and lower-income population, which is underserved in housing finance."[9]

"The Saudi government does have an arm that does some of this, but there's a twenty-year waiting list," Essex said.

In the spring of 2010, Deutsche Bank of Germany announced the creation of Deutsche Gulf Finance, a "Shariah-compliant home financing company." The bank owns 40 percent owned of the company, and Saudi investors led by the Al-Rajhi banking family control 60 percent. The bank said its research had determined that "the total outstanding home finance provided by the private sector in Saudi Arabia aggregates to less than 1 percent of GDP compared with well over 50 percent in most developed countries" and with 6–7 percent in Saudi Arabia's neighboring countries on the Gulf.[10] One of the new venture's first moves was to create a Facebook page.

The package of grants and other benefits that King Abdullah handed out in the winter of 2011 included several intended to alleviate the housing shortage: construction of 500,000 units of public housing all across the country; an infusion of 30 billion riyals into the government's housing loan funds; an increase in the ceiling for these interest-free loans from 300,000 riyals (about $80,000) to 500,000; and debt forgiveness for previous buyers who have died, to relieve their families of the payments. The king also elevated the General Housing Authority to a ministry, giving its director a seat in the cabinet.

At about the same time, the Majlis ash-Shoura (Consultative Assembly) completed work on a new mortgage law that it had been haggling over for years. The law contains measures designed to encourage private mortgage lending, permit lenders to secure their investments by taking property as collateral, expedite processing, and regulate the market. Opinion among bankers and housing specialists is divided over the potential impact.

"We expect the mortgage law could act as a key trigger for Saudi Arabia's home finance industry in the longer term," economists at Banque Saudi Fransi wrote in a 2010 analysis of the housing market, but "the short term implications of its passage will be minimal unless the government increases the availability of land, pushing down prices to levels that are more afford-able for common people. Even if land is made available at more affordable rates on the periphery of major cities, there are currently no public transport alternatives to accommodate this suburban expansion."[11] In Jeddah, the fast-growing metropolis on the Red Sea, shortages of water, sewage treatment, and electricity will hinder the king's order to build housing and plans for private-sector development for years. And as the economists pointed out, in all the cities, the absence of public transportation limits efforts to build hous-ing in outlying areas where land is cheaper.

Abdul Aziz Fahad, one of Riyadh's most prominent lawyers, is even more skeptical than the bank economists are about the potential of the mortgage law. "Mortgage financing is not the problem," he said. "The problem is that the state won't put families on the street. Under current law anyone can build and then sell on installments, in effect holding a mortgage, or can build to rent. But if the occupants don't pay there's no recourse. The law may be on your side but nobody is going to send marshals to enforce it."[12] The new law attempts to address this issue by specifying that the lender, not the borrower, owns the property and by clarifying the courts' authority to enforce these contracts. How these stipulations will work in practice remain to be seen be-cause there is virtually no market in Saudi Arabia for previously owned homes; therefore, the lender might find the value of a foreclosed property to be minimal.

The high cost of land is one of the most common sources of popular com-plaints about the corruption and lavish lifestyles of the royal and the well connected. People wonder, how did Prince X obtain title to that land he is selling to his developer friends? Combined with a shortage of buildable space in the cities, land prices dictate a trend toward construction of multistory apartment buildings, but Saudis don't like to live in them. The Saudis' pref-erence is to live in a house in a compound with the extended family, an arrangement that ensures privacy, maintains the sequestration of women, and subjects children to the discipline of watchful relatives. Living in a two-bedroom apartment on an upper floor of a building in which everyone rides the same elevator and relatives are far away may be an economic necessity in the new Saudi Arabia, but it will be a difficult adjustment and a potential cause of some social upheaval. A banker friend who is skeptical about the new law and about the king's order to build 500,000 units reminded me that when refugees from Kuwait flooded into Saudi Arabia after the Iraqi invasion in 1990, the Saudi government housed them in vacant apartment buildings. "Why were those buildings vacant?" my friend asked.

THE CHILDREN OF THE HELP CENTER

One place to see how Saudi society is being transformed and how the need for social services is exploding is the Help Center, a unique institution hidden in plain sight at a busy Jeddah intersection. Its anodyne name reveals nothing about what goes on inside. The bright, spotless facility is a combination school, clinic, gymnasium, and job-training center for 350 children with Down syndrome.

The children are in the care of the center's director, a relentlessly energetic and upbeat woman named Maha Juffali, and her staff of 150 teachers, doctors, nurses, physical therapists, and athletic coaches. The money to create the center and support its work came from the charitable foundation of her late father, Ahmed Juffali, an industrial tycoon.

The Help Center has classrooms, a gymnasium, a garden where the children grow vegetables, a model house where the children learn household tasks such as vacuuming, a miniature market where they learn how to shop for groceries, a wood shop with power tools, a pottery, a swimming pool, and a little animal farm where the children tend rabbits. All students, male and female, are taught how to cook. The objective is to develop these young Saudis, who would otherwise be permanently dependent social outcasts, into self-sufficient, productive citizens—and to find employers willing to give them jobs.

"Our oldest graduate is thirty now," Maha Juffali said. "He's working in a factory."

While enrolled at the Help Center, the children go home to their families at night. If they lived at the center, she said, "this place would be treated like an orphanage. Saudis wouldn't accept it" because it would bring shame on the families in a society that traditionally cares for its dependents, young and old, at home. Breaking down a taboo that inhibited families from even talking about the children's disability was one of the greatest challenges the Help Center faced when it was created, she said. "The children are happy. It's the parents who need work."

Another obstacle was the indifference of Saudi doctors, who were generally unsympathetic to the mentally disabled. "We had to work with the doctors, who were saying things like, 'He'll be a vegetable,' she said. "We talked about behavior modification, about mainstreaming."

Members of the Help Center staff, trained as family counselors, sometimes accompany the children when they go home to check family attitudes, to work with brothers and sisters, and to understand the living conditions of their students, even the family's dining habits. The reason all the children at the center are required to learn how to swim, the director said, is that "the swimming is the only thing in which they have an advantage over their siblings."

Breaking through society's aversion to the disabled is a slow process, accomplished one family at a time, Juffali said. "We recently had a father who took his son to the mosque with him for the first time. He was so proud."[13]

Maha Juffali is hardly the stereotypical, cloistered Saudi woman. I met her at a gender-integrated reception in the home of a famous architect at which the guest of honor was Jimmy Carter. She was educated at Mills College in California. Her staff and her students work together regardless of their sex. On her desk is a miniature plastic traffic cone bearing the words, "Of course I can handle any crisis. I'm a mom."

She said the Help Center has trained the children of 5,000 families since it began with 3 students in a small house in 1985 and today, with 350, has a waiting list. Why does this institution have a waiting list of clients? Because Saudi Arabia, for all its wealth and its spectacular physical development, has one of the world's highest rates of genetically caused birth defects, and the disabled are not welcome in the public schools. A March of Dimes worldwide survey published in 2006 found that only impoverished Sudan, with 82 such defects per thousand births, has more than Saudi Arabia, which has 81. The rate in France was 40, in Austria 42, and in the United States 48.[14] (The figures do not include birth defects attributable to postconception causes such as fetal alcohol syndrome or rubella.)

On Down syndrome specifically, five Saudi doctors published a study in a Saudi medical journal in 2008 that said the incidence in the kingdom was

1.8 per thousand live births.[15] By comparison, in Singapore, a highly developed city-state with a heterogeneous and well-educated population, the rate declined from 1.17 to 0.89 during the 1990s. (Abortion of Down syndrome fetuses may account for some of the decline.)[16]

Why are the rates of defect so high in Saudi Arabia, which now has a nationwide network of qualified doctors and enough money to provide essential medical care to every person? One standard answer is the high number of consanguineous marriages. Many Saudis marry first cousins, in arrangements long sanctioned by tribal custom.

According to the March of Dimes study, "Parental consanguinity increases the birth prevalence of autosomal recessive birth defects. The risk for neonatal and childhood death, intellectual disability and serious birth defects is almost doubled for first cousin unions."[17] In the Saudi doctors' study, "Consanguinity and Major Genetic Disorders in Saudi Children," 11,554 mothers were interviewed over two years. An astounding 56 percent of their marriages were consanguineous. With the consanguineous marriages, the Saudi doctors found a significant causal relationship with childhood heart diseases but less of a demonstrable link to other defects. Perhaps surprisingly, they wrote, "There was no significant association between first-cousin consanguinity and Down syndrome."[18]

Maha Juffali's years of work with Down syndrome children have led her to conclude otherwise. "Intermarriage is the biggest problem," she said. "Everybody is doing in vitro [fertilization] and they don't check the genes." The government now requires all couples to undergo genetic testing before marriage, but Juffali said many couples "ignore the results and get married anyway." She said one of her families had five Down syndrome babies and was still planning to have more children.

Saudi Arabia has an immense population of physically and mentally disabled people. A 2005 study at the University of East Anglia in England put the number at 720,000, or more than 2.5 percent of the population, and growing by 5 percent annually.[19] At another institution for the disabled, the Sultan bin Abdul Aziz Humanitarian City, in the desert north of Riyadh, staff members told me that genetic abnormalities are one of two major causes of the disabilities they see. The other is motor vehicle accidents.

CARNAGE ON THE ROADS

So many people are killed or maimed in road accidents in Saudi Arabia every year that the government has taken on this issue as an urgent public health problem, like diabetes, another fast-spreading affliction in a population that eats too much and exercises too little. (Obesity is endemic now. Those lean, leathery bedouin of the past have given way to a new generation that drives everywhere and wolfs down fast food as much out of boredom as hunger.)

Saudi Arabia's roads are among the most dangerous in the world. According to Maj. Gen. Fahd Al-Bishr, director-general of the government's Traffic Department, about 50,000 people were killed and more than 300,000 injured from 1999 to 2009, and the annual numbers were rising. "Every year we lose about 6,400 precious lives in road accidents," he said, noting that even in the worst period of the homegrown terrorist attacks that began in 2003, they killed no more than 200 people in any one year.[20] A recent British study calculated that every year Saudi Arabia suffers about 23 traffic fatalities per 100,000 inhabitants, which is fewer than Malaysia or South Korea but more than twice the number in Nigeria, Egypt, or China.[21] Put another way, the Saudi Ministry of Interior says there are an average of 18 traffic deaths a day in the kingdom, or one every hour and half. In 2009, according to the ministry, there were 485,931 reported accidents.[22]

The traffic toll has become a serious drain on the kingdom's economic resources and health care facilities. Dr. Ali Al-Ghamdi, a professor of traffic engineering at King Saud University and the country's most prominent academic expert on the subject, has calculated that road accidents cost the country almost $7 billion a year and that accident victims occupy one-third of the beds in government hospitals.

The numbers, of course, do not calculate the emotional toll. I saw some of it at the Prince Sultan Center, where members of the staff labored to teach maimed victims how to care for themselves. It is one thing to reach from a wheelchair and pull a can from a shelf. It is quite another to get out of the chair; kneel on the floor to pray, as Muslims do; and then get back in the chair.

In a paper published by the National Academy of Sciences in Washington, Al-Ghamdi calculated that the traffic accident problem is most serious on residential streets, where heedless, speeding drivers wipe out pedestrians. He estimated, "About half of the traffic fatalities during 2002 to 2003 in Riyadh, for example, were pedestrians who were hit by speeding drivers." More than half the victims were children under the age of sixteen.[23]

He reported that speeding is the biggest single cause of accidents, accounting for about 40 percent. He did not list the other causes, but anyone who has spent time in Saudi Arabia can see what some of them are. Drivers are often incompetent, inexperienced, or indifferent, and sometimes all three. Bored young men with nothing to do but race around in expensive cars are distracted by their electronic devices or by the sight of young women. They think seat belts are for babies. Drivers become impatient in the all-day traffic jams and drive the wrong way on narrow streets or on exit ramps. On the well-paved cross-country highways, there is nothing much to see. Some drivers speed to hasten the boring journey; others fall asleep. Taxi drivers, almost all from foreign countries, seldom know their way around except for the most prominent buildings and hotels, and they must navigate on the fly, usually by telephone. For the many Saudis with money, the loss of a car in an accident is just an inconvenience, not a serious economic concern.

The lack of public transportation forces everyone to get around by car. Arterial roads through the cities lack pedestrian crossings. There are no bicycle paths and in many places no sidewalks; even when the weather is pleasant, considerations of status inhibit walking or bicycle riding. Children ride bicycles in parks, but otherwise the only people who ride bicycles are South Asian laborers.

The lack of public transportation is a national scandal. Whereas next-door Dubai has a sparkling new metro train system and a reliable bus network with air-conditioned waiting shelters, Saudi cities have rattletrap jitneys and minibuses used mostly by foreign laborers. The only exception is a Chinese-built light rail line in Mecca that serves mostly pilgrims performing the annual pilgrimage. In the fall of 2010 Prince Khaled Al-Faisal, the governor of Mecca Province, which includes the city of Jeddah, announced plans for a 21-billion-riyal tram network with 201 stations. Even if it is completed as planned, however, it is not clear how Saudis can be persuaded to use it.[24]

Aside from the implications for health and commerce, conditions on the roads are a large part of the argument about whether women should be permitted to drive. How could a woman drive with her face veiled? What would happen if a woman got into an accident with a car driven by a man? Wouldn't we need female police officers and ambulance attendants?

Saudi officials understand that their cities will more closely resemble Cairo than Stockholm if they cannot impose some discipline on the traffic. In an effort to deal with the nightmarish conditions on the roads, the Ministry of Interior's Traffic Department is installing in the eight largest cities a massive electronic monitoring and enforcement system known as Saher. Through a network of cameras and radio links, it aims to speed information to police and accident crews, improve traffic flows, and record the license plate numbers of violators. Drivers who commit any of a long list of violations—speeding, running stop signs, failing to display license plates, passing a stopped school bus, ignoring a traffic officer's instructions, failing to use seat belts—will be tracked down through their plate numbers and fined. If they don't pay, their vehicles can be impounded.[25]

Even before Saher's installation had spread beyond Riyadh to the other seven cities, Saudi newspapers were reporting a fast-growing trade in devices that prevent the digital roadside cameras from deciphering plate numbers. As the Saher network spread through the major cities in 2010 and misbehaving drivers actually began to be hit with stiff fines, a new dodge was reported: using stolen license plates from neighboring countries in place of genuine Saudi plates. One young man who did it told *Arab News* that he was now free to speed around Riyadh with impunity, but he was "careful not to go over 150 kilometers per hour." That is 93 miles an hour. (This traffic speeding is not to be confused with *tafheet*, the late-night drag racing in stolen cars that has long been a favorite amusement of bored young men.)

Within a few months, resistance to Saher had escalated to the point that angry motorists who had been fined were attacking the cameras with rocks and iron bars. The police had to send out security squads to protect them.

CRIME WAVE

Hiding license plate numbers may frustrate the traffic authorities, but it is hardly the most serious kind of lawbreaking that Saudi authorities have to face. Once virtually free of violent crime other than domestic violence, Saudi Arabia now has street crime, criminal gangs, drug smugglers, and high-crime neighborhoods that are virtually outside the law.

The country also suffers from what might be called social crimes, or violations of the law committed by people trying to evade the country's stifling social restrictions. For young Saudis, even the ones with money, there is virtually nothing to do when school is not in session except hang around at coffee shops, make catcalls at passing women, and wear jeans and T-shirts instead of traditional attire to show off the muscles they develop at the gym. The country has creative young filmmakers, but their works are not shown in their own country because until late 2010 there were no public movie theaters. There are rock bands and jazz musicians but virtually no public concerts and no mixed-gender dancing. It is not that movies and music are prohibited as art forms—indeed, there are many video and music stores—but public performances are generally proscribed because they might attract mixed-sex audiences. At the one movie theater, a multiscreen complex in a shopping mall in Dammam, there are separate screenings for men, women, and families. A man can take a woman to a movie only if he is already married to her or she is a close relative.

As an example of social crime, in the first half of 2010 the Saudi media began reporting police raids on shops that sold illegal satellite television signal decoders that enable viewers to watch blocked pornographic channels. It was probably inevitable that there would be a thriving market for pornography in a country where young people have no access to sex, or even to sex-free romance, and legions of imported foreign laborers live in work camps without their families.

The rise in crime did not come as a surprise to the authorities. More than twenty years ago, officials at the old Ministry of Planning showed me their projections of the consequences of urbanization, and the onset of crime was one of them. In the village in the old days, young people were always under the watchful eye of a relative or the village imam. Who plays that role in a city of 3 million people where everyone has a car?

Saudi Arabia's harsh justice and fearsome prisons have not been adequate deterrents to the negative forces of poverty, family dislocation, and clandestine immigration of desperate people. In the spring of 2010, the police even reported that they had uncovered a prostitution ring of Asian women in Mecca, the holy city.

Here is a sampling of the headlines that appeared on the Web site of Jeddah's English-language *Arab News* on one day chosen at random, April 27, 2010:

Embezzlers Held in Riyadh
Decomposed Bodies Found
Smuggler Killed during Chase
Dozens of Cell Phones Stolen from Shop
Alcoholic Cop Impersonator Busted
Over 100 Kg of Hash Seized
High School Ransacked, Guard Attacked
Bootleggers Arrested
Burglar Arrested in Jeddah
Jail and Lashes for Bus-Driving Pervert
Rapist Gets Two Years, Lashes
11 Held following Street Brawl
Retired Official Gunned Down

This list is not to suggest that ordinary people live in fear. Those crimes reported in the headlines are still uncommon enough that they rate press coverage; citizens go about their business mostly without fear of anything other than the traffic. Carjackings are frequent now, but Riyadh is not to be confused with Ciudad Juárez, Mexico. Unlike crime in many countries, Saudi crime is not organized. It is a symptom of larger problems for which Saudi Arabia has not yet devised solutions: boredom; a lack of opportunity for young people; overcrowding in poor neighborhoods; growing populations of immigrants, legal and otherwise, who are not part of the Saudi value system and thus not reined in by family shame or grandfatherly disapproval; a dearth of community-based organizations and civic groups, which are regarded by the regime as politically suspect; and an antiquated justice system, rooted in Islamic law, that often appears arbitrary and unfair.

As with other afflictions of an urban, industrializing society such as environmental degradation, Saudi Arabia is changing as a new generation of better-educated, energetic young people finds opportunities and challenges in addressing the problem of crime in new ways. (In Jeddah there is even a group of volunteers organizing to help people with AIDS.) And as with other issues, the country is struggling to reconcile the need for new approaches with the inviolability of tradition and to match the performance of an unaccountable, top-down government with the demands of better-informed citizens looking for real solutions.

One way to understand this evolution is to look at how the country is slowly changing its attitude toward drug abuse and addiction. In the preceding headlines, the references to bootlegging and hashish smuggling are indicative of the problem. Trafficking in illegal substances is still a capital offense, as all visitors to the country are warned in stark language, but the smuggling, distribution, and use of illegal substances are now so widespread that the problem cannot be handled simply by executing people.

The police and customs authorities frequently report raids, mass arrests, and seizures of contraband, including hashish and manufactured drugs such as Captagon, a stimulant popular with young people throughout the Middle East. According to a 2008 report from the UN Office on Drugs and Crime, "Last year in Saudi Arabia 14 tonnes of amphetamine were seized, mostly in the form known as Captagon. That's one quarter of all amphetamines seized in the world. Seven years ago, Saudi Arabia accounted for only 1% of all such seizures."[26] In the past few years there have also been reports in the Saudi press about arrests for heroin distribution.

Dr. Mohammed Al-Turaiki is a professor of bioengineering at King Saud University, president of the Islamic World Council on Disability and Rehabilitation, inventor of a replacement ankle joint, and chief executive of a company that specializes in the rehabilitation of drug addicts and alcoholics. He does not work for the Saudi police or the Ministry of Health and thus is not locked into the official policy of regarding drugs as exclusively a law enforcement matter. In January 2010, he signed a "letter of intent" with Brighton Hospital, an addiction treatment facility in Michigan, to build and manage a 250-bed treatment center in Riyadh.

In announcing the agreement, Al-Turaiki said he had selected Brighton as a partner after a nine-month global search because of "its expertise, high success rate, clinical care model and 12-step approach."[27] Even if successful, a single facility in Riyadh will not put an end to the Captagon traffic—there are too many bored, young thrill seekers with money to spend—but the creation of such a center signals changing attitudes and greater flexibility in Saudi Arabia. Placing a child or other family member in a residential treatment hospital inside the country would be an acknowledgment of addiction and represent a big breakthrough in itself because seeking any form of institutionalized care other than conventional medicine is still uncomfortable for Saudi families.

THE ALCOHOL ISSUE

How can alcohol addiction be a problem in a country where alcoholic beverages are prohibited? Some name-brand liquor is smuggled in and sold (at very high prices) on the black market, but most of the alcohol is home brewed. There is a reason supermarkets stock fifty-kilogram bags of sugar and vats of grape juice. Years ago, I was invited to a party in a residence on the Aramco compound. A waiter asked me if I wanted "brown" or "white." I had no idea what he was talking about until another guest explained that the *sadiqi*, or homemade booze that was being served, was available in brown, which looked like bourbon, or white, which looked like gin.

In one of the secret diplomatic cables made public by WikiLeaks in December 2010, Martin Quinn, the U.S. consul general in Jeddah, described a Halloween party that members of his staff attended:

> The scene resembled a nightclub anywhere outside the Kingdom: plentiful alcohol, young couples dancing, a DJ at the turntables, and everyone in costume. Funding for the party came from a corporate sponsor, [name redacted] a U.S.-based energy-drink company, as well as from the princely host himself. Alcohol, though strictly prohibited by Saudi law and custom, was plentiful at the party's well-stocked bar, well-patronized by Halloween revelers. The hired Filipino bartenders served a cocktail punch using 'sadiqi,' a locally-made 'moonshine.' While top-shelf liquor bottles were on display throughout the bar area, the original contents were reportedly already consumed and replaced by sadiqi. On the black market, a bottle of Smirnoff can cost 1,500 riyals when available, compared to 100 riyals for the locally-made vodka. It was also learned through word-of-mouth that a number of the guests were in fact 'working girls,' not uncommon for such parties. Additionally, though not witnessed directly at this event, cocaine and hashish use is common in these social circles and has been seen on other occasions.[28]

It is illegal to transport alcohol into Saudi Arabia, but once it is inside the country, its consumption by foreigners in their homes is unofficially tolerated. Selling it to Saudis, however, brings prosecution and imprisonment. There is also no tolerance for drug trafficking, and as all visitors are warned, the penalty is death.

Capital punishment is likely to remain the policy toward the unfortunates who are captured smuggling and distributing amphetamines and other drugs. Most of those people are foreigners who have no advocates among the Saudi public and are left to their fate. But the Saudis are learning that such an approach is not effective with their own children, who are young, restless, and denied the ordinary social pleasures available to their counterparts in every other country. Which would be worse—letting a boy take a girl to a movie and hold her hand as they head home, or watching that boy pop amphetamines and drive his car at a hundred miles an hour? This is not a question that well-intentioned human rights advocates or any other outside force will answer. The Saudi people will have to answer it, because everyone understands that the current system is profoundly hypocritical. Indeed, most people attending clandestine parties in Jeddah, driving across the causeway to easygoing Bahrain, and filling the flights to wide-open Dubai on weekend nights are Saudis, partaking of the pleasures denied to those who have to stay home.

The plugged-in younger generation is forcing the issue. They are "pushing the barrels," a Saudi friend explained: If the border is not marked by a fence but only by barrels, you push the barrels a little way into the forbidden territory. If no one objects, you push them a little more. As long as you get away with it, you keep doing it.

The sponsors of an annual film festival in Jeddah pushed the barrels too far. For three years they excited young Saudis by putting on foreign and Arab movies in a Sundance-like event, which held the only public movie screenings in the country. For its fourth year, in 2009, filmmakers had arrived and tickets had been sold when the government abruptly pulled the plug on the eve of the event. Movie theaters are not technically illegal and no explanation was given, but the public took it for granted that the relentless opposition of the religious authorities was responsible. The following year, in 2010, the sponsors did not bother to try again. On the other hand, across the country in Dammam, a cinema complex has opened in a shopping mall with little controversy, showing adventure films and cartoons to separate male and female audiences.

Finding the right place for the barrels to come to rest will not be easy. Every time some liberal columnist or blogger advocates easing some social restriction, the response is a blizzard of denunciations from critics who talk of defending Islamic values and fending off the corrupting cultural influences of the West. The Arabic equivalents of "live and let live" and "mind your own business" are not in their lexicon because Islam teaches the opposite: All human activity is subject to God's law. What is actually required or forbidden by that law and therefore immutable—and what was added by human beings and is therefore subject to change—is the fundamental argument that Saudi Arabia is having with itself.

10

BAD NEIGHBORHOOD

The heartland of the Arabian Peninsula known as the Nejd is such a harsh environment, and in the past was so poor and thinly populated, that it has only once been successfully invaded by any foreign power. The Ottoman Turks held Mecca and the Red Sea coast and in the early nineteenth century the sultan dispatched an Egyptian force into the Nejd that laid waste to the desert capital of an earlier Al-Saud regime, but the conquerors did not linger, and left few traces. The modern kingdom would be a richer prize, but is it more vulnerable? Could the seemingly perpetual instability that plagues the Gulf region and its neighbors derail the modernization and development of the kingdom?

When the American military affairs expert Anthony Cordesman and the Saudi security analyst Nawaf Obaid published a detailed assessment of Saudi Arabia's national security a few years ago, they declared on the opening page that the greatest threat to the kingdom came from homegrown terrorists and extremists rather than any foreign menace. The rise of al-Qaeda as a force inside Saudi Arabia and its campaign to bring down the monarchy presented the "most urgent" threat and would require the kingdom to "pay far more attention to internal security than in the past," they wrote.[1]

That assessment was probably true when their book came out, in 2005, but it is not true today because the al-Qaeda campaign failed and the kingdom's internal security forces are far more powerful and competent than they were in 2005. The death of the regime's mortal enemy Osama bin Laden in 2011 was a dramatic ending to this chapter of Saudi history, but in truth al-Qaeda's relevance inside the kingdom had already dissipated. The greatest threat to Saudi Arabia's national security now comes from its neighbors around the Gulf, where forces that are beyond Saudi Arabia's control could cause chaos that would enflame the entire region.

Saudi Arabia lives in a bad neighborhood. The kingdom has more than fifty-five hundred miles of land that borders Iraq, Yemen, Jordan, Kuwait, Qatar, the United Arab Emirates, and Oman. Strife-riven Bahrain is a short drive away. Egypt at its closest point is just twelve miles across the Gulf of Aqaba, and the southern tip of Israel lies just beyond that. Across the Persian Gulf is Iran. Given the perennial turbulence of Middle East politics, Saudi Arabia has a difficult perimeter to manage.

Some combination of civil war in Iraq, state failure in Yemen, a regional conflict between Sunni and Shia Muslims, and the development of nuclear weapons by Iran could provoke turmoil in Saudi Arabia. None of those outcomes is inevitable, but all are possible. Add the prospect of trouble in Egypt, where the future is uncertain after the downfall of President Hosni Mubarak; the unending conflict between nearby Israel and the Palestinians; and the chaos just across the Red Sea in Somalia and Sudan, and the Saudis see the potential for trouble all around them. Terrorism, floods of refugees, and disruption of oil shipping lanes are not abstractions but recurring nightmares. Of all the uncertainties and challenges facing Saudi Arabia in the coming decade, this international dimension is the one in which the stakes are highest for the United States and the one in which the United States will play the most direct role. The American investment in Iraq, the protective U.S. relationship with Israel, and the security of Saudi Arabia itself, a long-standing ally and business partner of the United States, are on the line.

The Saudis are continually modernizing their weapons and beefing up their security forces, but they can influence developments around them only indirectly. On their own, they cannot stabilize Yemen; install a competent, friendly government in Iraq; ensure orderly succession in Egypt; or deter Iran from pursuing nuclear weapons.

Now that Iraq is no longer a military power, Saudi Arabia's armed forces, after decades of American training, are the largest and best equipped on the Arab side of the Gulf, with a total of about 300,000 men in uniform. They are probably good enough to hold off any direct attack long enough for the United States to come to their aid, but in reality there is little prospect of an invasion by any neighboring state. In any case the ability to win conventional battles is not the point; the kingdom's national security depends on avoiding battle and maintaining stability in the Gulf. Most of its oil exports go through the Gulf, and even the threat of war can disrupt the oil market. Most of Saudi Arabia's refineries, storage tanks, and processing terminals are on the Gulf coast, vulnerable to sabotage and short-range missiles. So are most of the water desalination plants, fat targets for missiles fired from ships in the Gulf.

The Saudis know that American interests in the Gulf closely parallel theirs and that the United States would support them in a crisis, as U.S. forces did when Iraq invaded Kuwait and threatened the kingdom in 1990. But the United States and Saudi Arabia have never had a binding mutual defense treaty, and it is doubtful that the U.S. Senate would ratify one if it were proposed. The Saudis know that the United States has interests and commitments worldwide, not just in the Gulf, and that its policies can vary with changes in American politics. Moreover, the Saudis' close relationship with the United States is a liability to them in the regional contest for influence with Iran, which presents itself as the true defender of regional independence and protector of Muslim interests. Charting a safe course through this minefield of threats and competing interests would be a great challenge even for leaders more robust and vigorous than those of Saudi Arabia.

It is probably in the area of security and foreign policy that the opacity of Saudi decision making and the lack of accountability in its government are most frustrating for its friends, to say nothing of its own citizens. It is not as if the Saudis have legislative committees with the power to ratify appointments and treaties, to appropriate funds, or to convene public hearings at which officials would be compelled to testify. A small circle of men, who are accountable only to themselves, make all the strategic decisions. They sometimes make speeches and give interviews, but they never discuss the decision-making process. There is no Saudi equivalent of the White House's "National Security Policy" document or the Pentagon's "Quadrennial Defense Review," which explain overall strategic policies to the public and provide a theoretical framework for American decision making.

One consequence of that structural gap is that Saudi Arabia often does not have a strategy that would provide guidance on what to do in a crisis. In the past it often appeared that the Saudis equated strategy with acquisition: Not knowing what to do, they bought weapons—"toys for boys," it was called in the defense trade—without regard for their cost or efficacy. This tendency of Saudi Arabia and some of its Arab neighbors may be changing as the Gulf states, under American tutelage, grow in military sophistication and focus on weapons that are actually useful in their defense. But, in Saudi Arabia at least, it is still not always clear what strategic objective is being addressed as this military buildup progresses.

Gregory Gause of the University of Vermont, one of the best-informed American analysts of Gulf affairs, has written that Saudi Arabia's long-term security strategy is "to maintain the security of the regime, in the face of conventional regional military threats and in the face of transnational challenges to the regime's domestic political stability and legitimacy."[2] True, but a determination to survive is not a strategy for doing so. Lacking the ability or the desire to project power by force of arms, the Saudis traditionally have sought to protect themselves through a combination of religious persuasion, cash, ad hoc alliances, and reliance on the United States. They have been successful in the sense that the House of Saud has held on to power and the country has not been invaded, but they have not been successful in stabilizing the region, quelling the threats that spring up around them, or ending the ideological war within Islam that has produced their most zealous foes. Nor have they succeeded in forging a coherent security strategy that would provide a framework for tactical decisions.

The kingdom has a National Security Council (NSC), which King Abdullah reorganized and expanded in 2005 with himself as chairman. The council's secretary-general is Prince Bandar bin Sultan, a son of the late defense minister and a former air force pilot. For many years he was the kingdom's ambassador to the United States. Bandar, who cut a flamboyant figure in Washington, has kept a very low profile since assuming his new position, and it is not clear exactly what the council does, if anything. Even Anthony Cordesman, who has been studying the region's armed forces for years, was unable to discern the scope of the National Security Council's mission and activities and concluded that "the real-world importance and effectiveness of the NSC may not be apparent for years to come."[3] Cordesman's list of "key Saudi national security decision makers" has twenty-three people on it, including the ministers of education, justice, and health.

The lack of strategy, or at least of a strategy known outside the royal palace, sometimes leaves the kingdom's allies unaware of major, game-changing decisions. For example, in 1988 Saudi Arabia's clandestine acquisition of

CSS-2 missiles from China—missiles that in other known deployments were nuclear capable—caught the United States flat-footed. Saudi Arabia's friends were caught off guard also when King Abdullah, in the fall of 2009, suddenly reached out to President Bashar Al-Assad of Syria. The king invited Assad to join him at the opening ceremony of his pet project, the university that bears his name, and then went to Damascus for a much-publicized state visit. Before that, the Saudis had shunned Assad because of Syria's support for extremist groups and its suspected involvement in the assassination of former Lebanese prime minister Rafiq Hariri, a longtime client of Riyadh's. It can be assumed that the king was trying to coax Syria out of its long-standing alliance with Iran, but he was under no obligation to explain this initiative to his subjects. Equally mystifying was the Saudi military intervention in a local insurgency across the border in Yemen in 2009, a bloody military adventure for which Riyadh never offered a convincing explanation.

Then the Saudis deployed troops to Bahrain in 2011. Many Saudis, including members of the Consultative Assembly, said that their country acted because it believed Iran was behind the troubles there and could not be allowed to meddle on the Arab side of the Gulf. The word "Iran," however, did not appear in official announcements about the intervention.

With Israel on one side of them and Iran on the other, Saudi Arabia and its Arab neighbors have never forged a common defense strategy or built a functioning regional security organization. Saudi Arabia, Oman, Qatar, Kuwait, Bahrain, and the United Arab Emirates are members of an organization called the Gulf Cooperation Council, but it is basically an economic grouping and was always on the margins of security matters until the violent spring of 2011. The members have neither a common defense strategy nor a functional joint defense force, because the smaller states fear Saudi Arabia would dominate it.

When he was the commanding officer of the U.S. Central Command (CENTCOM), which includes the Gulf, Gen. David Petraeus acknowledged publicly that the GCC countries were not going to achieve a unified strategy for confronting the threat from Iran or a potential threat from Iraq because of "some friction, certainly, to put it mildly, between a number of the different countries."[4] With no prospect of a joint strategy or joint operations doctrine, Petraeus said, CENTCOM worked with each GCC member individually to "integrate bilateral activities to achieve multilateral effects."[5]

Lt. Gen. John R. Allen of the U.S. Marine Corps, deputy commander of CENTCOM, told a Washington audience in October 2010 that "we have undertaken the development of a regional security architecture," which he said is "designed to serve as a construct in which our partners may strengthen national and regional defense capability." He added, however, that "participation in a regional security architecture is a sovereign decision of each participant. There are no treaties, there are no binding formal arrangements."[6]

The events of 2011 pushed the GCC monarchies to overcome their inability to establish a collective strategy. They installed an activist Bahraini, Abdul Latif Al-Zayyani, as the GCC secretary-general. Under the Saudi monarchs' rule, the organization's members, all ruled by Sunnis, ratified and expedited the Saudi deployment to Bahrain, accompanied by police detachments from the UAE, because of their collective fear of Shia Iran. They jointly crafted a proposed settlement for the upheaval in Yemen, which is not a GCC member but would threaten all GCC states if it disintegrated; and they united to torpedo a planned Arab summit conference in Baghdad because of their collective antipathy to the government of Nouri Al-Maliki, whom they regard as unduly influenced by Iran. When the crises in Bahrain and Yemen are resolved, the GCC might revert to its fractious ways, but in the short run at least, it is helpful for Saudi Arabia to have the cooperation of all its neighbors in its efforts to stabilize the region.

REPUBLICS NEED NOT APPLY

The preamble to the GCC's charter says the member states have "common characteristics and similar systems founded in the creed of Islam"—that is, they are all hereditary monarchies. This qualification excludes Iraq and thus creates an enduring political barrier between the monarchies and a large Arab Gulf littoral neighbor that is vital to all of their interests. It also excludes Yemen, which is neither a monarchy nor a Gulf littoral state but is nevertheless a critical element of the regional security picture. Unless Iraq disintegrates into a civil war that spills across the Saudi border or falls completely into the Iranian orbit of influence, the instability and lawlessness of Yemen, which long predated the upheaval of 2011, are likely to present Saudi Arabia with its most immediate security challenge for years to come, one that is more urgent than the theoretical nuclear threat from Iran.

Yemen, the poorest country on the Arabian Peninsula, has been an uncomfortable neighbor for Saudi Arabia ever since its ruling dynasty was overthrown in a military coup in 1962. It has never had a strong central government; in the hinterlands tribal loyalties trump state authority. For years Yemen was split into two countries, one of which was the only communist state in the Arab world. Yemen could be the first country in the region to run out of water, a development that could only exacerbate the problems along the Saudi border, where the smuggling of people, drugs, and guns has long been the principal economic activity. In addition to the rebellion in the north by the group known as the Houthis—the conflict in which Saudi Arabia intervened on the side of the government—Yemen faces a separatist insurgency in the south, which was formerly an independent country.

In some ways Yemen is to Saudi Arabia as Mexico is to the United States: a poor and violence-prone southern neighbor from which economically desperate people cross a long, porous border illegally in search of jobs. The difference is that Yemen has become a training ground and propaganda center for the Saudi regime's most dedicated foe, the extremist group known as al-Qaeda in the Arabian Peninsula. Bin Laden's death did not put an end to this threat.

Defeated and driven underground in Saudi Arabia itself, al-Qaeda regrouped in Yemen—the ancestral homeland of the bin Laden family—where it has easy access to weapons and ideological support among some of the tribes. Its presence in Yemen predates 9/11. In October 2000, radicals affiliated with al-Qaeda attacked the USS *Cole* in the Yemeni port of Aden, killing seventeen Americans.

Jeffrey D. Feltman, assistant secretary of state for Near Eastern Affairs, told the Senate Foreign Relations Committee in 2010 that "the Al-Qaeda threat emanating from Yemen directly threatens U.S. vital interests," including the security of Saudi Arabia. He noted that the United States provides "training and assistance to Yemen's key counterterrorism units" and plans to expand the range of its aid in the near future.[7]

Christopher Boucek and Marina Ottaway of the Carnegie Endowment for International Peace starkly depicted the situation in Yemen when they published *Yemen on the Brink* in September 2010. "Yemen is a nation in crisis. A civil war in the North, a secessionist movement in the South, and a resurgent al-Qaeda organization are active against a background of economic collapse, lack of state capacity, and governance and corruption issues. Without addressing Yemen's immediate security challenges, the country's long-term economic and governance issues cannot be resolved," they said. They described Yemen as "a failing state."[8]

Despite financial assistance from Saudi Arabia and logistical support from the United States, the central government in Yemen is not capable of eliminating al-Qaeda's cells or preventing cross-border attacks. These attacks are unlikely to bring down the House of Saud, but they are very likely to present a long-term security nuisance that will require constant vigilance. Combined with the nonideological crime long prevalent on the border, these attacks could undermine the stability of several provinces in southern Saudi Arabia, where fealty to the government in Riyadh is less than fervent. All these concerns shot up the Saudis' anxiety meter as the government of Yemen's longtime president Ali Abdullah Saleh, an ally in the struggle against al-Qaeda, disintegrated in 2011.

In the summer of 2009, Saudi Arabia awarded a five-year, $2.8 billion contract to the European defense contractor EADS for a massive high-technology project to secure its borders. The company's announcement about the contracts said, "The Saudi border guard will benefit from a leading edge solution, providing visibility and operational awareness for about 9000km of borderline (mountains, deserts and sea borders). The solution will ensure border coverage is visible and managed at the sector level, whilst simultaneously providing situational awareness at the regional and national level."[9] According to the trade journal *Defense Industry Daily*, the border guard is "a system of fences, watchtowers, radar, day/night cameras, and communications, with links back to command centers that can pool data at the local, regional and national levels."[10] The Saudis hope this network will help them regain control of the border not only with Yemen to the south but also with Iraq to the north, where they fear infiltration by al-Qaeda operatives—some of whom are Saudis—who fought in the sectarian conflict there.

With American help, and at American urging, the Saudis are also creating a 35,000-member "facilities security force" specifically to protect their oil installations and terminals, which are known targets of al-Qaeda in the Arabian Peninsula. This project, a joint venture of the United States and the Saudi Ministry of Interior, is being managed by a Pentagon–State Department team known as OPM MOI-FSF, which is military-speak for Office of

Program Management Ministry of Interior–Facilities Security Forces. American defense contractors will train and equip this force, under an arrangement similar to that in which Americans have been training the Saudi Arabian National Guard for almost four decades.[11]

Such measures may prove effective in securing the borders and deterring al-Qaeda infiltration and sabotage, but they do not offer a response to the potential nuclear threat from Iran.

A MENACING IRAN

Once the most powerful military organization in the region, Iran's conventional armed forces were depleted by its eight-year war with Iraq (1980–1988) and by international sanctions that have made it difficult to acquire weapons and parts. Indeed, it has often been noted in the region that Saudi Arabia was most secure when Iran and Iraq were fighting each other. Now Iran is rebuilding its forces, including its navy. According to Anthony Cordesman, Iran has reached the point where it is "the only regional military power that poses a serious conventional military threat to Saudi Arabia and Gulf stability."[12]

Does Iran really pose "a serious conventional military threat to Saudi Arabia"? Iran is different from all other states in the region except Egypt and Yemen in the sense that it is not a modern invention. It is has been a unified, recognizable entity for centuries. It has three times Saudi Arabia's population, extensive natural resources, and a battle-tested military establishment. But internal conflicts, inept economic management, deteriorating infrastructure, and international sanctions that make it difficult to purchase military equipment have undermined its strengths. It is extremely unlikely that Iran would attempt to attack Saudi Arabia by land because its troops would have to cross part of Iraq. Even if Iraq permitted it, such a movement would be visible to everyone, and there would be plenty of time for the United States to come to Saudi Arabia's aid.

Iran might be capable of disrupting Gulf shipping to the point where it throws the international oil market into turmoil, an outcome that would undermine Saudi Arabia's long-term commitment to keep oil markets stable. Media commentary about a possible confrontation between Iran and Saudi Arabia often focuses on the prospect that Iran would block or interdict shipping through the Strait of Hormuz, the narrow passage from the Gulf into the open sea.[13] Such an action is unlikely because closing the strait would cut off exports of Iranian oil as well as Arab oil and, in any case, would cause the U.S. Navy to intervene to reopen the waterway and secure friendly shipping, as it did during the so-called Tanker War in the 1980s. Iran's interest in the security of oil shipping lanes is as great as that of Saudi Arabia. The real threat posed to Saudi Arabia from Iran is political.

Iran is the only nation-state between the Mediterranean and the Indian Ocean that presents any serious challenge to the supremacy of Saudi interests in all three areas that matter most: oil, security, and religion. The people of Arabia's Nejd heartland and the Persians have been rivals since the Muslim Arab forces defeated the Persian Empire in the early years of Islam. Iran is the center of Shia Islam, while the Saudis represent the most conservative school of Sunni Islam. As noted in chapter 8, this schism has divided Muslims almost since the death of the Prophet in AD 632.

The Saudis have made no secret of their anxiety about the prospect of such a rival acquiring nuclear weapons, but they also recognize that for all their wealth they cannot do much to prevent it. They are incapable of halting the Iranian nuclear program by military means and probably would not do so even if they could because of Iran's ability to retaliate. There might be incentives that would induce Iran to take a different course, but neither Saudi Arabia nor anyone else has divined what those might be.

The Saudis did propose one creative initiative that would have given Iran a face-saving solution to its quest for uranium enrichment so that it would not be dependent on U.S. or European suppliers. In November 2007, on behalf of the GCC, the Saudis offered to finance the development of a jointly owned enrichment facility in a neutral country, such as Switzerland or Kazakhstan, that would serve all participants, including Iran, under the International Atomic Energy Agency's supervision. Iran spurned the offer, demonstrating that it wants the technology and not just the fuel, which is already available on the international open market.

As Tariq Khaitous wrote in a well-argued paper for the Washington Institute for Near East Policy, "There is no incentive package that Arabs can bring to the table that would persuade Iran to follow international demands and halt its uranium enrichment . . . Additionally, Arab states are unable to provide security to Iran in exchange for stopping the nuclear program." Dependent on the United States for their own security, they are in no position to offer

Iran any sort of guarantees or alliances that the Iranians would find sufficient even if Iran were receptive to such proposals.[14]

Perhaps the most important question about the long-term security of Saudi Arabia and the Gulf is, what will the Saudis do in the event that Iran develops, or is known to acquire, nuclear weapons and the means to deliver them? Will they try to acquire or develop their own nuclear arsenal to balance Iran's power? Will they participate in a regional nuclear arms race? Will they refrain from the nuclear temptation and seek new assurances from the longtime guarantor of their security, the United States? Or, most likely, do they not know what they would do because matters have not yet reached a point where they have to decide? Because of the opacity of Saudi Arabia's decision-making process, there is no way to know for sure.

Throughout 2010, as the Iranians pressed ahead with their nuclear program and regional fears about it deepened, armchair strategists and think tank analysts in Israel and in the United States advanced the notion that the perceived threat from Iran would prompt Saudi Arabia to make common cause on this subject with Israel, on the old theory that the enemy of my enemy is my friend.[15] Late in 2010 the antisecrecy Web site WikiLeaks fortified this wishful thinking when it made public secret cables that showed the GCC rulers were almost as anxious about Iran as Israeli leaders were. The Sunni Arab regimes' anxiety was elevated a few months later when the Shia-led conflict began in Bahrain, and they believed it was stoked by Iran. But joint Arab-Israeli action on this front is somewhere between unlikely and out of the question. The contest for regional influence between Iran and Saudi Arabia is based at least in part on popular regional perceptions about which is the more legitimate, more authentic power. Saudi Arabia could conceivably give a "wink and nod," or unannounced assistance, to a joint U.S.-Israeli campaign against Iran, but an overt partnership with the Jewish state would be political suicide.

For Saudi Arabia the contest with Iran is in some ways more difficult than was the struggle with Egypt's Gamal Abdel Nasser in the 1950s and 1960s. Nasser was a secular leader and a socialist who suppressed the Muslim Brotherhood and was an ally of the Soviet Union. It was easy for the Saudis to present themselves as anticommunist upholders of Islam, or the ideological opposites of Egypt, and a bulwark against Soviet inroads in the Muslim world.

The Islamic Republic of Iran, by contrast, presents itself as the legitimate force of the faith and depicts the Saudis as agents of the corrupt "crusaders" in the United States and as patsies for the encroachment of Western culture. Iran's appeal to the Muslim masses is fortified by its unwavering opposition to the existence of Israel, unlike Saudi Arabia, which has offered a plan for Arab peace with the Jewish state. This appeal to religious values, coming from a country run by Shiites—whom Saudis scorn as apostates—is a fundamental threat to the House of Saud's claims to legitimacy.

In broadest terms, this argument is about the nature of Islam itself and has divided the believers since the first decades after the death of Muhammad. Sunni Muslims, of whom the Saudis consider themselves the truest, believe that the prophet's early followers were correct when they decided that his successor, the caliph, should be chosen by consensus rather than by the line of descent. In the centuries since the original schism, the Sunnis generally accepted the authority of the caliph, whoever he was and however he attained the position, rather than that of imams descended from the Prophet, as in Shia Islam. For centuries the caliph was the Ottoman sultan in Constantinople, but Mustafa Kemal Atatürk abolished the caliphate after the collapse of the Ottoman Empire. While no one holds or claims that position today, Sunni Islam generally teaches that the duly constituted authority in the state—in this case, the Al-Saud rulers—commands allegiance.

Sunnis constitute the vast majority of the world's Muslims, but the ascent of the Islamic republic under the Ayatollah Khomeini's glowering visage energized the Shia throughout the region. In Lebanon, the formerly marginalized Shia are now probably the most powerful political force, and in Iraq, when U.S. forces ousted Saddam Hussein, the oppressed Shia majority were free to claim political supremacy. Saudi Arabia cannot afford to lose this competition.

Saudi Arabia and Iran are unlikely to confront each other in a conventional war. Neither is powerful enough to overcome the other, and both countries remember what happened when Saddam Hussein's Iraq invaded Iran: Hundreds of thousands died in an eight-year war that settled nothing. One reason the Saudis objected to the U.S. invasion of Iraq was that they were more comfortable with Saddam Hussein's secular Baathist Iraq providing a regional counterweight to Iran than with the Shia-dominated neighbor that they knew would emerge after his downfall.

Assuming that the Islamic Republic survives in its current form, Iran and Saudi Arabia can be expected to continue their rivalry in the arenas of religion and ideology. They will espouse irreconcilable views on the legitimacy of Israel's existence and the role of the United States in the region. The relationship might be called a managed rivalry, for they compete for influence in the region and throughout the Muslim world but avoid provocations that might lead to regional destabilization, which would damage both.

This managed rivalry is likely to continue unless there is some game-changing event, such as an Iranian nuclear test or a shift in the government in Tehran. Even when the Saudis intervened in Bahrain in 2011 to enforce what many Saudi officials called a "red line" against Iranian influence, they did not engage in open conflict with any Iranian forces, and the Gulf sea-lanes remained undisturbed.

Meanwhile, Iran has extensive economic interests on the Arab side of the Gulf, in Dubai and Qatar, especially, that it wants to protect. Iran and Saudi Arabia are still nominal partners in OPEC. Saudi Arabia has rejected suggestions that it break with OPEC formulas and quotas to drive down the price of oil as a way to undermine the Iranian economy, but there are indications that Saudi Arabia's effort to become the principal oil supplier to China and India through discounts and refining partnerships is intended in part to wean those countries from their dependence on Iran. According to analysts at Rice University's Baker Institute, "The initial result of the effort was dramatic, with Iran reporting in April 2010 as many as 25 cargoes of unsold oil—totaling 48 million barrels or the equivalent of 19 days worth of Iranian crude oil exports—floating adrift at sea, unable to find a buyer."[16]

According to messages from U.S. Ambassador James Smith in the WikeLeaks file, Saudi Arabia told the Chinese that it is willing to guarantee oil supplies in return for Chinese pressure on Iran not to develop nuclear weapons. That means diplomatic pressure in the UN Security Council. It is not the same thing as flooding the market to drive down the price of oil, and in any case Saudi Arabia is already committed to a long-term oil supply relationship with China. (See chapter 2.)

Saudi Arabia and Iran signed cooperation agreements a decade ago that are still in effect on terrorism, money laundering, drug trafficking, and illegal immigration. They have some mutual interests in South Asia, and they cooperate when Iranians journey to Mecca every year for the Muslim pilgrimage, a rite observed by Sunni and Shia alike. Iranian troublemakers rioted during the pilgrimage in 1987, provoking clashes that killed more than four hundred pilgrims and prompted the Saudis to cut off Iranian access to Islam's most sacred site. As competitors for religious supremacy, neither country wants to relive that episode.

RAND Corporation analysts in 2009 produced an illuminating study of relations between Saudi Arabia and Iran that concluded that the two countries bring different strengths to their rivalry. On the one hand, Iran is "more adept" at projecting power through non-state actors such as Hezbollah and "playing a rejectionist trump card on issues such as Palestine and U.S. presence in the region." Prior to the Bahrain episode, the Iranians had some success in courting a form of coexistence with some of the Arab sheikhdoms on Saudi Arabia's borders, including Dubai, Qatar, and Oman, where economic interests predominate. On the other hand, the Saudis have far greater financial resources, "control of pan-Arab media outlets," and the backing of the United States."[17] The Saudis also have much more modern and capable weapons and aircraft.

Iranian acquisition of nuclear weapons would change that delicate balance of forces to Saudi Arabia's disadvantage. The fear is not that Iran would actually use such weapons but that it would feel emboldened to throw its weight around. As Dr. Lewis Dunn put it in a 2009 paper for the U.S. Naval Postgraduate School, "Among virtually all of Iran's neighbors, there is considerable concern that once in possession of nuclear weapons, the Iranian leadership could intensify its interference in those neighbors' domestic politics, step up support for extremist groups, and use the shadow of nuclear weapons to shape regional relations in a manner more favorable to it."[18]

In the judgment of the RAND analysts, "The advent of a nuclear-armed Iran would likely be perceived as an existential threat to Riyadh, possibly pushing Saudi Arabia to acquire its own countervailing deterrent."[19] Dennis Ross, the Middle East peace negotiations veteran who became President Obama's chief adviser on Iran, told a Washington audience in the spring of 2010 that "a nuclear-armed Iran would almost certainly precipitate a dangerous arms race in the Middle East, where states are already hyper-sensitive in their competition for regional influence and security."[20]

In a 2009 diplomatic cable to Secretary of State Clinton, preparing her for an upcoming meeting with King Abdullah, Ambassador Smith said the king had told a senior White House official that "if Iran succeeded in developing nuclear weapons, everyone in the region would do the same, including Saudi Arabia."[21] That remark might seem conclusive, but it should not be taken as a definitive statement of a national commitment or a policy consensus within Saudi Arabia. The leaked cables show that the king had been steadily ratcheting up his alarmist rhetoric in an effort to prod Washington into taking a tougher stance on Iran and that most of his senior advisers were urging caution.

It is not inevitable that the Saudis would seek their own nuclear arsenal in response to Iran or for any other reason. There are powerful disincentives to any attempt by Saudi Arabia to acquire or develop nuclear weapons, even apart from its shortage of technical and engineering capability.

THE NUCLEAR TEMPTATION

The prospect of a nuclear-armed Saudi Arabia has been on the table since the United States discovered accidentally in 1988 that the kingdom had acquired CSS-2 missiles from China. Previously these missiles had always been seen in a nuclear configuration, and their relative inaccuracy allows no military value other than the delivery of weapons of mass destruction, nuclear or otherwise. The tension over that episode faded after Saudi Arabia acceded to the Nuclear Nonproliferation Treaty (NPT) and other events claimed the headlines. When President George W. Bush in 2008 committed the United States to help Saudi Arabia develop commercial nuclear energy, the announcement generated surprisingly little controversy because the media's attention at the time was focused almost entirely on the skyrocketing world price of oil and what Saudi Arabia was going to do about it. Bush had a reputation as perhaps the most supportive of Israel of American presidents, and as one who would not do anything to jeopardize that country's security.

Nevertheless, as the Saudis actually begin to move in the direction of nuclear power, the words "nuclear materials" and "Saudi Arabia" in the same sentence are bound to generate anxiety in Washington and Jerusalem. Questions about nuclear weapons and the possible diversion of nuclear materials to terrorists are sure to arise. When Bush made his commitment to the Saudis, the kingdom agreed to join the worldwide Proliferation Security Initiative, a multifaceted U.S. program to combat the threat of nuclear proliferation. The subsequent White House announcement listed many steps that Saudi Arabia had agreed to take as part of the Global Initiative to Combat Nuclear Terrorism and to ensure that nuclear materials be kept secure, such as "enhance its accountability and physical protection of nuclear systems."[22] But this commitment, of course, is based on the assumption that the signatory government remains in power and is dealing in good faith, an assumption Congress is unlikely to accept at face value.

In theory, certainly, the issues of nuclear power and nuclear weapons should be entirely separate, and often they are. In the case of Saudi Arabia, however, any plan to develop nuclear power will inevitably raise questions about the parallel issue of acquiring nuclear weapons—largely because of the perceived threat from Iran. Saudi Arabia is the largest military power on the Arab side of the Gulf and the only apparent counterweight to Iranian influence in the region in the absence of Iraq. It is Iran's historic rival because of the Sunni-Shia divide and claims to have unique security responsibilities because of the annual Muslim pilgrimage to Mecca and its stewardship of the Holy Places. The Saudis will not easily escape questions about whether their true intentions in pursuing nuclear energy reflect these considerations.

From the American perspective, the 1988 Chinese missile deal appeared dangerous and destabilizing in several ways, even apart from the potential menace to Israel. It accelerated a Middle East missile race that was already under way, demonstrated a streak of independence and duplicity that Washington did not anticipate from Riyadh, and introduced China as an arms supplier to a country that had made its opposition to communism a cornerstone of its long relationship with the United States. The discovery thus triggered an alarmed response from Washington. The Reagan administration basically forced the Saudis to accede to the Nuclear Nonproliferation Treaty as the price of keeping the missiles. Previously the Saudis had said they would accede to the NPT only when Israel did so, knowing perfectly well that Israel would not do that.

If the Saudi people had been able to vote on the matter, or if Saudi Arabia had had a legislature, its accession to the NPT without any corresponding commitment from Israel might have been rejected. As always the small circle of people who wield power in the kingdom made the decision without any public debate.

By signing the NPT, Saudi Arabia officially forswore nuclear weapons. It accepted the treaty's grand bargain, by which the five established nuclear powers, including the United States, agreed to take steps toward nuclear disarmament and to assist non-weapons countries in developing civilian nuclear energy programs. Nevertheless, some analysts have argued that acquiring nuclear weapons could make sense for Saudi Arabia because it is, after all, a vulnerable country. The competence of its armed forces is dubious, and violence-prone and sometimes threatening neighbors surround the country. Saudi Arabia has no strategic heartland into which its defensive forces could retreat and regroup, as the Russians did when Napoleon and Hitler invaded. The kingdom's greatest vulnerability lies along the Gulf coast, where the oil installations and desalination plants essential to national survival are located. What would the kingdom do if a superior force attacked those facilities? The obvious answer is call Washington, but can Saudi Arabia assume that the United States will always answer the phone?

Even before the U.S. invasion of Iraq removed the Saudis' buffer against Iranian ambition, the security analyst Richard L. Russell argued the case for the Saudis' acquisition of nuclear capability. He observed that "it would be imprudent, to say the least, for Riyadh to make the cornerstone of [its] national-security posture out of an assumption that the United States would come to the kingdom's defense under any and all circumstances."

"From Riyadh's perspective," wrote Russell, "the acquisition of nuclear weapons and secure delivery systems would appear logical and even necessary." Those "secure delivery systems," he argued, would not be aircraft, which are vulnerable to ground defenses, but "ballistic-missile delivery systems that would stand a near-invulnerable chance of penetrating enemy airspace"—namely, the Chinese missiles.[23]

Those missiles were obsolete even when Russell's essay was published in 2001, and as far as the United States knows, they have never been replaced or even upgraded. According to Anthony Cordesman,

> It is also far from clear that the CSS-2 missile is kept truly operational. Saudi Arabia has never conducted a meaningful operational test of the CSS-2 and is incapable of conducting the tests necessary to refine the missile's targeting. . . . The Kingdom has to make hard choices about the future of its CSS-2 missiles and whether it will buy a replacement. CSS-2 missiles are not a meaningful response to the Iranian CRBN [chemical, radiological, biological, nuclear] and missiles threat, and they have only token warfighting capability.[24]

Military experts say it is theoretically possible that the missiles could be made operational, modernized, and retrofitted with nuclear warheads acquired from China, Pakistan, or perhaps, within a few years, North Korea. Any attempt to do so, however, would present immense technical and political difficulties—so much so that Saudi Arabia might emerge even less secure.

Aside from the fact that such a nuclear program would violate the Nuclear Nonproliferation Treaty and place Saudi Arabia in the category of global nuclear outlaw along with North Korea, the Saudis' acquisition of warheads would encounter strenuous opposition from the United States and Israel. Having watched Washington's reaction to Pakistan's nuclear tests in 1998, the Saudis are well aware that U.S. law requires economic and military sanctions against nuclear proliferators. And whereas Pakistan and India had friends in Congress who were willing to help them escape the network of mandatory sanctions, Saudi Arabia does not. If an angry Congress cut off Saudi Arabia from future purchases of U.S. military equipment and Israel threatened a preemptive strike, the kingdom's position would be untenable.

Having committed itself to a long-term national development strategy that assumes full integration with the global economy and extensive foreign investment, Saudi Arabia would undermine its own interests if it turned into a nuclear rogue and alienated the industrialized nations. Moreover, however strong its antipathy to Iran, Saudi Arabia does not face any current or foreseeable domestic or external threat to its security to which the use of nuclear weapons would be a relevant response. No country is capable of invading the kingdom, especially while it is under U.S. protection, and nuclear weapons are useless against domestic troublemakers or border infiltrators. The benefits of acquiring nuclear weapons, if any, would be psychological and political rather than strategic, including a potential deterrent effect against reckless neighbors.

There appears to be no possibility that Saudi Arabia, so long as it is ruled by the Al-Saud family, would ever consider nuclear weapons for aggressive purposes because the kingdom has not threatened any of its neighbors since the last border issues were settled decades ago, but deterrence might be another matter. The kingdom's strategic weaknesses at the time of its Chinese missile acquisition—long porous borders, inviting targets, armed forces of untested capability, relatively small population—have not been overcome. For the possible deterrent effect alone, some analysts think the kingdom would feel compelled to seek nuclear weapons if Iran developed a nuclear arsenal.

Saudi Arabia's official position on this subject is unequivocal: It does not want nuclear weapons for itself, it would like to see the entire region declared by international agreement to be a zone free of weapons of mass destruction (WMD). That proposition is not so outlandish as it might seem; the idea has been discussed for many years in various conferences and forums. In the spring of 2010, the parties to the Nuclear Nonproliferation Treaty asked UN secretary-general Ban Ki-moon to organize a conference in 2012 that would attempt to forge such a regional agreement. This effort is not likely to succeed without a permanent solution to the Arab-Israeli conflict or the Iran issue, but the NPT Review Conference's decision to call for a conference that includes all Middle East states moved the Saudis' position into the diplomatic mainstream.

In the spring of 2010 in Washington, Saudi intelligence chief Prince Muqrin bin Abdul Aziz was a representative at a nuclear security summit convened by President Obama. Forcefully reiterating the kingdom's position in his official statement, he said Saudi Arabia endorses Iran's right to develop nuclear energy, as long as its purposes are peaceful and it complies with the rules of the International Atomic Energy Agency, which is the enforcer of the Nonproliferation Treaty. Peace, he said, "cannot be based on the possession of, or threat to use, nuclear weapons or the imposition of a policy of fait accompli and hegemony which would constitute a source of concern and pose a threat not only to the peoples of the region but to international peace and security as a whole." He was talking about Israel as much as he was talking about Iran, but the Saudis know quite well that Israel, while nuclear armed, is no threat to them because they do not represent any real threat to Israel. After all, Israel did not use nuclear weapons in its darkest hour, the first week of the 1973 war when Egyptian and Syrian troops were on the march. There is no conceivable reason why Israel would put Saudi Arabia on its nuclear target list today, but Israel's attitude would surely change if Saudi Arabia acquired nuclear weapons.

AN ARSENAL IN PAKISTAN

Some security analysts and U.S. diplomats hold that Saudi Arabia in effect already has nuclear weapons—in Pakistan. They believe that Saudi Arabia, a longtime friend of Pakistan's, put up a good bit of money to help Pakistan develop its nuclear arsenal and could summon those weapons to the kingdom on demand. This is extremely unlikely, especially now that the clandestine nuclear technology bazaar operated by the Pakistani scientist A. Q. Khan has been dismantled. A Pakistani transfer of nuclear weapons to Saudi Arabia would infuriate the United States and Israel and would jeopardize Saudi Arabia's growing friendship with India. The purpose of Pakistan's nuclear arsenal is to provide security against the far larger India, security that would be diminished, rather than enhanced, by moving its nuclear weapons out of the country. Besides, it is hard to see how Pakistan would benefit, except perhaps financially, by supplying Saudi Arabia with nuclear weapons as a way to protect the kingdom against a nuclear Iran. On the contrary, such a move could turn Iran into a second hostile nuclear-armed state on Pakistan's border.

Moreover, if Saudi Arabia possessed nuclear arms, or even the technology and materials to assemble a bomb without actually doing so, it would be seriously jeopardized should an extremist group obtain a nuclear device and use it against the United States or Israel. A nuclear-capable Saudi Arabia would be a suspect and a possible target for retaliation; without such capability it would not. On balance, then—and assuming, of course, that the U.S. commitment to the kingdom's security remains in place—it is unlikely that Saudi Arabia will seek nuclear weapons, no matter what happens with the Iranian program.

Given the numerous uncertainties and moving parts in Iraq, in Yemen, in Iran, and among extremist groups in the region, it is impossible to predict the outcome of the Iranian nuclear issue and its impact on Gulf security. The most likely eventuality is that Iran will develop the capability to construct nuclear weapons, if not the actual warheads, and that the countries around it will seek strategies to contain it—that is, to prevent Iran from using whatever additional power its nuclear capability might confer to bully its neighbors and influence regional developments. As the RAND analyst Robert Hunter put it, "Containment of Iran is doable, but it will be expensive and a long-term commitment."

While that proposition means a long-term commitment by the United States, Hunter said, the American people's "tolerance for the degree of engagement we have today is not unlimited. Can something be created that will enable the United States to protect its interests at lower cost, a lower cost in blood and treasure?"[25] In a book published by RAND, he offered the possibility that the answer might be no. "Of course, in this particular region," he wrote, "development of a comprehensive and effective security *structure* may not be possible: Differences among states and religious and other groupings may prove to be simply too deep and pervasive."[26]

Hunter proposed partial steps—similar to those developed with the Soviet Union during the Cold War, such as an "incidents at sea" agreement and "counter-piracy cooperation" in the Indian Ocean and the Gulf of Aden—that all countries in the region, including Iran, could accept in their own interest. Even if the Iranian nuclear issue were resolved to Washington's satisfaction, however, Hunter concluded unarguably that "the nature of U.S. and Western interests in the region—e.g. the secure export of energy, stability and predictability, counterterrorism, relations with other great powers, geopolitics and geoeconomics in general—means that the United States will have no choice but to remain a deeply engaged power in the region even though the terms, conditions, qualities, dimensions, and application of that power are subject to debate, decision, and responses to events that have not yet happened or, perhaps, even been imagined."[27]

From the Saudis' perspective, what matters is that they be perceived as a valuable and reliable partner of the United States in that endeavor. There is every reason to think that will be the case. If the security partnership between the United States and Saudi Arabia survived September 11, 2001, it is not in jeopardy now, despite the sharp disagreements over regional issues that surface from time to time.

11

AN EVOLVING ALLIANCE

The alliance of Saudi Arabia and the United States, forged during World War II, has proved to be as durable as it was unlikely.

At the time President Franklin D. Roosevelt and Saudi Arabia's founding king, Abdul Aziz Al-Saud, came together for their famous meeting in February 1945, the United States was the world's greatest industrial and economic power and the only combatant nation that would emerge from the war stronger than when it began. Saudi Arabia was a little-known, impoverished tribal state without schools, roads, ports, irrigation, electricity, or hospitals.

The two countries were as different as it was possible to be in religion, culture, social system, language, and political organization. Many Americans had ancestral ties to European countries and Asia, but few had ancestral ties to the Arabian Peninsula. The entire political system and social organization of Saudi Arabia were antithetical to American values.

Despite these vast differences, the two countries found themselves essential to each other. King Abdul Aziz, whose desperation for revenue obliged him to bring in foreign assistance over the objections of the religious fanatics around him, had awarded an oil exploration contract to the American company Chevron, which struck the Saudi bonanza in 1938. After the oil company opened the door, American industry rushed in. Throughout the second half of the twentieth century, Americans built power plants and transmission lines, refineries, airports, hospitals, roads, and a railroad. They also created and staffed the national airline, introduced television, mechanized Saudi agriculture, and trained and equipped the Saudi armed forces.

251

American technology was the foundation of modern Saudi Arabia, and American military power guaranteed the regime's security.

Saudi Arabia made itself indispensable to the United States as well, as a supplier of oil and as a reliable ally in the Cold War contest with communism. The kingdom represented stability in a turbulent region and supported the United States in conflicts from Afghanistan to Nicaragua.[1]

At President Roosevelt's behest, King Abdul Aziz actually declared war on the Axis powers in the waning months of World War II to meet the price Roosevelt set for admitting charter members to the United Nations. The bilateral alliance has never been formalized in a treaty—the supposed "oil for security" agreement forged between Roosevelt and the king is a myth, extrapolated from subsequent events—but every U.S. president since Harry S. Truman has undertaken one commitment or another to Saudi Arabia that collectively added up to the same arrangement.[2]

The strength and durability of the alliance can be seen in the fact that it has weathered crises and disputes that might have caused a long-term rupture between countries less firmly entwined: the disappointment of King Abdul Aziz and the fury of his most trusted son, Faisal, over President Truman's recognition of Israel in 1948; the Arab oil embargo prompted by U.S. support for Israel in the 1973 Middle East War; American outrage over Saudi participation in the terror attacks on New York and the Pentagon on September 11, 2001; and Saudi anger at the U.S. invasion of Iraq, which in Riyadh's view strengthened Iran and Shia Islam at Saudi expense. (King Abdullah shocked Washington with a 2007 speech at an Arab summit conference that denounced the "illegitimate foreign occupation" of Iraq.) When Barack Obama became president in January 2009, he inherited a bilateral relationship deeply strained by Saudi resentment over the policies of his predecessor, George W. Bush, especially Bush's ill-advised and ill-fated effort to move Saudi Arabia toward political liberalization as the price of continued U.S. friendship.

Saudi Arabia's association with the events of 9/11 brought to the surface a deep reservoir of popular antipathy in the United States. An outpouring of books, articles, political speeches, and movies excoriated the kingdom for its support of religious extremism and its dismal human rights record. During the extremist insurgency that began in 2003, thousands of Americans who had been living in Saudi Arabia left because of the rising security threat, a threat that was exaggerated by hair-raising warnings from the State Department. The Saudi insurgency also coincided with a rising Arab wave of anti-American sentiment over the U.S. invasion of Iraq. Those years represented one of the darkest periods in the history of the alliance.

Yet even then, there was no prospect of an outright rupture between Washington and Riyadh because neither side wanted or could afford such a development. The United States needed the Saudis' cooperation in the war on terrorism and in cutting off the flow of money to extremist groups. And Saudi Arabia continued to rely on the United States to confront the threat from the kingdom's most powerful rival, Iran. Differences over Iraq and the Israeli-Palestinian question could not be allowed to interfere with those strategic realities.

The Final Report of the National Commission on Terrorist Attacks upon the United States, popularly known as *The 9/11 Commission Report* and issued in 2004, gave Bush the political cover he needed to rebuild the relationship when it "found no evidence that the Saudi government as an institution or senior Saudi officials individually" funded the al-Qaeda network.[3] The commission did not absolve the Saudi government from responsibility for creating an atmosphere in which al-Qaeda could flourish and noted that individual Saudi citizens had been financial backers of the organization. The Bush administration and the Saudi government, however, chose to emphasize the report's positive findings as they strove to repair the damage done by the 9/11 attacks.

By the end of his second term, Bush had retreated from his efforts to democratize the Middle East, and on a last trip to Riyadh in May 2008 he signed a new package of bilateral agreements, including a U.S. commitment to help Saudi Arabia develop civilian nuclear energy. The White House's fact sheet describing the results of the president's visit said the agreements "further cement the longstanding U.S.-Saudi friendship and close cooperation to help bring peace and stability to the region and its people."[4]

Even in the darkest days, the extensive bilateral business relationships remained in place. American companies lowered their profile in the kingdom, but Saudi Arabia retained its standing as the largest U.S. trading partner in the Middle East. Although Bush worked hard in his last few years as president to pull the bilateral relationship back from the brink of disintegration, there was a palpable sense of relief in Riyadh when his presidency ended.

OPTIMISM ABOUT OBAMA

Saudi Arabia regarded President Obama optimistically, if only because he was not Bush, and Obama set out almost immediately upon becoming president to restore harmony to the relationship. On his first trip to the Middle East, he first stopped in Riyadh and met with King Abdullah before heading to Cairo to deliver his landmark speech about U.S. relations with the Muslim world. The Saudis appreciated the gesture, but Obama's relations with Abdullah got off to a rocky start when the president, who was poorly briefed, asked the king for unilateral gestures of goodwill toward Israel, such as extending to Israeli aircraft the right to fly over Saudi airspace. As was predictable, the king rebuffed the president. The Saudis' position is that they crafted, and persuaded all members of the League of Arab States to endorse, a comprehensive peace offer based on Israel's return to its pre-1967 borders. They feel they have no obligation to do more.

Saudi foreign minister Prince Saud Al-Faisal said as much a year later, after meeting with Secretary of State Hillary Rodham Clinton in Washington the eve of Abdullah's return visit. "The question is not what the Arab world will offer—that has been established: an end to the conflict, recognition, and full normal relations as exist between countries at peace," he said. "The question really is: what will Israel give in exchange for this comprehensive offer?"

But the prince also declared, "Our two nations have been friends and allies for over seven decades. We have seen the coming and breaking of many storms. Over time, the relationship has grown stronger, broader, and deeper. And our discussion today reflected the maturity of this relationship. It was frank, honest and open—just as it should be among friends."[5]

The open differences over policy toward the Israeli-Palestinian conflict are hardly new; indeed, they have been part of the bilateral discussion since Roosevelt's meeting with Abdul Aziz. The deep economic and strategic ties between the two countries remain in place despite those differences, as they always have. But the U.S.-Saudi relationship will never be what it was at its height in the 1980s because the kingdom and world around it have changed.

The disintegration of the Soviet Union and the end of the Cold War eliminated a cornerstone of the alliance. The threat that had united Washington and Riyadh against Egypt's Nasser and other pro-Soviet Arab nationalists, against Cuban influence in Africa, against the Sandinistas in Nicaragua, and finally against the Soviet Union itself in Afghanistan vaporized with the fall of the Berlin Wall. Now the only common enemy facing the United States and the Saudi regime, other than Iran, is Islamic radicalism, which is dangerous to both but an existential threat to neither. The end of the communist threat and the discrediting of secular Arab nationalism have liberated Saudi Arabia to stake out positions different from those of the United States on several international issues, including the Israeli-Palestinian question and Iraq, and to find new arms suppliers, including Russia.

In domestic terms, Saudi Arabia is a grown-up country now and is no longer dependent on Americans for its industrial development. After half a century of American tutelage, Saudi Arabia no longer needs Americans to operate its oil industry, construct its buildings, fly its airplanes, or staff its hospitals. The years when Saudi government agencies were staffed by American civil servants, through contracts managed by the U.S. Treasury Department, ended in 2000, because the Saudis decided that the arrangement had outlived its usefulness.

Saudi Arabia is a member of the World Trade Organization and the only Arab state in the G-20 group of economically developed countries. It has options in economic affairs that it did not have when the Americans were making most of the decisions, as evidenced by the rapid rise of its trade with China, South Korea, and other Asian countries.

In 2009 for the first time Saudi Arabia exported more oil to China than it did to the United States. It has financed the construction of refineries in China that can process the heavy crude that American refiners do not want. Saudi Arabia's quest for assured markets and reliable long-term customers fits neatly with China's need for ever-greater supplies.

Chinese construction contractors can be found all across Saudi Arabia, even in Mecca, where they have constructed a monorail to facilitate pilgrimage traffic. In trade volume, the United States remains Saudi Arabia's biggest partner, but its share of the market is declining while China's has more than doubled, rising from 4.1 percent in 2000 to 9.6 percent at the end of 2007.[6] Saudi officials have become frequent visitors to China and vice versa. King Abdullah's first foreign trip after he assumed the throne was to China. In short, a country with which Saudi Arabia refused to have any contact whatsoever before the late 1980s because it was communist has become a major, growing trade partner and a cornerstone of Saudi Arabia's industrialization plans.

THE CHINA SYNDROME

So wide and deep have the economic links between Saudi Arabia and China become over the past decade that some American and European analysts predict that China will supplant the United States as the kingdom's principal security guarantor. To cite just one example, two analysts at the Institute for Near East and Gulf Military Analysis in Dubai wrote in April 2010 that "the pendulum is clearly shifting toward the Chinese camp. In time, as the Kingdom's economic ties grow firmer with China, their military relationship will expand. As China's military power comes to match its political and economic power globally, it will become Saudi Arabia's strongest military ally."[7]

There is a certain superficial logic to such arguments. An alliance with China could be appealing to Saudi Arabia because China, like the United States, is a nuclear power and a permanent member of the UN Security Council. Because of China's need for oil, it also has an abiding interest in maintaining stability in the Gulf. It has been expanding its armed forces, especially its navy, while the United States has been bogged down in Iraq and Afghanistan. It does not harangue its trading partners about their human rights policies or religious preferences. It has no history of colonial interference in the Middle East and no territorial ambitions in the region. It carries none of the Israeli baggage that makes dependence on Washington a political liability for the Saudi rulers.

Nevertheless, China is not about to assume the principal role in securing the Gulf's stability, or the unique responsibility for the security of Saudi Arabia, that the United States has held for decades. China has neither the capability nor the desire to do so. Its economic ties to Saudi Arabia match its economic ties to Iran, and it is reluctant to jeopardize either relationship. China has massive security concerns right in its own neighborhood, with Taiwan, North Korea, Russia, Vietnam, and Tibet. As Japan did in an earlier era, it can reap economic benefits from all around the Gulf, including Iran, without having to assume responsibility for maintaining order.

China is not going to match the 230,000 members of the U.S. armed forces, equipped with the most sophisticated aircraft, ships, and weapons, that the United States maintains in the area of CENTCOM's responsibility, which includes the Gulf and South Asia.[8] There is no prospect that China will develop a carrier-based fleet and station it in Bahrain to patrol the Gulf, as the United States does. Nor can it easily supplant seven decades of American influence with the Saudi armed forces, painstakingly constructed through training, operational cooperation, and shared experiences such as the 1991 Gulf War.

As Library of Congress researchers reported to Congress in late 2009, "The United Sates has long been Saudi Arabia's leading arms supplier. From 1950 through 2006, Saudi Arabia purchased and received from the United States weapons, military equipment, and related services through Foreign Military Sales worth over $62.7 billion and foreign military construction services worth over $17.1 billion (figures in historical dollars.)"[9]

President Bush in his second term added millions more, and the Obama administration, in office less than a year at the time of that report, had already notified Congress of pending sales worth an additional $2 billion. More, much more, was soon to come.

The only foreigners directly involved in securing internal stability within the kingdom are Americans. Under bilateral agreements, the United States provides contractors to train and equip the National Guard and the Interior Ministry's new Facilities Security Force. It would take decades for China to achieve a similar position in Saudi Arabia's security apparatus, even if it were so inclined.

Alarmist essays by academics notwithstanding, there is scant evidence that the people in the U.S. government who are responsible for the country's national security feel urgent concern about a possible Chinese threat to U.S. strategic dominance in the Gulf region. In the *National Security Strategy* document issued by the White House in May 2010, for instance, the word "China" does not even appear in the section covering the Middle East.[10]

The Pentagon's "Quadrennial Defense Review," issued in February 2010, notes that "as part of its long-term, comprehensive military modernization, China is developing and fielding large numbers of advanced medium-range ballistic and cruise missiles, new attack submarines equipped with advanced weapons, increasingly capable long-range air defense systems, electronic warfare and computer network attack capabilities, advanced fighter aircraft, and counter-space systems. China has shared only limited information about the pace, scope, and ultimate aims of its military modernization programs, raising a number of legitimate questions regarding its long-term intentions." It also says, however, that "the United States remains the only nation able to project and sustain large-scale operations over extended distances." It adds that China's newfound economic interests in the Middle East might turn out to be a positive development if Beijing pursues stability and long-term security there.[11]

A few months after publication of the "Quadrennial Defense Review," the Pentagon sent to Congress its annual report on Chinese military capabilities and national security policy, the most comprehensive unclassified document available on the subject. It noted the rapid escalation of China's military capability, including an expansion of its deep-sea navy and its missile arsenal. It also said, however, that the Chinese buildup—and Chinese policy—are focused on regional concerns in the Taiwan Strait, the South China Sea, and the Strait of Malacca. The report also cited an expanding range and depth of Chinese military cooperation with the United States and depicted China not as a threat to U.S. interests in the Gulf but as an asset in promoting regional stability. "China's military engagement with other countries," such as its participation in the multinational antipiracy patrols in the Gulf of Aden, "seeks to enhance China's national power by improving foreign relationships, bolstering its international image, and assuaging other countries' concerns about China's rise," the report said.[12]

China is the beneficiary of a changing global energy picture and of the ambitions of a rising class of Saudi entrepreneurs looking for new opportunities. China's development of substantial economic ties to Saudi Arabia and other countries in the region need not be detrimental to the United States or to the U.S.-Saudi relationship. On the contrary, it gives China incentive to help the United States stave off instability all around the Gulf.

PRESERVING THE REGIME

This entire discussion assumes, of course, that the House of Saud will continue to rule the kingdom. All the sons who have followed King Abdul Aziz on the throne have upheld, with varying degrees of enthusiasm, the alliance that he forged. None of the potential successors to King Abdullah, in his generation or the next, would be likely to break away.

If some other person or group were to come to power in Riyadh, the alliance could well come to an end. After overthrowing their monarchies, Egypt in 1952, Iraq in 1958, Libya in 1969, and Iran in 1979 all jettisoned their alignments with Western countries. Given the widespread unpopularity of the United States in the Arab world, any new regime in Saudi Arabia might follow that pattern, especially if that new ruler came from an Islamist movement.

A rupture would not necessarily be total unless the new ruler or rulers came from the most radical fringe of Islamic extremism, but a new regime might well believe that its legitimacy would be enhanced if it developed new security arrangements that were less dependent on Washington. The often-expressed fear in the West of an oil cutoff is unfounded. Anyone running Saudi Arabia, regardless of ideology, will have to sell oil in the global market because the country has no other way to pay for food or to support the state.

In any case, for reasons explained in chapter 1, there is no reason to think that any such upheaval is on the horizon in Saudi Arabia. Critics of the Saudi regime have been predicting its downfall ever since Abdul Aziz's death in 1953, and it has not yet come close to happening. There is no domestic or external threat visible today that could bring an end to Al-Saud rule. It is a truism of intelligence work that "you don't know what you don't know"—nobody had heard of Gamal Abdel Nasser before the Egyptian revolution—but the House of Saud seems to be in full control.

Therefore, the U.S.-Saudi alliance, which is crucial to both countries, is likely to continue, and to continue evolving, as it has for several decades. That evolution is likely to be based on ad hoc and informal arrangements rather than on any formal, treaty-based mutual defense commitment.

When the possibility that Iran might acquire nuclear weapons became part of Gulf regional security calculations several years ago, one concern that naturally arose in Washington was that it might ignite a regional nuclear arms race, in which Saudi Arabia, Egypt, and others might take part. In addition to thinking about how to deter or dissuade Iran from pursuing nuclear weapons, analysts began to consider how to avert a rush by other countries to match it if Iran broke through to nuclear warhead deliverability.

Think tank–sponsored conferences and papers offered one answer: The United States should formally bring friendly countries in the region under its protection and create a Persian Gulf version of the North Atlantic Treaty Organization (NATO). The idea was that sheltering Saudi Arabia and other friendly states under what is known as the U.S. nuclear umbrella would convince them they did not need to acquire such weapons on their own and scare off any potential attackers. NATO members that might have developed nuclear weapons—in particular, Germany and Turkey—refrained from doing so and adhered to the Nuclear Nonproliferation Treaty because they were under the U.S. umbrella. Japan followed the same course in Asia.

Obama's secretary of state, Hillary Clinton, took this concept from the theoretical into the possible in 2009. When asked about Iran during a news conference in Thailand, she said,

> We will hold the door open [to Iran], but we also have made it clear that we'll take actions, as I've said time and again, crippling actions working to upgrade the defense of our partners in the region. We want Iran to calculate what I think is a fair assessment, that if the United States extends a defense umbrella over the region, if we do even more to support the military capacity of those in the Gulf, it's unlikely that Iran will be any stronger or safer, because they won't be able to intimidate and dominate, as they apparently believe they can, once they have a nuclear weapon.[13]

Her remarks were widely interpreted as a signal that the Obama administration was contemplating the sort of defense treaty initiative that had been the subject of academic speculation in the past about opening the "nuclear umbrella" over friendly Gulf states such as Saudi Arabia. But Clinton did not use the word "nuclear" and with good reason. A commitment to use nuclear weapons in the defense of Saudi Arabia would require a treaty and its ratification by the Senate. Having been a senator, Clinton surely knew that such a development is highly unlikely if not out of the question. Given the low esteem in which many Americans hold Saudi Arabia, it would be extremely difficult politically for any president to sign such a treaty or for any senator to vote for it.

The Saudis know that. They stopped asking for a formal mutual defense treaty long ago. Instead, they have settled for American support that has included arms sales, military training, public statements, consultations, and troop deployments when necessary, as in Operation Desert Shield after Iraq's 1990 invasion of Kuwait.

When Congress authorized military assistance to Middle East countries in 1950, President Truman formally declared that military aid to Saudi Arabia was "essential" to American national security. "In making this determination," his statement said, "I find that (1) the strategic location of Saudi Arabia makes it of direct importance to the defense of the Near East area, (2) the assistance to be furnished is of critical importance to the defense of free nations, and (3) the immediately increased ability of Saudi Arabia to defend itself is important to the preservation of the peace and security of the Near East area, and to the security of the United States."[14] Every subsequent president has taken more or less the same position, without the formality of a mutual defense treaty. President Obama has followed the template.

On October 20, 2010, the Obama administration notified Congress of plans for a major new arms sale to Saudi Arabia, probably the biggest ever once all transactions are completed over the next decade or so, with a potential value of $60 billion. Congress can disapprove such transactions, and there had been strong objections to previous proposed sales to Saudi Arabia because of its hostility to Israel. To gauge sentiment in advance of the formal notification, the Obama administration briefed members of key committees and their staffs and leaked information about the planned sale to the news media. Only token opposition surfaced, and by the time of formal notification, officials at the Pentagon and the State Department were convinced that the deal would be approved, as indeed it was.

That Obama would send this arms sale notification to Congress less than two weeks before his party faced mid-term elections, which polls indicated would not go well, was a sure sign that 9/11 was off the table as a political issue. Saudi Arabia's campaign over the previous nine years to sanitize its reputation had succeeded to the point where Obama and his advisers did not fear preelection accusations of being soft on terrorism. On Capitol Hill, it was clear to most legislators and to staff members of the relevant committees that the arms sale was a matter of Gulf security and the presumed threat from Iran and that it did not pose any danger to Israel.

Absent compelling reasons to do otherwise, members of Congress tend to favor arms sales because they mean jobs for American workers and reduce the overall per-unit cost of developing weapons systems for the U.S. armed forces. In its official notification to Congress about the planned Saudi sale, the Pentagon's Defense Security Cooperation Agency listed the contractors that would manufacture the weapons and aircraft to be delivered. It included such defense industry giants as Boeing, Lockheed Martin, General Electric, and Sikorsky Aircraft.

The hardware package included:

- 84 F-15A combat jets and upgrades of the kingdom's existing fleet of 70 F-15S fighters to the F-15A configuration, with additional capabilities
- 190 helicopters, including 66 Apaches and Black Hawks
- 6,568 surface-to-surface, air-to-surface, and air-to-air missiles, such as Harpoons, Sidewinders, high-speed anti-radiation missiles (HARMs), and Hellfire IIs
- assorted bombs, machine guns, and cannons
- radar and air detection equipment and night vision gear

In addition, hundreds of Americans, both active-duty military personnel and contractors, would be deployed to Saudi Arabia for years to supervise the delivery and installation of the aircraft and weapons.

From Washington's perspective, these transactions could have several benefits beyond the assembly-line jobs they would generate. They could reinforce the ability of an important ally to defend itself and strengthen that ally's need to stay on good terms with the United States. They could discourage Iranian adventurism in the region and help Saudi Arabia secure itself against troublesome infiltration from Yemen. And they could give Washington more leverage than it already has in discouraging any ambitions Saudi Arabia might develop to follow Iran down the road to nuclear weapons.

Technically the sale will be made in four separate packages to the air force; the army; the National Guard, which is the principal domestic security force; and the Royal Guard, an army regiment assigned to protect the ruling family. Each piece, the Pentagon said in its notification documents, "will contribute to the foreign policy and national security of the United States by helping to improve the security of a friendly country which has been and continues to be an important force for political stability and economic progress in the Middle East."[15]

"We welcome Saudi Arabia's decision to continue to strategically align itself with the United States," Assistant Defense Secretary Alexander Vershbow said at a briefing for reporters. "If approved, this program will be implemented over 15 to 20 years, which means that our defense bond with the Saudis will only continue to grow deeper and stronger."

"We are undertaking this sale because it supports our wider regional security goals in the Gulf by deepening our security relationship with a key partner with whom we've enjoyed a solid security relationship for nearly 70 years," Assistant Secretary of State Andrew J. Shapiro said at the same briefing. He said the planned sale "will send a strong message to countries in the region that we are committed to support the security of our key partners and allies in the Arabian Gulf and the broader Middle East. And it will enhance Saudi Arabia's ability to deter and defend against threats to its borders and to its oil infrastructure, which is critical to our economic interests."

The sale is "not solely about Iran," Vershbow said. The Saudis "live in a dangerous neighborhood, and we're helping them preserve and protect their security in a dangerous neighborhood against legitimate security threats."[16]

Neither Shapiro nor Vershbow addressed the question of whether the Saudis are capable of using such weapons effectively or even keeping them operational. Defense contractors who have lived in the kingdom and worked with its armed forces have told me that the Saudis are chronically deficient in maintenance and operational readiness, but those issues have not been a deterrent to equipment sales.

William Hartung, director of the Arms and Security Initiative of the New America Foundation, was one of the few voices raised in opposition to the latest proposed sale. "Is the Middle East really suffering from a dearth of advanced weaponry?" he asked. "In addition, how stable is Saudi Arabia? In the short run, there may be no major cause for concern, but the combat planes, helicopters, missiles, and bombs that are part of the deal will last for decades. Would anyone have predicted in the mid-1970s that the heavily armed regime of the Shah of Iran would be toppled by a group of Islamic fundamentalists?"[17]

No, few predicted the Iranian regime change, but the position of the House of Saud is not comparable to that of the shah, as explained in chapter 1. And in any case, the gamble to which Hartung objected is the same one that the United States has been making since the Truman administration. A self-confident Saudi Arabia, equipped with weapons powerful enough to help keep peace in the Gulf but not powerful enough to threaten Israel or, in the unlikely event of a change in regime, to threaten the United States, is much more of an asset than it is a potential liability. Thus this combination of long-term U.S. commitment and ad hoc implementation can be expected to continue indefinitely.

On September 22, 2010, Saudi Arabia celebrated National Day, a holiday that King Abdullah created in 2005 to commemorate the modern kingdom's unification in 1932. That this holiday even exists is a testament to Abdullah's willingness to defy the religious establishment in favor of the nation-state. The religious hierarchy has always opposed the celebration of any holidays other than those specifically associated with religious events such as Ramadan, and National Day is an entirely secular event.

To mark the occasion, Secretary of State Clinton issued a congratulatory message that went well beyond the usual polite banalities. Her proclamation said,

> King Abdullah's leadership on key challenges, from developing the Kingdom's institutions and economy to establishing an enduring dialogue promoting moderation and tolerance, has put Saudi Arabia and the region on a path towards a stronger, more prosperous, and more secure future. We also honor King Abdullah's steadfast support for the Arab Peace Initiative [with Israel]. This groundbreaking initiative provided a far-sighted vision for comprehensive regional peace when the King first proposed it. As we continue working to support direct talks between the Israelis and the Palestinians, the principles enshrined in the Arab Peace Initiative are more important than ever.

That statement was custom-tailored to appeal to Abdullah personally, because before his meeting with President Obama in June 2010, he had felt that his peace initiative was not taken seriously in Washington.

Clinton went on to praise U.S.-Saudi cooperation on matters as varied as the health of Haj pilgrims to Mecca and expanded opportunities for women. "As we join in celebrating this special day," she concluded, "we reaffirm the commitment of the United States to broaden and deepen our partnership with Saudi Arabia in the years to come."[18]

Many Americans might not recognize in those comments the country that they associate with backwardness and cruelty. That dichotomy in the relationship has always existed, though, as leaders of the American foreign policy and business establishment have valued Saudi Arabia for what it is and not for what they wish it were.

A month after Hillary Clinton's salute to the national day holiday, Ambassador Smith happily told a Washington audience that many of the security issues that had soured the relationship in the 1990s had been re-solved. As the threat of terrorist violence has receded, U.S. diplomats and other officials assigned to the kingdom are again permitted to take their fam-ilies with them, and the length of their tours has been restored to two years instead of one. Embassy personnel are leaving their secure but isolated build-ing in increasing numbers to interact with the local population. Student and business visas—which after 9/11 had been virtually shut off, to the anger of Saudis who considered themselves longtime friends of the United States—are once again available. "And we have not compromised security at all," Smith said.[19] He omitted any mention of the long-running struggle to have Saudi Arabia toughen its policy on those who export funds to extremist groups, a lingering irritant in the bilateral relationship. (See chapter 8.)

The dramatic events that transformed the Arab world in the winter of 2011, however, brought new tensions over new issues. The Saudis felt that the United States contributed to the humiliation of their longtime ally, Egyptian president Hosni Mubarak. They also resented American criticism of their decision to intervene in Bahrain. And they were angry after Secretary Clinton gave a speech at a conference in Qatar in which she criticized cor-rupt Arab leaders. In this spat, the Saudis actually declined to receive Clinton and Defense Secretary Robert Gates. They soon relented on Gates, who vis-ited Riyadh, and welcomed a week later Obama's national security adviser, Tom Donilon. I was in Riyadh at the time of Donilon's visit. While my con-versations with Saudis and Americans alike clearly indicated that the coun-tries' disagreements were serious, they would not threaten the fundamental strategic and economic relationship because each country continued to need the other. A few weeks earlier, the U.S.–Saudi Arabian Business Council had reported that the volume of bilateral trade reached $43 billion in 2010, or a 31 percent increase from the year before, as the global economy began re-covering from recession. Cooperation in combating terrorism continued without interruption.

Obviously a radical transformation of the government of Saudi Arabia would shatter this harmony, but there is no reason to expect any such de-velopment and nobody in Washington can plan for it. For better or for worse, the United States and Saudi Arabia are closely intertwined on matters of de-fense and security, as they have been for nearly seven decades. Whatever the outcome of Saudi Arabia's long-term economic restructuring, its educational reform, and its social evolution, the kingdom can pursue those endeavors secure in the knowledge that it can do so largely undisturbed by external threats to its peace and security. As long as oil is the fuel of the global economy, the United States will see to Saudi Arabia's security.

NOTES

INTRODUCTION

1 Saad Sowayan, "Saudis Bring Reform by Stealth as Society Takes the Lead in Forging Modernity," an essay written in 2007 for a now-defunct Web site and reprinted in *The Kingdom: Saudi Arabia and the Challenge of the 21st Century*, ed. Joshua Craze and Mark Huband (New York: Columbia University Press, 2009), 87ff.

2 *Arab News* (daily English-language print and online newspaper), November 26, 2010.

3 Paul Gamble, "Saudi Population Growth Slows; Expats Jump," *Monthly Bulletin*, Jadwa Investment Group, September 2010, http://www.susris.com/documents/2010/101001-jadwa-september-bulletin.pdf.

4 Grant C. Butler, *Kings and Camels: An American in Saudi Arabia* (New York: Devin-Adair, 1960).

CHAPTER 1. KINGS AND COUNTRY

1 Jack Goldstone, "Understanding the Revolutions of 2011: Weakness and Resilience in Middle Eastern Autocracies," *Foreign Affairs* 90, no. 3 (May–June 2011): 8.

2 The popular blogger known as Saudi Jeans, at saudijeans.org, provided an English version of this document.

3 Carnegie Endowment for International Peace, "News and Views: Saudi Reform Petition," *Arab Reform Bulletin* 1, no. 4 (October 2003), http://www.carnegieendowment.org/publications/index.cfm?fa=view&id=1370&prog=zgp&proj=zdrl#petition.

4 Author's interview, Riyadh, April 2011.

5 Author's interview, Washington, November 19, 2008.

6   Gwenn Okruhlik, "The Irony of *Islah* (Reform)," *Washington Quarterly* 28, no. 4 (Autumn 2005): 153–70.

7   Author's interview, Riyadh, May 2010.

8   Jamal Khashoggi, "An Insight into Education Reform in Saudi Arabia," August 15, 2006, http://www.saudi-us-relations.org/articles/2006/ioi/060815-jamal-textbooks.html.

9   Interview with the author, Dubai, May 2010.

10 Asad Abukhalil, *The Battle for Saudi Arabia: Royalty, Fundamentalism, and Global Power* (New York: Seven Stories Press, 2004), 127.

11 The English text of the Basic Law is in Anders Jerichow, *The Saudi File: People, Power, Politics* (New York: St. Martin's, 1998), 10.

12 Interview with the author, Washington, November 19, 2008.

13 A thorough and accessible summary of how the government is structured and how it functions, compiled by the Carnegie Endowment for International Peace and a partner group in Spain, Fundación par las Relaciones Internacionales y el Diálogo Exterior (FRIDE), is *Arab Political Systems: Baseline Information and Reforms*, March 6, 2008, http://www.carnegieendowment.org/arabpoliticalsystems.

14 This brief narrative greatly oversimplifies a complicated history. See F. Gregory Gause III, "Official Wahhabism and the Sanctioning of Saudi-U.S. Relations," in *Religion and Politics in Saudi Arabia: Wahhabism and the State,* ed. Mohammed Ayoob and Hasan Kosebalaban (Boulder, CO: Lynne Rienner, 2009), 136–37; and H. St. John Philby, *Saudi Arabia* (Beirut: Librairie du Liban, 1968 edition), 313.

15 See chapter 7 of this volume.

16 Abdulaziz O. Sager, "Political Opposition in Saudi Arabia," in *Saudi Arabia in the Balance: Political Economy, Society, Foreign Affairs,* ed. Paul Aarts and Gerd Nonneman (New York: New York University Press, 2005), 235.

17 Interview with the author, Washington, May 13, 2009.

18 This comment was made during an informal conversation in Washington.

19 Caryle Murphy, "Tiny Saudi Democracy Movement Sends King Blueprint for Reform," *Christian Science Monitor*, May 15, 2009.

20 Sager, "Political Opposition in Saudi Arabia," 248.

21 International Crisis Group, "Can Saudi Arabia Reform Itself?," 2004. The International Crisis Group has representatives in many countries, but it usually does not name the authors of its reports.

22 Text of the August 3, 2003, speech is available online at http://saudinf.com/display_news.php?id=859.

23 Interview with the author, Riyadh, October 2009.

24 See the extensive critical assessment of the National Society for Human Rights, "Second Report on the Status of Human Rights in the Kingdom of Saudi Arabia," 2008, http://nshr.org.sa/FKCFiles/Second_Report_on_the_Status _of_Human_Rights(3).pdf.

25 Human Rights Watch, "Precarious Justice," March 24, 2008, http://www.hrw.org/en/node/62304/section/1.

26 Andrew Hammond, "Reading Lohaidan in Riyadh: Media and the Struggle for Judicial Power in Saudi Arabia," *Arab Media and Society*, St. Antony's College, Oxford University, no. 7 (January 2009), http://www.arabmediasociety.com /?article=702.

27 Ibid.

28 Address to the Tenth Session of the UN Human Rights Committee, March 20, 2009. The spelling and punctuation are from the printed text that Al-Aiban gave to the author.

29 Human Rights Watch, "Looser Reign, Uncertain Gain," September 27, 2010, http://www.hrw.org/en/reports/2010/09/27/looser-rein-uncertain-gain.

30 Okruhlik, "The Irony of *Islah* (Reform)," 153–70, note 9.

31 Jones's comments appeared in the Middle East blog of foreignpolicy.com on June 2, 2010.

32 Remarks at the National Council on U.S.-Arab Relations' Fifteenth Annual Arab-U.S. Policymakers Conference, Washington, October 2006.

33 Aarts and Nonneman, "Conclusions," in *Saudi Arabia in the Balance*, 453–54.

34 On the Great Mosque episode and its aftermath, see chapter 8 of this volume.

CHAPTER 2. OIL RICH, ENERGY SHORT

1 International Energy Agency, *World Energy Outlook 2010* (Paris: International Energy Agency, 2010), 4–6.

2 U.S. National Intelligence Council, *Global Trends 2025: A Transformed World* (Washington: U.S. Government Printing Office, 2008), 46.

3 Unless otherwise specified, all quotations from current and former Saudi Aramco personnel in this chapter are from interviews conducted by the author in Dhahran, Saudi Arabia, in October 2009.

4 Turki Al-Faisal, "Don't Be Crude," *Foreign Policy*, September–October 2009.

5 "Saudi Arabia Preparing for Oil Demand to Peak," *Houston Chronicle*, January 15, 2010.

6 Remarks at Washington Institute for Near East Policy, Washington, March 27, 2010.

7 International Energy Agency, *Oil Market Report*, April 2010.

8   Economist Intelligence Unit report, "The GCC in 2020: Resources for the Future," http://viewswire.eiu.com/report_dl.asp?mode=fi&fi=427089827.PDF&rf=0.

9   "Saudi Arabia's Coming Oil and Fiscal Challenge," Saudi-US Relations Information Service, http://www.susris.com/2011/07/30/saudi-arabias-coming -oil-and-fiscal-challenge/.

10 See the International Energy Agency's *World Energy Outlook 2010: Key Graphs*, http://www.worldenergyoutlook.org/docs/weo2010/key_graphs.pdf.

11 John Busby, "Oil and Gas Net Exports," June 29, 2008, http://www.after -oil.co.uk/oil_and_gas_net_exports.htm.

12 David Victor and Linda Yueh, "The New Energy Order," *Foreign Affairs*, January–February 2010, http://www.foreignaffairs.com/articles/65897/david-g -victor-and-linda-yueh/the-new-energy-order.

13 Remarks at private dinner, Washington, May 6, 2009.

14 Organization of the Petroleum Exporting Countries (OPEC), *World Oil Outlook 2009* (Vienna, Austria: OPEC Secretariat, 2009).

15 Matthew Simmons, *Twilight in the Desert: The Coming Saudi Oil Shock and the World Economy* (Hoboken, NJ: John Wiley, 2005).

16 Simmons's remarks can be found online at http://www.oilcrisis.com/simmons/. Emphasis is in the original.

17 See Steve Andrews and Randy Udall, "Sense and Nonsense from Nansen Saleri," Association for the Study of Peak Oil & Gas–USA, March 10, 2008, http://www.aspo-usa.com/archives/index.php?option=com_content&task =view&id=333&Itemid=93.

18 Private e-mail message.

19 Michael Lynch, "'Peak Oil' Is a Waste of Energy," *New York Times*, August 25, 2009.

20 Peter Jackson, "The Future of Global Oil Supply: Understanding the Building Blocks," IHS Cambridge Energy Research Associates, November 2, 2009, http://www.cera.com/aspx/cda/client/report/report.aspx?KID=5&CID=10720#top.

21 U.S. Energy Information Administration, *International Energy Outlook 2009* (Washington: Energy Information Administration, May 2009), http://www.eia.doe.gov/oiaf/ieo/pdf/0484(2009).pdf.

22 Telephone interview with the author, August 10, 2009.

23 Luke Pachymuthu and Rania El Gamal, "Saudi Hails 'Perfect' Price at Arab Oil Meeting," Reuters, December 5, 2009, http://www.reuters.com/article/idUSTRE5B338S20091205.

24 Nawaf E. Obaid, *The Oil Kingdom at 100: Petroleum Policymaking in Saudi Arabia,* policy paper 55 (Washington: Washington Institute for Near East Policy, 2000), 18.

25 See *Oil Daily*, January 20, 2010.

26 The text of his remarks was distributed by the official Saudi Press Agency on March 16, 2009.

27 *Arab News*, January 25, 2010.

28 The World Bank's figures, derived from National Oceanic and Atmospheric Administration (NOAA) satellite data, are in "Unlocking the Value of Flared Natural Gas" at http://siteresources.worldbank.org/EXTGGFR/Resources /IGUarticle-Unlockingvalue(Jan09).pdf.

29 Al-Naimi's remarks from a talk titled "The Role of Oil in Saudi Arabia's Economy and Its Global and U.S. Relations," at the U.S.-Saudi Business Opportunities Forum, Chicago, April 29, 2010.

30 See "Shortage of Ethane Feedstock in Several Middle East Countries Forcing Strategic Rethink," Plastemart.com, October 14, 2010, http://www.plastemart.com /Plastic-Technical-Article.asp?LiteratureID=1507.

31 Ibid.

32 Thomas Cottier et al., "Energy in WTO Law and Policy," *World Trade Report 2010*, at http://www.wto.org/english/res_e/publications_e/wtr10_forum_e /wtr10_7may10_e.htm#fnt1.

33 See the Energy Information Administration's assessment at http://www.eia.doe.gov/emeu/cabs/Saudi_Arabia/NaturalGas.html.

34 Interview with the author, Riyadh, October 2009.

35 Interview with the author, Riyadh, May 2010.

36 Office of the Press Secretary, "Fact Sheet: Strengthening Diplomatic Ties with Saudi Arabia," White House, May 16, 2008, Text of White House announcement at http://georgewbush-whitehouse.archives.gov/news/releases /2008/05/20080516-1.html. The actual text of the MOU has never been made public.

37 Text distributed by Saudi Press Agency, April 17, 2010.

38 Interview with the author, Riyadh, April 2011.

39 Pöyry company news release, "Pöyry Awarded Nuclear and Renewable Energy Strategy Project in Saudi Arabia," June 10, 2010.

40 See Utilities ME Staff, "Saudi Arabia May Turn to Uranium Enrichment," June 17, 2010, http://www.utilities-me.com/article-60l-saudi-arabia-may-turn-to -uranium-enrichment/.

41 International Energy Agency, *Monthly Oil and Gas Report*, April 2010.

CHAPTER 3. HUNGRY PEOPLE, THIRSTY LAND

1 U.S.–Saudi Arabian Business Council (USSABC), *The Agriculture Sector in the Kingdom of Saudi Arabia* (Washington: USSABC, 2008), 1. See also the council's *A Business Guide to Saudi Arabia 2010*, 122.

2 CIA, *The World Factbook*, https://www.cia.gov/library/publications/the-world-factbook/geos/sa.html.

3 Alexei Vassiliev, *The History of Saudi Arabia* (London: Saqi Books, 2000), 455. For a fuller discussion, see Thomas W. Lippman, *Inside the Mirage: America's Fragile Partnership with Saudi Arabia* (Boulder, CO: Westview Press, 2004), chapter 10.

4 Unless otherwise noted, population figures and estimates are from the Population Reference Bureau, Washington, at http://www.prb.org.

5 Based on news articles at http://www.riceonline.com/.

6 USSABC, *The Agriculture Sector in the Kingdom*, 2.

7 For an overview of poverty in Saudi Arabia see Kim Murphy, "Saudis' Quicksand of Poverty," *Los Angeles Times*, May 16, 2003. According to Abdelmohsen Al-Akkas, former minister of social welfare, more than 2 million Saudi citizens subsist entirely on cash payments from the government. (Interview with the author, Riyadh, May 2008.)

8 See Jon B. Alterman and Michael Dziuban, "Clear Gold: Water as a Strategic Resource in the Middle East" (Washington: Center for Strategic and International Studies, 2010).

9 The quotation appears in "Cultivating Sustainable Agriculture," an article in a special advertising section of *Foreign Affairs*, November–December 2007.

10 U.S. National Intelligence Council, *Global Trends 2025*.

11 "Arab World Needs $144 Billion to Meet Food Needs, Official Says," *Bloomberg News*, May 7, 2010.

12 Jarmo T. Kotilaine, chief economist, NCB Capital, "Bridging the Food Gap," NCB Capital economic research unit, Jeddah, March 2010.

13 Ministry of Economy and Planning, "Saudi Arabia: Long-Term Strategy 2025" (UN Development Programme Saudi Arabia, September 2007), section 3.1.2, part d.ii, http://www.undp.org.SA/SA/documents/ourwork/pr/long_term_strategy_2025.pdf.

14 Eng. Taha A. Alshareef, "King Abdullah's Initiative for Agricultural Investment Abroad," at the International Policy Council's Conference on Food and Environmental Security: The Role of Food and Agricultural Trade Policy, Salzburg, May 10–11, 2009, http://www.agritrade.org/events/Spring2009Seminar.html.

15 See "Custodian of the Two Holy Mosques Receives Minister of Commerce and Industry," Ministry of Foreign Affairs, January 27, 2009, http://www.mofa.gov.sa/sites/mofaen/ServicesAndInformation/news/statements/Pages/NewsArticleID88796.aspx.

16 The Saudi Star project was widely reported in the regional press; see, for example, "Les visées de l'Arabie saoudite sur les terres fertiles du continent," *Jeune Afrique*, December 1, 2009. Collected articles are at http://farmlandgrab.org.

17 The quotation is from Alshareef, "King Abdullah's Initiative," slide 4.

18 Javier Blas, "Saudis Get First Taste of Foreign Harvest," *Financial Times*, March 4, 2009.

19 Margaret Pagano, "Land Grab: The Race for the World's Farmland," *The Independent*, May 3, 2009.

20 Neil MacFarquhar, "African Farmers Displaced as Investors Move In," *New York Times*, December 22, 2010.

21 Interview with the author, Riyadh, October 2009.

22 Abdullah Al-Hamoudi's remarks during Special Workshop: Saudi Arabia's Agricultural Initiative, U.S.-Saudi Business Opportunities Forum, Chicago, April 29, 2010.

23 Interview with the author, Riyadh, October 2009.

24 Food and Agriculture Organization of the United Nations, "Foreign Direct Investment: Win-Win or Land Grab?," World Summit on Food Security, November 18–23, 2009, Rome, http://farmlandgrab.org/8833.

25 "How to Feed the World in 2050" (paper), High-Level Expert Forum, Food and Agriculture Organization of the United Nations, http://www.fao.org/wsfs/forum2050/en/.

26 See the concluding section of the FAO assessment in FAO, International Fund for Agricultural Development (FAD), and International Institute for Environment and Development (IIED), *Land Grab or Development Opportunity? Agricultural Investment and International Land Deals in Africa*, 2009, 101–2, ftp://ftp.fao.org/docrep/fao/011/ak241e/ak241e04.pdf.

27 Eng. Taha A. Al-Shareef, remarks at U.S.-Saudi Business Opportunities Forum, Chicago, April 29, 2010.

28 U.S. National Intelligence Council, *Global Trends 2025*.

29 Carin Smaller and Howard Mann, *A Thirst for Distant Lands: Foreign Investment in Agricultural Land and Water* (Winnipeg, Canada: International Institute for Sustainable Development, 2009), 3.

30 From *U.S.-Saudi Business Brief* 14, no. 5 (2009): 11.

31 See Liz Sly, "Iraq in Throes of Environmental Catastrophe, Experts Say," *Los Angeles Times*, July 30, 2009. See also Chris Toensing, "Iraq's Water Woes," *Middle East Report* 254 (Spring 2010): 19.

32 For details see Helen Metz, *Saudi Arabia: A Country Study* (Washington: Government Printing Office for the Library of Congress, 1992); and Lippman, *Inside the Mirage*, chapter 10.

33 Hussein Mousa, "Saudi Arabia Grain and Feed: Saudi Arabia to Import Wheat in 2009," GAIN Report no. SA8003, U.S. Department of Agriculture, Foreign Agricultural Service, February 19, 2008.

34 USSABC, *The Agriculture Sector in the Kingdom*, 1.

35 Interview with the author, Riyadh, October 2009.

36 Interview with the author, Riyadh, October 2009.

37 Interviews with the author, Riyadh, October 2009.

38 Smaller and Mann, "A Thirst for Distant Lands," 4, note 105.

39 Slides of the Saudi presentation at the Conference on Food and Environmental Security were previously posted at http://www.agritrade.org/events/Spring2009Seminar.html.

40 Al-Shareef's remarks, U.S.-Saudi Business Opportunities Forum.

41 "In Russia, Fire Sows Grain Shortage," *Washington Post*, August 6, 2010.

42 On rice, see Daniel Workman, "Rice Import Dependent Countries," International Trade, April 16, 2008, http://internationaltradecommodities.suite101.com/article.cfm/rice_import_dep endent_countries. On barley, see Al-Shareef's slide presentation, "King Abdullah's Initiative," Conference on Food and Evironmental Security.

43 Kotilaine, "Bridging the Food Gap," note 11.

44 Jane Kinninmont, "The GCC in 2020: Resources for the Future" (Geneva: Economist Intelligence Unit, 2010), http://viewswire.eiu.com/report_dl.asp?mode=fi&fi=427089827.PDF&rf=0.

45 James A. Russell, "Environmental Security and Regional Stability in the Persian Gulf," *Middle East Policy* 16, no. 4 (Winter 2009): 90.

46 Alan George, "Water Scandals: Saudi Arabia," *The Middle East*, October 1, 1994.

47 John Sfakianakis, Turki Al Hugail, and Daliah Merzaban, "Full Steam Ahead: Saudi Power, Water Sectors Occupy Centre Stage as Demand Soars," Banque Saudi Fransi (Saudi French Bank) Saudia Arabia Sector Analysis, March 14, 2010, available at the "Economic Reports" section of the bank's Web site, http://www.alfransi.com.sa/en/section/about-us/economic-reports.

48 Ibid.

49 Jon B. Alterman, "Middle East Notes and Comment," Center for Strategic and International Studies, April 15, 2010.

50 "Water Issues in the Middle East: When SUEZ Environment Puts Its Technology to Work for Large-Scale Development Projects," Suez Environment corporate press kit, May 2008, 5.

51 USSABC, *A Business Guide to Saudi Arabia 2010*, 121.

52 Arthur Clark and Muhammad Tahlawi, eds., *A Land Transformed: The Arabian Peninsula, Saudi Arabia, and Saudi Aramco* (Houston: Aramco Services, 2006), 14–15.

CHAPTER 4. A NEW ECONOMIC MODEL

1 Interview with the author, Dubai, May 2010.

2 Sfakianakis, Hugail, and Merzaban, "Full Steam Ahead."

3 The plan can be read online in English at http://www.undp.org.sa/sa/documents /ourwork/pr/long_term_strategy_2025.pdf.

4 "Long-Term Strategy for the Saudi Economy," at http://www.mep.gov.sa/index.jsp;jsessionid=7964BB428DF64DD5D897FE5A4 F1DDC31.beta?event=ArticleView&Article.ObjectID=53.

5 In this volume, for information on water, see chapter 3; on electricity, see chapter 2; and on education, see chapter 6.

6 This document is at http://www.mci.gov.sa/industrial.

7 Interview with the author, Riyadh, May 2010.

8 "Cluster Industries to Stimulate Growth," *Saudi Aramco Dimensions*, Spring 2009, 3.

9 Interview with the author, Riyadh, October 2009.

10 *International Oil Daily*, December 10, 2009.

11 The Saudi Arabian General Investment Authority's plan for the cities is at http://www.sagia.gov.sa/en/Why-Saudi-Arabia/Economic-cities/.

12 Interview with the author, Riyadh, May 2010.

13 Interview with the author, Riyadh, October 2009.

14 *Saudi Gazette*, May 6, 2010.

15 See Steve Gelsi, "Alcoa to Team on Aluminum Project in Saudi Arabia," *Wall Street Journal*, MarketWatch file, December 21, 2009, http://www.marketwatch.com/story/alcoa-saudi-arabia-in-108-billion -aluminum-pact-2009-12-21.

16 Nicolai Ouroussoff, "Saudi Urban Projects Are a Window to Modernity," *New York Times*, December 13, 2010.

17 "Incubating the Future: Entrepreneurship in Saudi Arabia," *US-Arab Tradeline*, newsletter of the National U.S.-Arab Chamber of Commerce, Spring 2010.

18 Initiative details at "2010 Saudi Fast Growth 100 Winners," Allworld Network, http://www.allworldlive.com/saudi-arabia-100/winners/2010.

19 "Incubating the Future: Entrepreneurship in Saudi Arabia," *US-Arab Tradeline*.

20 Interview with the author, Riyadh, October 2009.

21 Gene W. Heck and Omar Bahlaiwa, *Saudi Arabia: An Evolving Modern Economy* (Riyadh: privately printed, 2005), 15.

22 On mining, see "Mining Industry to Become the Kingdom's Third Pillar," *U.S.-Saudi Business Brief*, distributed to members by the U.S.–Saudi Arabian Business Council, 14, no. 1, November 1, 2009.

23 GE signed a memorandum of understanding to that effect with the Ministry of Commerce and Industry in Chicago in April 2010.

24 *U.S.-Saudi Business Brief* 11, no. 2 (2006).

25 "KEC Signs with DeepCloud SA for Development of DeepCloud Madinah Technology Center," AMEinfo.com, press release, May 24, 2010, http://www.ameinfo.com/233461.html.

26 Brad Bourland, "Saudi Arabia and the WTO," SAMBA Economic Report, March 18, 2006, http://www.saudi-us-relations.org/articles/2006/ioi/060318 -samba-wto.html.

27 Ahmed Al-Sadhan's PowerPoint presentation "2020 Vision for the Kingdom of Saudi Arabia," December 7, 2004. is available online at http://www.mci.gov.sa/industrial/4.%20Vision%2020202%20for%20KSA.ppt. Emphasis is in the original. On Hamad, see Glen Carey, "GE Sees Saudi Arabia as Manufacturing, Supply-chain Hub in Islamic World," Bloomberg News, June 30, 2010.

28 For details of the Acer agreement, see "Acer Signs with Advanced Electronics Company (AEC) for PC Plant," Business Intelligence Middle East, February 13, 2006, http://www.bi-me.com/main.php?id=3115&t=1.

29 USSABC, *A Business Guide to Saudi Arabia 2010*, 187.

30 Interview with the author, Riyadh, October 2009.

CHAPTER 5. THE LABOR MARKET AND ITS DISCONTENTS

1 Saudi unemployment figures are notoriously unreliable and differ from department to department within the government. I am indebted to Patrice Flynn, an American labor economist who lived in Jeddah and studied the Saudi labor market, for her help with these estimates.

2   See John Sfakianakis, Banque Saudi Fransi, "Saudi Arabia Economics—
    Employment Quandary," February 21, 2011, at http://www.thegulfintelligence
    .com/Docs.Viewer/8ad91021-1053-43d7-b8a8-d250151257ab/default.aspx.

3   Many obituaries recounted this anecdote when the minister died in 2010.

4   Steffen Hertog, "A Rentier Social Contract: The Saudi Political Economy since
    1979," in *The Kingdom of Saudi Arabia, 1979–2009: Evolution of a Pivotal
    State* (Washington: Middle East Institute, 2009), http://mei.edu/Portals/0
    /Publications/SaudiArabiaViewpoints.pdf.

5   Interview with the author, Riyadh, October 2009.

6   Joy Winkie Viola, *Human Resources Development in Saudi Arabia:
    Multinationals and Saudization* (Boston: International Human Resources
    Development Corporation, 1986), 177. This book is the most extensive
    treatment of the subject in English.

7   Al-Humaid was interviewed in Riyadh in May 2010. On women's issues more
    generally, see chapter 7.

8   These figures are from a slide show on the commission's Web site at scta.gov.sa
    and from *Arab News*, March 27, 2011.

9   Interview with the author, Jeddah, October 2009.

10 Author's telephone interview, July 21, 2009.

11 These figures are from the "Manpower and Employment" section of the *Saudi
    Arabia: Long-Term Strategy 2025* master economic plan, which can be read
    online in English at http://www.undp.org.sa/sa/documents/ourwork/pr/long
    _term_strategy_2025.pdf.

12 Interview with the author, Riyadh, May 2010.

13 See text of Banque Saudi Fransi's report "Slow but Sure: Saudi Arabia Set for
    Steady 2010 Recovery," January 13, 2010, at http://www.susris.com
    /2010/01/13/steady-recovery/.

14 Paul Gamble, "The Saudi Economy in 2010," Jadwa Investment, February
    2010, http://www.jadwa.com/Research/store/Econ%20outlook%202010.pdf.

15 USSABC, *A Business Guide to Saudi Arabia 2010*, 218.

16 *Arab News*, May 15, 2010.

17 Gamble, "Saudi Population Growth Slows; Expats Jump."

CHAPTER 6. THE EDUCATION REVOLUTION

1   The TIMSS scores are online at http://timss.bc.edu/timss2007/index.html,
    under the International Database heading.

2   Author's telephone interview, June 16, 2009.

3   The authority's Web site is http://www.sagia.gov.sa.

4   Interview with the author, Riyadh, October 2009.

5   This study may be downloaded from the Web site of the Investment Authority's National Competitiveness Center, http://www.saudincc.org.sa/CMSPages /GetFile.aspx?guid=b31d593f-be06-4b62-9ff4-45915b712b59. Unless otherwise noted, all statistics in this chapter are from this study.

6   The Webometrics rankings, as of January 2011, are available at http://www.webometrics.info/rank_by_country.asp?country=sa.

7   "Ninth Development Plan (2010–2014) Approved, August 9, 2010," http://www.saudiembassy.net/latest–news/news08091005.aspx.

8   The English text of the Basic Law is in Jerichow, *The Saudi File*, 10.

9   Eleanor A. Doumato, "Saudi Arabia: From 'Wahhabi' Roots to Contemporary Revisionism," in *Teaching Islam: Textbooks and Religion in the Middle East*, ed. Eleanor Doumato and Gregory Starrett (Boulder, CO: Lynne Rienner, 2007), 153.

10   Author's telephone interview, October 19, 2010.

11   U.S.–Saudi Arabian Business Council, *The Education Sector in the Kingdom of Saudi Arabia* (Washington: USSABC, 2009), 26. This report includes a useful summary of how the entire system is structured and organized.

12   Madawi Al-Rasheed, *A History of Saudi Arabia* (New York: Cambridge University Press, 2002), 189–96.

13   Michaela Prokop, "The War of Ideas: Education in Saudi Arabia," in Aarts and Nonneman, *Saudi Arabia in the Balance*, 57.

14   Doumato, "Saudi Arabia," 155.

15   In a statement accompanying the release of this report, Weiner said the quotations were from required texts that had been "smuggled out of Saudi Arabia" and translated by the Institute for Gulf Affairs, which he said was a "nonpartisan organization that produces political analysis of the Gulf region." That description is accurate as far as it goes, but it does not go far enough. The Institute for Gulf Affairs is a one-man outfit in Washington; the one man is Ali Al-Ahmed, a dissident Saudi journalist of the minority Shiite branch of Islam, whose life's work is denunciation of the Al-Saud regime. His background does not negate the accuracy of his findings, but Weiner ought to have acknowledged that Al-Ahmed always endeavors to put the Saudi rulers in the worst possible light. Al-Ahmed was also the principal source for the Hudson Institute study cited in the following note. Saudi officials have denied that textbooks have to be "smuggled" out of the country.

16   Center for Religious Freedom of the Hudson Institute with the Institute or Gulf Affairs, "Saudi Arabia's Curriculum of Intolerance: 2008 Update," (Washington: Center for Religious Freedom, 2008), http://www.hudson.org /files/pdf_upload/saudi_textbooks_final.pdf.

17 These and many other comments to the same effect have been posted on the Saudi Embassy's Web site in Washington, http://www.saudiembassy.net.

18 This text is at http://www.saudiembassy.net/files/PDF/Reports/2008Reports /Reform_Report_May08.pdf.

19 Doumato, "Saudi Arabia," 163.

20 U.S. Commission on International Religious Freedom, *Annual Report 2010* (Washington: U.S. Commission on International Religious Freedom, 2010), 136, http://www.uscirf.gov/images/annual%20report%202010.pdf.

21 U.S. Department of State, Bureau of Democracy, Human Rights, and Labor, "2009 Human Rights Report: Saudi Arabia," March 11, 2010, http://www.state.gov /g/drl/rls/hrrpt/2009/nea/136079.htm.

22 Prokop, "The War of Ideas," 59.

23 Interview with the author, Riyadh, October 2009.

24 Interview with the author, Riyadh, May 2010.

25 For an extensive review of the gender segregation issue in school and the workplace and the intensity of the debate about it, see Roel Meijer, "Reform in Saudi Arabia: The Gender-Segregation Debate," *Middle East Policy* 17, no. 4 (Winter 2010): 80.

26 Jeff Weintraub, "KAUST Announces Partnership with UC San Diego to Build World's Most Advanced Visualization Center," EurekAlert!, October 21, 2008, http://www.eurekalert.org/pub_releases/2008-10/kauo-kap102108.php.

27 Interview with the author, KAUST campus, October 2009.

CHAPTER 7. WOMEN: THE COMING BREAKOUT

1   The report is online at http://www.wunrn.com/news/2009/10_09/10_12 _09/101209_undp.htm.

2   Interview with the author, Riyadh, May 2010.

3   Dr. Muna Al-Munajjed, "Women's Employment in Saudi Arabia: A Major Challenge," Booz & Co., 2010, http://www.booz.com/media/uploads/Womens _Employment_in_Saudi_Arabia.pdf.

4   Zainah Almihdar, "Human Rights of Women and Children under the Islamic Law of Personal Status and Its Application in Saudi Arabia," *Muslim World Journal of Human Rights* 5, no. 1 (2008): 4.

5   Koran 33:35.

6   Koran 43:18, 4:34.

7   Eleanor Abdella Doumato, "Obstacles to Equality for Saudi Woman," Middle East Institute Viewpoints: *The Kingdom of Saudi Arabia, 1979–2009: Evolution of a Pivotal State* (Washington: Middle East Institute, October 2009), 23–26, http://mei.edu/Portals/0/Publications/SaudiArabiaViewpoints.pdf.

8   Qanta A. Ahmed, *In the Land of Invisible Women: A Female Doctor's Journey in the Saudi Kingdom* (Naperville, IL: Sourcebooks, 2008), 77.

9   She wrote in Arabic. An English version of her piece "Can You Put Yourself in a Woman's Shoes for One Day?" was posted by the popular blogger known as Saudi Jeans at http://saudijeans.org/2009/11/21/fawzia-albakr/.

10 See Robert Lacey, *Inside the Kingdom: Kings, Clerics, Modernists, Terrorists, and the Struggle for Saudi Arabia* (New York: Viking, 2009), 135–39; and Lippman, *Inside the Mirage*, 308–309.

11 Walaa Hawari, "Five Women Died as Car Driven by One of Them Overturns," *Arab News*, November 22, 2010.

12 This newsletter is http://www.ameinfo.com.

13 Jafar Alshayeb, "Women's Rights Gain Focus in Saudi Arabia," Carnegie Middle East Center of the Carnegie Endowment for International Peace, Beirut, May 27, 2010.

14 See, for example, the report by Human Rights Watch, "Perpetual Minors; Human Rights Abuses Stemming from Male Guardianship and Sex Segregation in Saudi Arabia," April 2008, http://www.hrw.org/en/reports/2008/04/19/perpetual-minors-0.

15 Interview with the author, Riyadh, October 2009.

16 Samar Fatany, "Bright Future Awaits Saudi Women with Vision and Courage," *Arab News*, September 23, 2006.

17 *Arab News*, October 15, 2008.

18 Reported by the Arabic newspaper *Okaz* on August 10, 2010.

19 E-mail message to the author, August 20, 2010.

20 On the muttawain and their role, see chapter 8.

21 Nimah Ismail Nawwab, *The Unfurling* (Vista, CA: Selwa Press, 2004), 2.

22 Wajeha Al-Huwaider, "Saudi Women Can Drive: Just Let Them," *Washington Post*, August 16, 2009.

23 She was interviewed by Katherine Zoepf. See "Talk of Women's Rights Divides Saudi Arabia," *New York Times*, May 31, 2010.

24 "Much Ado about Women," Saudiwoman's Weblog, May 4, 2010, http://saudiwoman.wordpress.com/2010/05/04/much-ado-about-women/.

25 "Some People Never Change," Saudiwoman's Weblog, April 10, 2010, http://saudiwoman.wordpress.com/2010/04/10/some-people-never-change/.

26 "Heila Al Qusayer," Saudiwoman's Weblog, June 18, 2010, http://saudiwoman.wordpress.com/page/6/?pages-list.

27 Interview with the author, Riyadh, May 2010.

28 Muna Abusulayman, "Women and Millennium Development Goals," United Nations Development Program, country office for Saudi Arabia, November 2005.

29 Rajaa Alsanea, *Girls of Riyadh* (New York: Penguin Press, 2007), 78.

30 Mark Weston, *Prophets and Princes: Saudi Arabia from Muhammad to the Present* (Hoboken, NJ: John Wiley, 2008), 440.

31 "Saudi Businesswomen Play Major Role at Jeddah Economic Forum," January 3, 2004, with English text at http://www.ameinfo.com/32998.html.

CHAPTER 8. ISLAM, SOCIETY, AND THE STATE

1 See Natana J. DeLong-Bas, "Wahhabism and the Question of Religious Tolerance," in Ayoub and Kosebalaban, *Religion and Politics in Saudi Arabia*, 11.

2 English text in Jerichow, *The Saudi File*, 10.

3 Abdullah Al-Fawzan, "What Does His Eminence the Mufti Mean by the Bond Between the 'Ulama and the Leadership?" *al-Watan*, August 29, 2009 (in Arabic).

4 The most extensive account of this episode is in Yaroslav Trofimov, *The Siege of Mecca: The Forgotten Uprising in Islam's Holiest Shrine and the Birth of Al Qaeda* (New York: Doubleday, 2007).

5 See Weston, *Prophets and Princes*, 422; and Lacey, *Inside the Kingdom*, 244.

6 The word "jihad" is routinely translated in the United States as "holy war," but it is a complicated concept. It means righteous struggle or effort on behalf of the faith. Whether the obligation to pursue jihad conveys a commitment to violence, or to attacks on non-Muslims just because they are not Muslims, is an argument that has been going on for centuries and filled entire books. See, for example, Carl W. Ernst, *Following Muhammad: Rethinking Islam in the Contemporary World* (Chapel Hill: University of North Carolina Press, 2003), 117–18.

7 Thomas Hegghammer, "The Failure of Jihad in Saudi Arabia," Combating Terrorism Center occasional paper (West Point, NY: Combating Terrorism Center, February 25, 2010).

8 An English text, "Shaykh Salman al-Oudah's Ramadan Letter to Osama Bin Laden, September 18, 2007," can be found online at http://muslimmatters.org/2007/09/18/shaykh-salman-al-oudahs-ramadan-letter -to-osama-bin-laden-on-nbc/.

9 See Marc Lynch's "Abu Aardvark" blog entry, "People of the Year 2009: Middle East Edition," Foreignpolicy.com, December 16, 2009, http://lynch.foreignpolicy.com/posts/2009/12/16/people_of_the_year_2009 _middle_east_edition.

10 Thomas Hegghammer, "Islamist Violence and Regime Stability in Saudi Arabia," *International Affairs* 84, no. 4 (2008): 701.

11 Interview with the author, Riyadh, October 2009.

12 *Asharq al-Awsat*, October 26, 2010.

13 He was profiled on NPR's *On the Media* program on June 25, 2009, and in the *New York Times* on January 3, 2009.

14 Final communiqué, Third Extraordinary Session of the Islamic Summit Conference, Mecca, December 7–8, 2005.

15 The official Saudi Press Agency disseminated this document on August 12, 2010, in news media and otherwise.

16 Text distributed by Saudi Press Agency, March 7, 2011.

17 Christopher Blanchard, *Saudi Arabia: Background and U.S. Relations*, Congressional Research Service report to Congress (Washington: Congressional Research Service, June 14, 2010).

18 See William McCants, ed., *Militant Ideology Atlas* (West Point, NY: Combating Terrorism Center, November 1, 2006), http://www.ctc.usma.edu/posts/militant -ideology-atlas.

19 These Wikileaks cables can be found at http://www.guardian.co.uk/world/the -us-embassy-cables?INTCMP=SRCH.

20 Ibid.

21 Testimony before the House International Relations Subcommittee on International Terrorism and Nonproliferation, May 4, 2005.

22 Written responses to questions from the Senate Select Committee on Intelligence, February 12, 2009.

23 Address to International Counter-Terrorism Conference, Riyadh, February 5, 2005.

24 An English text was posted at http://www.saudiembassy.net/print /announcement/announcement05071001.aspx.

25 The text of this statement is at http://www.assakina.com/news/3069.html, in Arabic.

26 Christopher Boucek, "Extremist Reeducation and Rehabilitation in Saudi Arabia," Jamestown Foundation's *Terrorism Monitor* 5, no. 16 (August 14, 2007). See also Katherine Zoepf, "Deprogramming Jihadists," *New York Times Magazine*, November 7, 2008.

27 Interview with the author, Washington, July 20, 2009.

28 In Arabic at http://www.alwatan.com.sa/Articles/Detail.aspx?ArticleID=742.

29 Vali Nasr, *The Shia Revival: How Conflicts within Islam Will Shape the Future* (New York: W. W. Norton, 2006), 24.

30 On the strategic rivalry with Iran, see this volume's chapter 10.

31 Weston, *Prophets and Princes*, 247.

32 International Crisis Group, "The Shiite Question in Saudi Arabia," *Middle East Report* no. 45, September 19, 2005, http://www.crisisgroup.org/en/regions/middle-east-north-africa/iran-gulf/saudi -arabia/045-the-shiite-question-in-saudi-arabia.aspx.

33 See the informative account, Toby Matthiesen, "The Shia of Saudi Arabia at a Crossroads," *Middle East Report*, May 6, 2009, http://www.merip.org/mero/mero050609. On the oil wealth issue, see "Awamiyah Shia Demand Oil Rights," *al-Watan*, August 4, 2007 (in Arabic).

34 Statement issued by the International Islamic Conference at the conclusion of a meeting in Amman, Jordan, July 4–6, 2005.

35 *Al-Hayat*, March 25, 2009 (in Arabic).

36 Human Rights Watch, "Saudi Arabia: Free Advocate for Shia Rights," March 23, 2010, http://www.hrw.org/en/news/2010/03/23/saudi-arabia-free-advocate -shia-rights.

37 U.S. Commission on International Religious Freedom, *Annual Report 2010*. See the section on Saudi Arabia, 123–38.

38 Interview with the author, Qatif, October 2009.

CHAPTER 9. SOCIAL UPHEAVAL, SOCIAL WELFARE

1 Samar Fatany, "Youth Problems Need Everyone's Attention," *Arab News,* June 10, 2008.

2 These figures can be found on various charts at the Web site for the Population Reference Bureau, http://www.prb.org.

3 See Gamble, "Saudi Population Growth Slows; Expats Jump."

4 John R. Bradley, *Saudi Arabia Exposed: Inside a Kingdom in Crisis* (New York: Palgrave Macmillan, 2005), 148.

5 Interview with the author, Riyadh, May 2008.

6 Online at http://www.hsbc.com/retirement.

7 This estimate has appeared in many studies. See, for example, Abeer Allam, "Saudi Arabia Holds Out for Mortgage Reform," Beyond Brics, June 4, 2010, http://blogs.ft.com/beyond-brics/2010/06/04/saudi/.

8 Author's telephone interview from Cairo, August 5, 2009.

9 "IFC Promotes Home Ownership in Saudi Arabia," news release, April 5, 2007.

10 *Saudi Gazette*, April 18, 2010.

11 John Sfakianakis, Turki Al Hugail, and Daliah Merzaban, "Real Estate, Saudi Arabia: Building Momentum," Banque Saudi Fransi Saudia Arabia Sector Analysis, April 6, 2010, available at the "Economic Reports" section of the bank's Web site, http://www.alfransi.com.sa/en/secton/about-us/economic -reports.

12 Interview with the author, Riyadh, May 2010.

13 Interview with the author at Help Center, Jeddah, October 28, 2009.

14 The March of Dimes' global report on birth defects is online at http://www.marchofdimes.com/mission/globalprogram_birthdefectstoll.html.

15 Mohammad I. El Mouzan et al., "Consanguinity and Major Genetic Disorders in Saudi Children: A Community-based Cross-sectional Study," *Annals of Saudi Medicine* 28, no. 3 (2008): 169.

16 F. M. Lai et al., "Birth Prevalence of Down Syndrome in Singapore from 1993 to 1998," *Singapore Medical Journal* 43, no. 2 (2002).

17 March of Dimes global report.

18 El Mouzan et al., "Consanguinity and Major Genetic Disorders," note 15.

19 This study is online at https://docs.google.com/viewer?a=v&q=cache :BjktkKFLAA8J:www.ejeg.com/issue/download.html?idArticle%3D48+abdulm ohsen+saudi+disabled+anglia&hl=en&gl=us&pid=bl&srcid=ADGEESjCRwb2 OqiO9cL2nuOPLoNrvr-D4PHE0igAlauyBiRMqWptt-JWLWyZY602rgH8hE Bahm2m3pI6dM1M0vAg_Ws27I7_xA0js3mJrKlmIwUuwGRF6v6WlvPh9WS NVgbtpBftJt-G&sig=AHIEtbQYO44FjhJL6-Fm-isG71nU_U8VYQ&pli=1.

20 P. K. Abdul Ghafour, "A Decade of Deaths!" *Arab News*, April 16, 2009.

21 This study by G. D. Jacobs and Amy Aeron-Thomas is online at http://www.transport-links.org/transport_links/filearea/publications/1_771 _Pa3568.pdf.

22 The ministry's statistics, in Arabic, are at http://www.moi.gov.sa/wps/portal /traffic/!ut/p/c1/hY7NDoIwEISfxQcwu1Ba8YhFaGP4VwQuhBhCSPjxYIy -vVU8GCNx9vjNzA4UoG6orm1TXdpxqDrIoGCl66cJcQXRcMs4yoiKYEcP KE1N8ZyVlIdcmp7idMNRT31O432ILKV_0kk9wPH586PD5YZyGVqKCaeE xMbE51pcMnEMdM_WIm45GAnDpmuBb331_9j4ys_IQvDF2NeQQ7GaXR EwyLu6qU53OPfZTbZy6ViLxQPcS9Tx/dl2/d1/L0lJSklna2shL0lCakFBQ3lBQ kVSQ0lBISEvWUZOZQTFOSTUwLXchLzdfR05WUzNHSDMxMEU2QzBJUT VIT0s1VTBJTzY!/?WCM_PORTLET=PC_7_GNVS3GH310E6C0IQ5HOK5U 0IO6_WCM&WCM_GLOBAL_CONTEXT=/wps/wcm/connect/main/Traffic /Main/Statistics/.

23 Ali S. Al-Ghamdi, "Analysis of Speeding in Saudi Arabia and Effectiveness of Enforcement Methods," *Transportation Research Record 1969* (2006).

24 *Arab News*, October 5, 2010.

25 Details of this program are at its Web site, http://www.saher.gov.sa.

26 This UN study is online at http://www.unodc.org/unodc/en/data-and-analysis /WDR-2008.html.

27 These comments are from a news release by the hospital announcing the agreement in January 2010, http://www.brightonhospital.org/wp-content /uploads/2010/05/Brighton-Hospital-Saudi-Story.pdf.

28 Formerly available at http://wikileaks.ch/cable/2009/11/09JEDDAH443.html. See http://www.guardian.co.uk/world/2010/dec/07/wikileaks-cables-saudi -princes-parties.

CHAPTER 10. BAD NEIGHBORHOOD

1 Anthony H. Cordesman and Nawaf Obaid, *National Security in Saudi Arabia: Threats, Responses, and Challenges* (Westport, CT: Praeger Security International, 2005), xxi.

2 F. Gregory Gause III, "Saudi Arabia's Regional Security Strategy," in *The International Relations of the Gulf*, Working Group Summary Report (Doha, Qatar: Center for International and Regional Security Studies of the Georgetown University School of Foreign Service, 2009).

3 Anthony H. Cordesman, *Saudi Arabia: National Security in a Troubled Region* (Santa Barbara, CA: Praeger Security International, 2009), 121.

4 Remarks at the Institute for the Study of War, Washington, January 22, 2010.

5 Remarks at the International Institute for Strategic Studies (IISS) Security Summit, Sixth Manama Dialogue, Manama, Bahrain, December 13, 2009.

6 Remarks at Nineteenth Annual Arab-U.S. Policymakers Conference, Washington, October 22, 2010.

7 Prepared testimony submitted to the Senate Foreign Relations Committee, January 20, 2010.

8 The quotation is from the Carnegie Endowment's news release announcing the book's publication, September 30, 2010.

9 The text of the press release, dated June 30, 2009, can be found at the company's Web site, http://www.eads.com/eads/int/en/news/press.cef29648 -298b-4ca0-844b-de95bf3657ec.08af92a7-2c53-400a-8429-8b135733cbcc .html?queryStr=saudi%20border%20guard&pid=1.

10 "Fencing the Kingdom: EADS Lands Huge Saudi Border Deal," *Defense Industry Daily*, July 19, 2009.

11 For details see Christopher Blanchard, *Saudi Arabia: Background and U.S. Relations.* Congressional Research Service report to Congress (Washington: Congressional Research Service, December 16, 2009).

12 Cordesman, *Saudi Arabia: National Security*, 16.

13 Nima Adelkhah, "Iranian Naval Capabilities and the Security of the Hormuz
    Strait," *Terrorism Monitor* 8, no. 30 (July 29, 2010), http://www.jamestown.org
    /single/?no_cache=1&tx_ttnews[swords]=8fd5893941d69d0be3f378576261
    ae3e&tx_ttnews[any_of_the_words]=hormuz%20iran%20&tx_ttnews[tt
    _news]=36682&tx_ttnews[backPid]=7&cHash=05d42bdfd7.

14 Tariq Khaitous, "Arab Reactions to a Nuclear Armed Iran," Washington
    Institute for Near East Policy, *Policy Focus* 94 (June 2009).

15 See, for example, Lee Smith, "Our Proxy War in the Middle East," *Newsweek*,
    August 13, 2010, http://www.newsweek.com/2010/08/13/the-israeli-saudi
    -american-alliance-against-iran.html?from=rss.

16 Jareer Elass and Amy Myers Jaffe, "The History of U.S. Relations with OPEC:
    Lessons to Policymakers," in *Energy Market Consequences of an Emerging
    U.S. Carbon Management Strategy* (Houston: Energy Forum of the James A.
    Baker III Institute for Public Policy, Rice University, September 2010), 24.

17 Frederic Wehrey et al., *Saudi-Iranian Relations since the Fall of Saddam:
    Rivalry, Cooperation, and Implications for U.S. Policy* (Santa Monica, CA:
    RAND, 2009), xii.

18 Dr. Lewis A Dunn, "Strategic Reassurance if Iran 'Goes Nuclear': A
    Framework and Some Propositions," *Strategic Insights* 7, no. 5 (December
    2009).

19 Wehrey et al., *Saudi-Iranian Relations*, xv.

20 Address to Anti-Defamation League, Washington, May 3, 2010.

21 WikiLeaks cable, previously at
    http://cablegate.wikileaks.org/cable/2010/02/10RIYADH178.html.

22 Office of the Press Secretary, "Fact Sheet: Strengthening Diplomatic Ties."

23 Richard L. Russell, "A Saudi Nuclear Option?" *Survival* 43, no. 2 (Summer
    2001): 70.

24 Cordesman, *Saudi Arabia: National Security*, 257.

25 Remarks at Middle East Institute, Washington, September 28, 2010.

26 Robert E. Hunter, *Building Security in the Persian Gulf* (Santa Monica, CA:
    RAND, 2010), iv.

27 Ibid., xxi.

CHAPTER 11. AN EVOLVING ALLIANCE

1   For details of this history, see Rachel Bronson, *Thicker Than Oil: America's Uneasy Partnership with Saudi Arabia* (New York: Oxford University Press, 2006), and Lippman, *Inside the Mirage.*

2   The most extensive account of the meeting between Roosevelt and Abdul Aziz is in Thomas W. Lippman, *Arabian Knight: Colonel Bill Eddy USMC and the Rise of American Power in the Middle East* (Vista, CA: Selwa Press, 2008), 127–50.

3   *The 9/11 Commission Report: Final Report of the National Commission on Terrorist Attacks upon the United States* (New York: W. W. Norton, 2004), 171.

4   Office of the Press Secretary, "Fact Sheet: Strengthening Diplomatic Ties."

5   Text of Prince Saud Al-Faisal's statement at the State Department, Washington, July 31, 2009, is available at http://www.saudiembassy.net/announcement /announcement07310901.aspx.

6   SABB Notes, an occasional publication of Saudi-British Bank, June 3, 2009.

7   Daniel Wagner and Theodore Karasik, "The Maturing Saudi-China Alliance," Real Clear World, April 7, 2010, http://www.realclearworld.com/articles/2010/04/07/the_maturing_saudi-china _alliance_98904.html.

8   Gen. David Petraeus gave the troop figure in remarks at the IISS Manama Dialogue in Bahrain, December 13, 2009.

9   Blanchard, *Saudi Arabia* (December 16, 2009, report).

10 The text of this document is at http://www.whitehouse.gov/sites/default/files/rss_viewer/national_security _strategy.pdf

11 The text of this document is at http://www.defense.gov/qdr/.

12 Office of the Secretary of Defense, *Annual Report to Congress: Military and Security Developments Involving the People's Republic of China, 2010*, online at http://www.defense.gov/pubs/pdfs/2010_CMPR_Final.pdf.

13 "Clinton Says US Considers 'Defense Umbrella' to Deter a Nuclear Iran," VOA News, July 22, 2009, http://www1.voanews.com/english/news/a-13-2009-07 -22-voa8-68653952.html.

14 U.S. Department of State, *Foreign Relations of the United States, 1952–54*, vol. 9, *Near and Middle East* (Washington: U.S. Government Printing Office, 1986), 2438.

15 The notification documents are at http://www.dsca.mil.

16 Vershbow and Shapiro spoke at a press briefing conducted at the State Department on October 20, 2010.

17 William Hartung's comments are from Deborah Jerome, ed., *Is the Big Saudi Arms Sale a Good Idea?* (Washington: Council on Foreign Relations, September 27, 2010), http://www.cfr.org/defensehomeland-security/big-saudi-arms-sale-good-idea/p23019.

18 Hillary Rodham Clinton, press statement, "Kingdom of Saudi Arabia's National Day," Washington, September 22, 2010, http://www.state.gov/secretary/rm/2010/09/147533.htm.

19 Remarks at Nineteenth Annual Arab-U.S. Policymakers Conference, 2010.

FURTHER READING

The literature on modern Saudi Arabia, skimpy before 9/11, is now extensive, but much of it is unreliable. This list includes books that are cited in the text and those that could be useful to readers who want additional information.

Aarts, Paul, and Gerd Nonneman, eds. *Saudi Arabia in the Balance: Political Economy, Society, Foreign Affairs.* New York: New York University Press, 2005.

Abukhalil, Asad. *The Battle for Saudi Arabia: Royalty, Fundamentalism, and Global Power.* New York: Seven Stories Press, 2004.

Ahmed, Qanta A. *In the Land of Invisible Women: A Female Doctor's Journey in the Saudi Kingdom.* Naperville, IL: Sourcebooks, 2008.

Alsanea, Rajaa. *Girls of Riyadh.* New York: Penguin Press, 2007.

Ayoob, Mohammed, and Hasan Kosebalaban, eds. *Religion and Politics in Saudi Arabia: Wahhabism and the State.* Boulder, CO: Lynne Rienner, 2009.

Bradley, John R. *Saudi Arabia Exposed: Inside a Kingdom in Crisis.* New York: Palgrave Macmillan, 2005.

Bronson, Rachel. *Thicker Than Oil: America's Uneasy Partnership with Saudi Arabia.* New York: Oxford University Press, 2006.

Butler, Grant C. *Kings and Camels: An American in Saudi Arabia*. New York: Devin-Adair, 1960.

Clark, Arthur, and Muhammad Tahlawi, eds. *A Land Transformed: The Arabian Peninsula, Saudi Arabia, and Saudi Aramco*. Houston: Aramco Services Co., 2006.

Cordesman, Anthony. *Saudi Arabia: National Security in a Troubled Region*. Santa Barbara, CA: Praeger Security International, 2009.

Cordesman, Anthony, and Nawaf Obaid. *National Security in Saudi Arabia: Threats, Responses, and Challenges*. Westport, CT: Praeger Security International, 2005.

Craze, Joshua, and Mark Huband, eds. *The Kingdom: Saudi Arabia and the Challenge of the 21st Century*. New York: Columbia University Press, 2009.

DeLong-Bas, Natana J. *Wahhabi Islam: From Revival and Reform to Global Jihad*. New York: Oxford University Press, 2004.

Doumato, Eleanor, and Gregory Starrett, eds. *Teaching Islam: Textbooks and Religion in the Middle East*. Boulder, CO: Lynne Rienner, 2007.

Ernst, Carl W. *Following Muhammad: Rethinking Islam in the Contemporary World*. Chapel Hill: University of North Carolina Press, 2003.

Fandy, Mamoun. *Saudi Arabia and the Politics of Dissent*. New York: St. Martin's Press, 1999.

Gause, F. Gregory, III. *The International Relations of the Persian Gulf*. New York: Cambridge University Press, 2010.

Heck, Gene W., and Omar Bahlaiwa. *Saudi Arabia: An Evolving Modern Economy*. Riyadh: privately printed, 2005.

Hunter, Robert E. *Building Security in the Persian Gulf*. Santa Monica, CA: RAND, 2010.

Jerichow, Anders. *The Saudi File: People, Power, Politics*. New York: St. Martin's, 1998.

Jones, Toby C. *Desert Kingdom: How Oil and Water Forged Modern Saudi Arabia*. Cambridge, MA: Harvard University Press, 2010.

Lacey, Robert. *Inside the Kingdom: Kings, Clerics, Modernists, Terrorists, and the Struggle for Saudi Arabia*. New York: Viking, 2009.

Lippman, Thomas W. *Inside the Mirage: America's Fragile Partnership with Saudi Arabia*. Boulder, CO: Westview Press, 2004.

Nasr, Vali. *The Shia Revival: How Conflicts within Islam Will Shape the Future*. New York: W. W. Norton, 2006.

Niblock, Tim. *Saudi Arabia: Power, Legitimacy and Survival*. London: Routledge, 2006.

Obaid, Nawaf E. *The Oil Kingdom at 100: Petroleum Policymaking in Saudi Arabia*. Washington: Washington Institute for Near-East Policy, 2000.

Ottaway, David B. *The King's Messenger: Prince Bandar bin Sultan and America's Tangled Relationship with Saudi Arabia*. New York: Walker, 2008.

Philby, H. St. John. *Saudi Arabia*. Beirut: Librairie du Liban, 1968.

Rasheed, Madawi Al-. *A History of Saudi Arabia*. New York: Cambridge University Press, 2002.

Simmons, Matthew. *Twilight in the Desert: The Coming Saudi Oil Shock and the World Economy*. Hoboken, NJ: John Wiley, 2005.

Tripp, Harvey, and Peter North. *Culture Shock! Saudi Arabia*. Portland, OR: Graphic Arts Center Publishing, 2003.

Trofimov, Yaroslav. *The Siege of Mecca: The Forgotten Uprising in Islam's Holiest Shrine and the Birth of Al Qaeda*. New York: Doubleday, 2007.

U.S.–Saudi Arabian Business Council (USSABC). *A Business Guide to Saudi Arabia 2010*. Washington: USSABC, 2010.

Vassiliev, Alexei. *The History of Saudi Arabia*. London: Saqi Books, 2000.

Viola, Joy Winkie. *Human Resources Development in Saudi Arabia: Multinationals and Saudization.* Boston: International Human Resources Development Corporation, 1986.

Wehrey, Frederic, Theodore W. Karasik, Alireza Nader, Jeremy J. Ghez, Lydia Hansell, and Robert A. Guffey. *Saudi-Iranian Relations since the Fall of Saddam: Rivalry, Cooperation, and Implications for U.S. Policy.* Santa Monica, CA: RAND, 2009.

Weston, Mark. *Prophets and Princes: Saudi Arabia from Muhammad to the Present.* Hoboken, NJ: John Wiley, 2008.

INDEX

imported labor, foreign workers, 5, 88, 90, 97, 105–7, 117, 121, 171

Independent, 70

India, 66, 84, 91, 128, 164, 215, 246, 248; and oil demand, 38, 46, 241

Indiana University, 165

Institute for Near East and Gulf Military Analysis, 256

"Interfaith Dialogue," 189, 207

International Agriculture and Food Investment Company, 71

International Atomic Energy Agency, 238, 247

International Crisis Group, 24, 206

International Energy Agency (IEA), 38, 42–43, 62

International Finance Corporation, 214–15

International Institute for Sustainable Development (Canada), 78

International Monetary Fund, 212

Iran, 2–3, 15–16, 39, 43, 53, 55, 68, 79, 103, 126, 141, 180, 198, 209, 230–31, 233–34, 238, 240–41, 245–46, 252–53, 255–56, 258, 261, 263; armed forces of, 237; and nuclear weapons, 230, 238–39, 241–42, 246–48, 262; Shah of, 15, 263; and Shia Islam, 196, 205–8, 238–39, 242, 259–60

Iraq, 2–3, 21, 23, 49, 53, 55, 68, 75, 80, 140, 163, 205–6, 208, 230, 233–34, 239, 244, 248, 255, 258; invasion of Kuwait, 185, 206, 217, 231, 260; U.S. invasion of, 6, 206, 240, 245, 252–53, 256, 260; war with Iran, 237, 240. *See also* Operation Desert Storm

Islamic World Council on Disability and Rehabilitation, 225

Israel, 2, 16, 53, 83, 101, 230, 233, 239–40, 243–44, 246–48, 252, 254, 261, 263–64. *See also* Arab-Israeli conflict

Isuzu Motors Co., 104

Jackson, Peter, 48

Jadwa Investment Group, 5, 42, 59, 78, 104, 120, 122, 212

Japan, 61, 79, 90, 103, 192–93, 256, 260

Jeddah, 41, 61, 81–82, 96, 104, 108, 109–11, 115–17, 120, 160–62, 164, 192, 213, 216–17, 221, 224, 226–27; floods in, 35, 82

Jeddah Chamber of Commerce and Industry, 161

Jeddah Economic Forum, 174–75

Jehani, Abdullah Al-, 112–14, 117

jihad, jihadists, 3, 7, 23, 24, 184–85, 187, 191, 193, 202–4

Jizan, 53–54, 95–96

Jobs, Steve, 91

Johnson, Paul, 186

Jones, Toby, 30

Jordan, 116, 128, 230

Juffali, Maha, 217–19

Kantrow, Alan, 127, 130

Kenana Sugar Company, 77

Kent State University, 99

Khadija, wife of Prophet Muhammad, 153

Khaitous, Tareq, 238

Khalid Al-Faisal, Prince, 158

Khan, A. Q., 248